FERRIE

BRITISH ISLES AND NORT

Ferry
Publications

ISBN 978-1-906608-72-9

Ferry Publications, PO Box 33,
Ramsey, Isle of Man IM99 4LP

Email: ferrypubs@manx.net   Website: www.ferrypubs.co.uk

europe's **leading** guide to the ferry industry

contents...

Stena Carisma (Miles Cowsill)

europe's **leading** guide to the ferry industry

introduction...

This is the twenty-sixth edition of this book, which first appeared in 1983 as the 24-page 'home published' *'Car Ferries from Great Britain and Ireland'*. The book aims to list every passenger/vehicle ferry in Great Britain and Ireland, ro-ro freight vessels which operate regular services between Great Britain and Ireland and to nearby Continental destinations and major passenger/vehicle ferries in other parts of Northern Europe. The coverage of Northern Europe is not fully comprehensive (to make it so would probably triple the size of the book) and does not include freight-only operations and vessels - although freight-only vessels have been included where the operators also run passenger services. Ro-ro vessels engaged in 'deep-sea' trade and those operated solely for the carriage of trade cars or paper are also not included.

Each operator is listed alphabetically within sections - major operators, minor operators, freight-only operators, chain, cable and float ferries, passenger-only ferries, other North European passenger operators and vehicle/passenger vessels owned by companies not currently engaged in operating services. After details relating to each company's management, address, telephone numbers, email, website and services, there is a fleet list with technical data and then a potted history of each vessel with previous names and dates.

Once again, 2013 was a mixture of good and bad news. The demise of SeaFrance, reborn as MyFerryLink was a major event of the year and that of TransEuropa Ferries, unlikely to be reborn in any form, has again emphasised how completive the English Channel is and how difficult it is to make money. The rise and rise of DFDS, now a major player in the Channel, demonstrates that this company sees the potential, although they must be disappointed that they failed to secure the two SeaFrance vessels. In the Baltic the private equity owners of Scandlines, ever in pursuit of short term profitability, sold a large part of the company to Stena Line and are seeking to sell the rest of the company. The debacle over the new ships for Gedser - Rostock can scarcely have aroused their enthusiasm for the ferry market.

However, there are sparks of light. Viking Line's new *Viking Grace* represents a major development and Eckerö Line's rebuilding of the Moby Freedom as the *Finlandia* has provided a splendid 'new' ferry at a much lower cost than a newbuild.

On the freight-only side, CLdN/Cobelfret Ferries, although withdrawing their Ipswich - Rotterdam service, have, in a relatively short time, developed as a major chartering company with no less than nine vessels now on charter to other operators. Fewer new ships were delivered and are currently are on order than in recent years but now practically all the 1970s built roros have been replaced a slow down was to be expected.

How the ferry industry will develop in 2014 is uncertain; what is certain is that there will be surprises and the ferry industry will continue to be fascinating.

Nick Widdows

Whitstable, Kent

July 2013

europe's **leading** guide to the ferry industry

foreword...

The ferry industry during 2013 has gone through another very pessimistic period again with the recession, severe competition from cheap airlines and pending legislation by the European Union on emissions, all being a dominating factor restricting the industry to move forward in a positive fashion. As I write this foreword in July only four ferries are currently under construction for the British ferry industry, two for Caledonian MacBrayne and Western Ferries.

The ferry industry in Scandinavia is showing a more positive view with the introduction of Viking Line's new LNG ship, the *Viking Grace*, which is featured in this edition of the publication and Fjord Line's new ships which will operate between Denmark and Norway.

The cruise industry continues to be a threat to ferry operators like Tallink/Silja line and Viking Line who have built their businesses over the last 40 years on short trips in the Baltic. The cruise industry, like the ferry industry ten years ago, has seen a downturn in their markets and there are early signs that they see a market to be tapped in the Baltic from the established ferry companies, which may only be a short-term marketing strategy but will not help the ferry companies to make long-term investments in new tonnage.

With the continued recession in the UK, despite two new ships being built for Caledonian MacBrayne, the Scottish company is faced with an ageing fleet, especially with their larger style tonnage which will need to be replaced. There remains a lot of insecurity with the offshore islands' ferry services following various venture capitalists companies leaving no cash reserve for the building of new ships. Condor Ferries will need to replace their trio of fast-craft in the very near future; the Steam Packet are faced with the replacement problem of the *Ben-my-Chree* and indecision as to where their long-term strategy and services will be to in the UK. Wightlink, meanwhile, will have to replace their tonnage on the Portsmouth-Fishbourne service and again lack any capital reserve for new tonnage. The larger companies, like Brittany Ferries and P&O Ferries, also will have to replace tonnage in the near future but with difficult market conditions and especially the proposed emissions policy of the EU, it appears in the short-term this is unlikely to happen.

If the proposed legislation by Brussels is implemented with regard to emissions from vessels, not only will it drive up the cost of travel but it will inevitably see the reduction of ferry services, especially on the North Sea and western sector of Britain.

There are early signs of recovery of the UK economy and likewise in 'Euroland' but the levels of passenger traffic are unlikely to return to that at the turn of this century.

As usual this publication brings you a comprehensive list of all information on all ferry operators in the UK and Europe and includes a detailed list of all ships that have been withdrawn in the last 12 months.

Miles Cowsill
Managing Editor

a **guide** to using
this book

A GUIDE TO USING THIS BOOK

Sections Listing is in seven sections. *Section 1* - Services from Great Britain and Ireland to the Continent and between Great Britain and Ireland (including services to/from the Isle of Man and Channel Islands), *Section 2* - Domestic services within Great Britain and Ireland, *Section 3* - Freight-only services from Great Britain and Ireland and domestic routes, *Section 4* - Minor vehicle ferries in Great Britain and Ireland (chain and cable ferries etc), *Section 5* - Major passenger-only operators, *Section 6* - Major car ferry operators in Northern Europe, *Section 7* - Companies not operating regular services possessing vehicle ferries which may be chartered or sold to other operators.

Order The company order within each section is alphabetical. Note that the definite article and words meaning 'company' or 'shipping company' (eg. 'AG', 'Reederei') do not count. However, where this is part of a ship's name it does count. Sorting is by normal English convention eg. 'Å' is treated the same as 'A' and comes at the start, not as a separate character which comes at the end of the alphabet as is the Scandinavian convention. Where ships are numbered, order is by number whether the number is expressed in Arabic or Latin digits.

Listing of Ships When a ship owned by a company listed in this book is on charter to another company listed, then she is shown under the company which operates her. When a ship owned by a company listed in this book is on charter to another company not listed, then she is shown under the company which owns her.

IMO Number All ships of 100t or greater (except vessels solely engaged in fishing, ships without mechanical means of propulsion (eg. chain ferries), pleasure yachts, ships engaged on special service (eg. lightships), hopper barges, hydrofoils, air cushion vehicles, floating docks and structures classified in a similar manner, warships and troopships, wooden ships) are required to be registered by the International Maritime Organisation (IMO), an agency of the United Nations. The number is retained by the ship throughout her life, however much the vessel is rebuilt. This number is now required to be displayed on the ship externally and on top so that it can be read from the air. The scheme is administered by Lloyd's Register-Fairplay, who maintain a database of all ships in excess of 100t (with some exceptions), not just those classified through them.

Company Information This section gives general information regarding the status of the company. That is, nationality, whether it is public or private sector and whether it is part of a larger group.

Management The Managing Director and Marketing Director or Manager of each company are listed. Where these posts do not exist, other equivalent people are listed. Where only initials are given, that person is, as far as is known, male.

Address This is the address of the company's administrative headquarters. In the case of some international companies, British and overseas addresses are given.

Telephone and Fax Numbers are expressed as follows: + [*number*] (this is the international dialling code which is dialled in combination with the number dialled for international calls (00 in the UK, Ireland and most other European countries); it is not used for calling within the country), ([*number*]) (this is the number which precedes area codes when making long-distance domestic calls - it is not dialled when calling from another country or making local calls (not all countries have this)), [*number*] (this is the rest of the number including, where appropriate, the area dialling code). UK '08' numbers are sometimes not available from overseas and the full number must be dialled in all circumstances.

Internet Email addresses and **Website** URLs are given where these are available; the language(s) used is shown. The language listed first is that which appears on the home page when accessed from a UK based computer; the others follow in alphabetical order. In a few cases Email facility is only available through the Website. To avoid confusion, there is no other punctuation on the Internet line.

Routes operated After each route there are, in brackets, details of 1 normal journey time, 2 regular vessel(s) used on the route (number as in list of vessels) and 3 frequencies (where a number per day is given, this relates to return sailings). In the case of freight-only sailings which operate to a regular schedule, departure times are given where they have been supplied. Please note that times are subject to quite frequent change and cancellation.

Winter and Summer In this book, Winter generally means the period between October and Easter while Summer means Easter to October. The peak Summer period is generally June, July and August. In Scandinavia, the Summer peak ends in mid-August whilst in the UK it starts rather later and generally stretches into the first or second week of September. Dates vary according to operator.

Spelling The convention is used in respect of town and country names is that English names are used for towns and areas of countries where such names exist (eg. Gothenburg rather than Göteborg) and English names for countries (eg. Germany rather than Deutschland). Otherwise local names are used, accented as appropriate. In a few cases, English names have slipped out of common usage and the local name is more commonly used in Britain, ie Dunkerque not Dunkirk, Helsingør not Elsinore and Vlissingen not Flushing. Many towns in Finland have both Finnish and Swedish names; we have used the Finnish name except in the case of Åland which is a Swedish-speaking area. In the case of Danish towns, the alternative use of 'å' or 'aa' follows local convention. The following towns, islands and territories are expressed using their English names - the local name is shown following: Antwerp - Antwerpen/Anvers, Fyn - Funen, Genoa - Génova, Ghent - Gent, Gothenburg - Göteborg, Hook of Holland - Hoek van Holland, Jutland - Jylland, Copenhagen - København, Ostend - Oostende, Oporto - Porto, Seville - Sevilla, Sealand - Sjælland and Venice - Venezia.

Terms The following words mean *'shipping company'* in various languages: Redereja (Latvian), Rederi (Danish, Norwegian, Swedish), Rederij (Dutch), Reederei (German) and Zegluga (Polish). The following words mean *'limited company'*: AB - Aktiebolaget (Swedish) (Finnish companies who use both the Finnish and Swedish terms sometimes express it as Ab), AG - Aktiengesellschaft (German), AS - Aksjeselskap (Norwegian), A/S - Aktie Selskabet (Danish), BV - Besloten Vennootschap (Dutch), GmbH - Gesellschaft mit beschränkter Haftung (German), NV - Naamloze Vennootschap (Dutch), Oy - (Finnish), Oyj - (Finnish (plc)) and SA - Société Anonyme (French).

Types of Ferry

These distinctions are necessarily general and many ships will have features of more than one category.

Car Ferry Until about 1970, most vehicle ferries were primarily designed for the conveyance of cars and their passengers and foot passengers. Little regard was paid to the conveyance of lorries and trailers, since this sort of traffic had not begun to develop. Few vessels of this type are still in service.

Multi-purpose Ferry From about 1970 onwards vehicle ferries began to make more provision for freight traffic, sharing the same ship with passengers and cars. Features usually include higher vehicle decks, often with retractable mezzanine decks, enabling two levels of cars or one level of freight and coaches, and separate facilities (including cabins on quite short crossings) for freight drivers.

Cruise Ferry In the 1980s the idea of travelling on a ferry, not just to get from A to B but for the pleasure of the travel experience, became more and more popular and ferries were built with increasingly luxurious and varied passenger accommodation. Such vessels also convey cars and freight but the emphasis is on passenger accommodation with a high level of berths (sometimes providing berths for all passengers).

Ro-pax Ferry A vessel designed primarily for the carriage of freight traffic but which also carries a limited number of ordinary passengers. Features generally include a moderate passenger capacity - up to about 500 passengers - and a partly open upper vehicle deck. Modern ro-pax vessels are becoming increasingly luxurious with facilities approaching those of a cruise ferry.

Ro-ro Ferry A vessel designed for the conveyance of road freight, unaccompanied trailers and containers on low trailers (known as 'Mafis' although often made by other manufacturers). Some such vessels have no passenger accommodation but the majority can accommodate up to 12 passengers - the maximum allowed without a passenger certificate. On routes where there is a low level of driver-accompanied traffic (mainly the longer ones), ordinary passengers, with or without cars, can sometimes be conveyed. On routes with a high level of driver-accompanied traffic, passenger capacity will sometimes be higher but facilities tend to be geared to the needs of freight drivers eg. lounge with video, high level of cabins on routes of three hours or more.

Con-ro Many ro-ro vessels are capable of having ISO (International Standards Organisation) containers crane-loaded on the upper 'weather' deck. In this book the term con-ro applies only to vessels whose upper deck can only take containers and has no vehicle access.

Fast Ferry Streamlined vessel of catamaran or monohull construction, speed in excess of 30 knots, water jet propulsion, generally aluminium-built but some have steel hulls, little or no freight capacity and no cabins.

Timescale Although the book goes to press in July 2013, I have sought to reflect the situation as it will exist in early Summer 2013 with regard to the introduction of new ships or other known changes. Vessels due to enter service after July 2013 are shown as '**Under Construction**'. The book is updated at all stages of the production process where this is feasible, although major changes once the text has been paginated are not possible; there is also a 'Late News' section on page 216 for changes which cannot be incorporated into the text.

List of vessels

NO (A)	GROSS TONNAGE (B)	SERVICE SPEED (KNOTS)	NUMBER OF PASSENGERS			VEHICLE ACCESS DECK (D)	IMO NUMBER
1 NAME	‡26433t 87	22.0k	150m 290P	650C	100L	BA2 UK	1234567
NAME	YEAR BUILT	LENGTH OVERALL	VEHICLE (C) DECK CAPACITY	FLAG (E)			

(A) » = fast ferry, • = vessel laid up, F = freight-only vessel (max 12 passengers), F‡ = freight-only vessel (with passenger certificate), p = passenger-only vessel

(B) C = Cars, L = Lorries (**15m**), T = Trailers (**13.5m**), r = can also take rail wagons, - = No figure quoted.

(C) B = Bow, A = Aft, S = Side, Q = Quarterdeck, R = Slewing ramp, 2 = Two decks can be loaded at the same time, C = Vehicles must be crane-loaded aboard, t = turntable ferry.

(D) The following abbreviations are used:

AG	= Antigua and Barbuda	EE	= Estonia	LU	= Luxembourg	PT	= Portugal
BB	= Barbados	ES	= Spain	LT	= Lithuania	PL	= Poland
BE	= Belgium	FO	= Faroes	LV	= Latvia	RU	= Russia
BM	= Bermuda	FI	= Finland	MI	= Marshall Islands	SG	= Singapore
BS	= Bahamas	FR	= France			SE	= Sweden
CY	= Cyprus	GI	= Gibraltar	MT	= Malta	UK	= United Kingdom
DE	= Germany	IM	= Isle of Man	NL	= Netherlands		
DK	= Denmark	IT	= Italy	NO	= Norway		
		IR	= Irish Republic	PA	= Panama		

In the notes ships are in CAPITAL LETTERS, shipping lines and other institutions are in *italics*.

Capacity In this book, capacities shown are the maxima. Sometimes vessels operate at less than their maximum passenger capacity due to reduced crewing or to operating on a route on which they are not permitted to operate above a certain level. Car and lorry/trailer capacities are the maximum for either type. The two figures are not directly comparable. Some parts of a vessel may allow cars on two levels to occupy the space that a trailer or lorry occupies on one level, some may not; some parts of a vessel with low headroom may only be accessible to cars. All figures have to be approximate.

Ownership The ownership of many vessels is very complicated. Some are actually owned by finance companies and banks, some by subsidiary companies of the shipping lines, some by subsidiary companies of a holding company of which the shipping company is also a subsidiary and some by companies which are jointly owned by the shipping company and other interests like a bank, set up specifically to own one ship or a group of ships. In all these cases the vessel is technically chartered to the shipping company. However, in this book, only those vessels chartered from one shipping company to another or from a ship-owning company unconnected with the shipping line are recorded as being on charter. Vessels are listed under the current operator rather than the owner. Charter is 'bareboat' (without crew) unless otherwise stated. If chartered with crew, vessels are 'time-chartered'.

Gross Tonnage This is a measure of enclosed capacity rather than weight, based on a formula of one gross ton = 100 cubic feet. Even small alterations can alter the gross tonnage. Under old measurement systems, the capacity of enclosed car decks was not included but, under the 1969 Convention, all vessels laid down after 1982 have been measured by a new system which includes enclosed vehicle decks as enclosed space, thereby considerably increasing the tonnage of vehicle ferries. Under this Convention, from 1st January 1995 all vessels were due to be re-measured under this system. Tonnages quoted here are, where possible, those given by the shipping companies themselves.

The following people are gratefully thanked for their assistance with this publication, many of them in ferry companies in the UK and abroad: John Bryant, Cees de Bijl, Andrew Cooke, Matthew Davies, Ian Hall, William Mayes, Willie Mackay, Matthew Punter, Pekka Ruponen, Ian Smith (The Camrose Organisation) and Gomer Press.

Whilst every effort has been made to ensure that the facts contained here are correct, neither the publishers nor the writer can accept any responsibility for errors contained herein. We would, however, appreciate comments from readers, which we will endeavour to reflect in the next edition which we plan to publish in summer 2014.

HAPPY BIRTHDAY, HURTIGRUTEN!

On 2nd July 2013 the Hurtigruten officially celebrated its 120th birthday. From its modest beginnings in 1893, when Captain Richard With established the service (literally the 'fast route') as a year round transport link between the north and south of Norway, it has grown out of all recognition, revolutionising the infrastructure and communication for those who live along the 'world's most beautiful coastline' between Bergen and Kirkenes which has made Norway a magnet for international tourism.

Now in the hands of Hurtigruten ASA, the Coastal Express or Hurtigruten (the names are interchangeable) generates an annual turnover of approximately NOK 3.5 billion (£400m), employing around 1,600 persons. The company currently operates 11 ships to provide a daily service offering a broad and unique range of transport for both local travellers and international guests. In addition, the 'explorer' ship *Fram* (2007) cruises both Greenland and Svalbard between May and September before migrating to the Southern Hemisphere and Antarctica for her November to February itineraries.

The Hurtigruten's early history has been well documented; the rich herring fisheries industry of the Vesterålen and Lofoten Islands had, as early as the 1860s, petitioned for better transport services in order to distribute their catch more efficiently. Growing pressure led on 10th November 1881 to the formation of Det Vesteraalens Dampskibsselskap (VDS) based at Stokmarknes, by Captain Richard With, who raised 4,000 kroner to purchase the steamship *Arendal*, renaming it *Vesteraalen*.

By 1890 the *Vesteraalen* was becoming a victim of its own success as she was now far too small for the traffic on offer. Finding nothing suitable in the second hand tonnage market VDS ordered a new and larger combined passenger and cargo vessel from Akers Mek, Oslo which was delivered in January 1891. She, too, was named *Vesteraalen*.

That same year August Kreigsman Gran, national steamship advisor for Norway, began to actively promote the idea of an express service between Trondheim and Hammerfest. There were a number of factors behind this submission. The growth of the 'kombinerte' (cargo/passenger/mail) services meant

Richard With *(Trond G Johnson/Hurtigruten ASA)*

Vesteraalen (1891) *(Hurtigruten ASA)*

Lofoten (1932) *(Hurtigruten ASA)*

Erling Jarl (1949) *(Mike Bent)*

Lofoten (1964) *(Mike Bent)*

that there were now 58 ports between Bergen and Hammerfest (48 of which were north of Trondheim), as a consequence travel was very slow as operators wanted to call at as many ports as possible in order to maximise their profits. The opening of the Christiania (Oslo) to Trondheim Railway in 1880 meant that the two cities were now only 12 hours apart and travellers now wanted to see this improvement translated further north. For freight businesses the protracted sailing times also tended to reduce the value of perishable goods, particularly fish. By limiting the calls to nine intermediate ports it was felt that such a service could succeed.

Det Nordenfjeldske Dampskibsselskab (NFDS) and Det Bergenske Dampskibsselskab (BDS) were offered the route by Gran, but turned it down on the grounds that sailing during darkness in such stormy waters was too risky. At that time only two marine charts existed and there were only 28 lighthouses north of Trondheim. VDS, however, were willing to take up the challenge. Captain Richard With had, with his pilot, Anders Holte, kept accurate records of courses, speeds and times taken to sail the route and was confident that such a service was viable. The *Vesteraalen* underwent a hasty rebuild with additional cabins and a spacious mailroom, raising her tonnage to 623 gross tons.

On 2nd July 1893, just after 08.00 the *Vesteraalen* departed the Brattøra Quay, Trondheim, for Hammerfest, with intermediate calls scheduled for Rørvik, Brønnøysund, Sandnessjøen, Bodø, Svolvær, Lødingen, Harstad, Tromsø and Skjervøy. She arrived at Hammerfest some 67½ hours later on Wednesday, 5th July at 03.30, some thirty minutes ahead of schedule. The 'Express' had been born! The following year, 1894, both NFDS and BDS joined the venture (the contract now extended until 30th June 1898) as a complementary service, each providing one ship every alternate year. Gradually the service developed in both importance and frequency; Bergen became the southern terminus, whilst northwards it was extended beyond Hammerfest and on to Kirkenes.

No new ships were built during the first decade and a half of the Hurtigruten operation; the shipping companies preferring to cascade older vessels on to the route. The Coastal Express with its all year round service was still quite understandably viewed as a high risk operation. Only after suffering war losses between 1914 and 1918 did ship owners actually start to insure their vessels. Older ships were obviously more expendable than younger ones.

It was not until 1909 that the first of four new purpose built ships (each approximately 1,000 gross tons; 200 feet) were introduced; the *Richard With* (VDS), *Midnatsol* (BDS), *Polarlys* (BDS) and *Finmarken* (VDS). All were to have long and distinguished careers. Whilst the *Richard With* was torpedoed and sunk off Rolfsøya, north of Hammerfest with much loss of life in September 1941, the others survived both World Wars: the *Midnatsol* until October 1950 when she was sold for scrapping in Antwerp; the *Polarlys* (taken out of service a year later), was to have a new career as the Royal Norwegian Navy's KNM *Valkyrie* acting as a 'mother ship' to their MTB fleet, finally being scrapped in 1963, a career which lasted 51 years. The *Finmarken*, withdrawn in 1956, also saw further service as the youth training ship *Gann* until 1960, when she was scrapped in the Netherlands. However, in 2003, some of her furnishings and rooms which had been sold on were returned to Norway and now feature prominently at the Hurtigruten Museum in Stokmarknes; her spirit lives on!

In 1919, after the First World War, the Coastal Express was enhanced with a sixth weekly round trip. With this expansion came a new company to the route, Det Stavangerske Dampskibsselskab (DSD). Their involvement meant a further extension of the route to Stavanger and although this ceased in 1936 the company remained as part of the Hurtigruten organisation until 1979.

Only five new builds came on stream during the inter-war years; the *Dronning Maud* (NFDS 1924), *Sanct Svithun* (DSD 1925), *Prinsesse Ragnhild* (NFDS 1931), *Lofoten* (VDS 1932) and *Nordstjernen* (BDS 1937). Whilst each was a further development of the pre war quartet (1,500 gross tons; 250 feet) all were still coal fired. A daily service was finally introduced in 1936, made possible by the Narvik based Det Ofotens Dampskibsselskab (ODS) joining the consortium, using the smaller coastal ship *Nordnorge* (1924) as their contribution. This small company was later to play a significant role in moulding the Hurtigruten into the enterprise we know today.

The Second World War was to have a devastating effect on the Coastal Express as no less than 14 ships were to be lost. Of the inter-war new builds only the *Lofoten* and *Nordstjernen* would survive. As the fortunes of war changed the service was reduced to five per week; two from Bergen and three from

Trondheim, all terminating at Tromsø. Northwards, there was a replacement operation, the Erstatningshurtigruten, using smaller local craft.

After hostilities a number of ships from other routes were pressed into service. They possessed an incredible range of ages, dimensions and capacities making the whole service quite inefficient as schedules had to be drawn up to match the performance of the slowest ship. The new building programme in 1946 set out to address this lack of standardisation, but with raw materials in short supply, it would be three years before the first of the new builds would arrive from Italy. Cantieri Navale Riuniti dell'Adriatico, Ancona, Italy, was awarded the first contract for four ships, which was followed by a similar one with Aalborg Verft, Aalborg, Denmark, for a further three ships.

The first of the four near identical 'Italia-Båtene' was the *Erling Jarl* built for NFDS. She was handed over in August 1949, followed by the *Midnatsol* (BDS), *Vesterålen* (VDS) and *Sanct Svithun* (DSD). Two class ships (2,098 gross tons and 286 feet), their prime mover was an 8-cylinder 2,500 bhp Fiat diesel, driving a four-bladed Ka-Me-Wa variable pitch propeller and giving a service speed of 16.5 knots. Today such propellers are the norm, but when the *Midnatsol* departed from Bergen on her maiden Hurtigruten voyage in December 1949, it was reported that the variable pitch propeller had inadvertently been left in the 'going astern' position with the ship having to drop both anchors very quickly in order to avoid ramming the quay behind her! The quartet did gain a reputation for being notorious 'rollers' and many a journey could become rather too lively for passenger comfort.

The 'Aalborg Trio', *Nordlys* (BDS), *Håkon Jarl* (NFDS) and *Polarlys* (BDS) followed in 1951/2 and whilst, similar in design, were far better sea boats. The building programme didn't stop there; for in 1956 a new *Nordstjernen* (BDS) was delivered from Blohm and Voss, Hamburg, replacing her 1937 built namesake which had foundered in the Raftsundet in September 1954.

The *Nordstjernen* was very similar to the Aalborg trio, whilst two other Coastal Express vessels, *Finnmarken* (VDS) and *Ragnvald Jarl* (NFDS), which were being built concurrently at the same Hamburg shipyard were designed with the engine room located towards the stern which released more space for cabins. Their radical appearance took a lot of people by surprise invoking a good deal of adverse comment. Both, however, were excellent sea boats, very practical and easier to maintain, but many found it hard to get used to their squat streamlined funnel astern and amidships foremast.

The *Harald Jarl* which followed in 1960, was a larger (2,568 gross tons) and better proportioned version with a combined mast and funnel positioned just aft of amidships. These improvements were to be further developed in the next three Coastal Express ships ordered in February 1962 from Akers Mek at Oslo and Bergen. However, before these were delivered, in late October of that year, there was the disastrous loss of the *Sanct Svithun*, off course and on the rocks at Nordøyan, near Rørvik, 42 losing their lives. It shook the whole of Norway, and even today, over 50 years later, the same questions are still being raised: how could such an accident happen with modern navigational aids and under normal weather conditions? How could experienced people not notice that the ship was on the wrong course? Sadly, the only people who could answer the questions, the duty pilot, mate and helmsman, all perished in the incident.

The new *Lofoten* (VDS) and *Nordnorge* (ODS) were constructed by Akers at their Oslo shipyard with the *Kong Olav* (DSD) built at their Bergen facility. The latter two ships sported a dummy funnel with the engine exhaust discharged through the mainmast located aft. There is little doubt that the *Kong Olav* in both her DSD and later VDS funnel livery was probably the finest looking of all the first generation post war motor ships on the Hurtigruten. Their delivery in 1964 signified the end of a 15 ship regeneration programme and at only 15 years, the *Erling Jarl* was now the oldest in the fleet. It would be another 18 years before any more new ships would enter service on the Hurtigruten.

Post war Hurtigruten ships in general have a reputation for longevity: other than the *Sanct Svithun*, all of the 'Italia-Båtene' and Aalborg Trio' would see over 30 years service; the *Polarlys* managing 40 years before seeing another decade of use as Mercy Ships' floating medical centre 'Caribbean Mercy'. The *Håkon Jarl* is still afloat, but awaiting probable scrapping, having spent her last years as a (somewhat disfigured) hotel/restaurant in Antwerp.

Of the 1956 trio, the *Finnmarken*, with 37 years of service behind her, is preserved out of the water as Norway's largest land based museum exhibit at the Hurtigruten Museum in Stokmarknes. Her sister

Narvik (1982) (John Bryant)

Trollfjord (2002) (Bryan Kennedy)

Richard With (1993) (*Bryan Kennedy*)

Polarlys (1996) (*Mike Louagie*)

Nordlys (1994) *(Dennis Tricker/Hurtigruten ASA)*

Nordstjernen (1956) *(Hurtigruten ASA)*

ship, the *Ragnvald Jarl* (39 years of service) still sails as the *Sjøkurs*, a sea cadet training ship, based at Kristiansand.

The *Nordstjernen* is the great survivor, designated as a 'cultural heritage' vessel and was only retired in late 2012 after an incredible 56 years on the Hurtigruten. She will continue to grace the fjords, sailing for Indre Nordhordland Dampbåtlag of Bergen.

The *Harald Jarl* too remains active, for having completed forty years service, she was refurbished as the cruise ship *Andrea* for Elegant Cruises and today operates as Premier Cruises *Serenissima*.

Of the final trio of ships, the *Lofoten* also enjoys 'cultural heritage' status and remains in Hurtigruten service, still in excellent condition and provides a unique travel experience. The *Kong Olav* and *Nordnorge* too had over 30 years on the Coastal Express and whilst the latter is no more, the former sadly languishes in the Southern Thailand Anchorage off Ranong, out of use since 1997 after a failed plan to use her as a cruise ship.

Despite all the new ships the performance of the Hurtigruten was not good. Freight levels were down and air services had captured most of the business travellers who hitherto had used the coastal steamers; even light mail now went by air. The transition of freight carriage from load-on load-off shipping services to roll-on roll-off ferry services led to far greater flexibility with drastically reduced journey times. Pallet loading, using forklift trucks driven on and off vessels via doors in the sides of the ship's hull, had also reduced turn-round times in port and labour costs. The Hurtigruten ships were now at a distinct disadvantage and indeed, from a cargo handling point of operation, they had been out of date from the day they were built. In addition, some of the fleet were beginning to show not just wear and tear but their overall standard of accommodation was well below what could be experienced elsewhere.

New ships therefore of similar size and design were perhaps not the right solution and a radical rethink was needed. With link spans only suitable at the major ports, the solution lay in having large doors in the sides of the ships' hulls, through which vehicles and cargo could be loaded. On-board lifts would be able to cope with any variations in height between quay and vehicle deck. Larger cargo could be craned onto a container deck. This concept emerged in the 'mid generation' ships of the early 1980s.

In 1978, DSD, who were facing financial problems, sold their *Kong Olav* to VDS. The sale triggered off a takeover bid when, in great secrecy, Troms Fylkes Dampskibsselskap (TFDS) approached BDS with an offer to purchase their four Hurtigruten ships. In a similar position to DSD, the Bergen group felt that their resources could be better utilised in other areas of their business.

During 1980, NFDS were also looking for a buyer for their *Håkon Jarl*. After negotiations with Det Saltens Dampskibsselskab (SDS) fell through, ODS purchased the ship. At the same time NFDS transferred its new Hurtigruten contract to ODS, whilst still continuing to operate the *Ragnvald Jarl* and the *Harald Jarl*.

The wheel had turned full circle, as for the first time since 1894, control of Hurtigruten operations was now with northern coastal companies. The new mix of Hurtigruten operators promised fresh ideas and a greater commitment to maintaining the service. ODS, VDS and TFDS were in a much more suitable position geographically to understand and cater for the transport needs of communities in the far north. It was a new era. No doubt Richard With would have had a smile on his face.

January 1st 1983 was a sad day in the history of the Hurtigruten as all on-board post offices were closed, and the transport of mail by sea continued only where no alternative existed. However, in the 1990s the Coastal Express ships were once more allowed to fly the postal flag in recognition of the special status the Hurtigruten has in Norway.

Before that, the first two of the 'mid generation' ships to entered service in 1982, the *Midnatsol* (BDS) followed by the *Narvik* (ODS) and in 1983, the *Vesterålen* (VDS). The ships were quite unlike anything seen before, at 4,131 gross tons (1,300 dwt) with an overall length of 108.55m (357 feet) they were in effect twice the size of their predecessors with three times the cargo capacity. Extremely functional in design they were hardly likely to win many plaudits, with the exhaust uptakes concealed in a box-like structure on the starboard side aft of the superstructure, the ships looked unbalanced.

It was not long before the complaints poured in, the accommodation was just too small! The restaurant received the greatest amount of adverse comment as, on busy days in summer, up to three sittings had to be provided.

From the winter of 1987/8, at a cost of NOK 40 million per ship, each was sent to Motorenwerke at Bremerhaven for a prefabricated passenger accommodation module to be fitted over the aft cargo deck. Two new funnel casings were constructed, one being a dummy, this gave the ships a better balance. The restaurant was doubled in size and in the new stern section there was a bar and lounge as well as further cabin accommodation. The ships now measured 6,167 gross tons.

On 1st January 1988, ODS merged with VDS to form Det Ofotens og Vesteraalens Dampskibsselskab (OVDS). The upshot was that the *Vesterålen* lost her attractive blue, white and black funnel livery together with the distinctive blue stripe along her hull. OVDS then sold the *Lofoten* to Finnmark Fylkesrederi (FFR), bringing in another company to the Hurtigruten table. However, this was short lived as only eight years later the ship was resold to OVDS.

Whilst all three ships have performed reliably, only the *Vesterålen* remains in service on the Hurtigruten. Fitting her with stabilizers is seen as a sure sign that she will remain on the route for some years to come. The *Midnatsol* was withdrawn from service after only 20 years to be replaced by a new ship of the same name; she did briefly reappear in 2005-07 as the *Lyngen* to cover a tonnage shortage but now sails as the expedition ship *National Geographic Explorer*. Similarly, the *Narvik* was sold at the end of 2006 to the Young Christian Seafarers Association (Rogaland Videregående Sjøaspirantskole), Stavanger and renamed ms *Gann* which provides training for young mariners as well as undertaking public summer cruises.

It was becoming clear as the 1990s began that if the Hurtigruten were to survive then it would have to markedly expand its tourism role and to provide suitable facilities and experiences accordingly. The 1950s built ships were in urgent need of replacement and a whole decade had passed since any new ships had been ordered. Passenger numbers had fallen from well over 500,000 in the early 1970s to half this amount in 1988. A fresh specification was drawn up with Meyer Werft (Papenburg) submitting the successful design. The actual building contract went to Volkswerft GmbH Stralsund, based in the former East Germany, whose bid was NOK 100 million per ship lower than any tender from a Norwegian shipyard.

The three (11,204 gross tons, 121.8m length) 'new generation' vessels, *Kong Harald* (TFDS), *Richard With* (OVDS) and *Nordlys* (TFDS), entered service in 1993/94 and made an immediate impact setting new standards both in terms of passenger comfort and interior design, ushering in a new era in Hurtigruten operation. One class ships, with spacious communal areas, bars, observation lounge, cafeteria, restaurant and conference rooms, no less than 212 of their 230 en suite cabins have outside views.

Such was their impact that three more ships in the series were ordered from the Ulsteinvik (Norway) shipyards; *Polarlys* (TFDS), *Nordkapp* and *Nordnorge* (both OVDS) being delivered in 1996/97. In 1998 passenger numbers were recorded at 441,000, a 64% rise over the 268,000 recorded in 1992.

Capitalising on this success, permission was given for a further trio of new ships which became known as the 'millennium class' and delivered in 2002/03. Whilst the *Finnmarken* (OVDS) was an enlarged version of the 'new generation' class vessels, the *Trollfjord* and *Midnatsol* were quite different, built very much with the wider cruise market in mind. In addition, both the *Finnmarken* and *Midnatsol* can serve as hospital ships having the capability to be at sea for extended periods.

The introduction of these new ships gave OVDS the opportunity to deploy the *Nordnorge* on a programme of Antarctic cruises each winter from 2002/3 through to 2006/7. For 2005/6 and 2006/7 she was joined by the *Nordkapp*, their meeting together in Antarctica was always one of the highlights. Positioning cruises were also available as the ships 'migrated' from north to south and vice versa.

The success of the Antarctic venture encouraged OVDS in 2005 to order a dedicated 'explorer' ship suited for such waters. This was to be the *Fram*; in essence a smaller version of the '*Finnmarken*' but with the capability, if ever necessary, to operate on the Hurtigruten. However, before she could enter service, OVDS and TFDS merged on 1st March 2006, to form Hurtigruten ASA. Named after Fridtjof Nansen's famous polar vessel, the *Fram* was built at Fincantieri's shipyard near Trieste and delivered as scheduled on 23rd April 2007. Her interiors reflect the culture and language of Greenland (where she shares her

Trollfjord (2002) *(Knut Jensen/Hurtigruten ASA)*

Nordkapp (1996) *(Trym Ivar Bergsmo/Hurtigruten ASA)*

Fram (2007) *(Tomas Mauch/Hurtigruten ASA)*

summers with further cruises around Svalbard); the public areas bear Inuit words of symbolic meaning, for example; Qilak (sky) Lounge, Imaq (sea) Restaurant, Nunami (land) Lobby. Having completed her final Greenland cruise, she then sails south to begin her Antarctic season based on Ushuaia, Southern Chile. The *Fram* enjoys high rates of occupancy particularly on her Antarctic cruises, varying her European ports of call each year on the positioning voyages between the Arctic and Antarctic regions and vice versa.

Today's Hurtigruten ASA operation fully recognises the mission and duty it has which extends well beyond just bringing tourists to its destinations. The ships play an important role along the Norwegian coast every single day and are an integral part of the coastal community from which it gains its livelihood. Passenger numbers have stabilised around the 450,000 mark of which 80% are port to port travellers; in many places the Hurtigruten service is still the quickest means of transport.

Operating all year round inevitably brings issues of how to deal with over capacity outside of the peak summer months, hence Hurtigruten's strong emphasis on the 'Hunting the Light' (winter), 'Arctic Awakening' (spring) and 'Autumn Gold' experiences. Not surprisingly, the most important markets are to be found in Germany, Norway, the UK, the USA, France and Sweden. The conference element, including two and three day 'short hop' packages and even 'off peak' whole ship charters is also strongly promoted aimed at corporate business, public sector groups and associations across Norway.

Each year in excess of 100,000 tonnes of freight is carried by the Hurtigruten ships along the Norwegian coast, reducing the burden on the road network by the equivalent of about 10,000 lorries per year. Rising environmental awareness in the community has seen growing numbers using the Hurtigruten for freight, particularly the large grocery chains on the section north of Tromsø; the only effective option open to the coastal population for the regular transport of fresh produce and products.

Now a very much slimmer organisation than before, having divested itself of other transport services (local ferries and buses) and with new headquarters in Tromsø, the company is able to concentrate solely on its core businesses. Hurtigruten ASA's current contract with the Norwegian Government runs until 31st December 2019, for daily departures from all the 34 ports of call throughout the year, with the government having an option to extend the contract for one year after it expires. The eleven ships on the route are scheduled to make no less than 25,000 port calls every year. It is a demanding business as weather and unforeseen incidents can play a major part in the company's fortunes.

The high regard in which the Hurtigruten is held by both employees and public alike, was ably demonstrated in June 2011 when the Norwegian Broadcasting Corporation (NRK) dedicated its second-largest TV channel to 134 hours of live transmission of the *Nordnorge's* voyage from Bergen to Kirkenes. The weather was almost perfect, thousands came to greet the ship, and NRK2, which normally attracts four per cent of Norwegian viewers, suddenly became the country's biggest TV channel with a 36 per cent share.

Under the helm of its new CEO, Daniel Skjeldam, Hurtigruten ASA will continue to evolve; the fine tuning of length of stays at ports, introducing new experiences as needs change and there is even the hint of one or two new builds before 2020. Notwithstanding the current challenging market, the company believe that there is a strong basis for growth and for favourable progress in the time to come.

John Bryant

THE BALTIC'S SAVING GRACE
Spotlight Turku

The principal trans-Baltic service linking Stockholm and Helsinki has long been at the vanguard of European ferry developments and the stage for vibrant competition between the main rivals Silja and Viking Line over the years. This reached its zenith during the golden era of the cruiseferries in the 1980s when the booming economies of Scandinavia along with a determination to support local ship-building led to ever more superlative vessels arriving, culminating in the *Silja Serenade* and *Silja Symphony* in 1990/91.

The secondary route between Stockholm and Turku has always operated in something of the shadow of the main capital cities service. Although indubitably part of the same ferry industry ecosystem with ships frequently transferring between the two routes for both operators, since the route emerged during the early 1960s it has tended to receive less investment and attention. During the 1980s and early 1990s, the most significant new tonnage tended to go straight onto the Helsinki run and by the time each of the operators invested in Turku tonnage, the ships were usually out-classed by better developed fleetmates on the more southerly route.

However, this longstanding trend was abruptly and impressively halted in December 2010 when Viking Line announced a major new order with STX for the Turku service that was to become the largest Baltic cruiseferry to date. To be constructed at Turku, the €240m vessel would set new standards in luxury and design for the second decade of the 21st century. Additionally, and perhaps even more revolutionary is her power plant, making her the first large LNG fuelled ferry in the world. This vessel entered service as the *Viking Grace* on 13th January 2013 to critical acclaim, immediately focusing the attention on the Turku service and soon having a major impact on the passenger numbers and market share of the route. The *Viking Grace* not only represented the most significant ferry arrival in the region since the Silja twins more than two decades previously, but with most of the recent investment coming from the Estonian Tallink, she struck a blow for Finnish national pride, both for her builder as well as her owner.

Stockholm - Turku through the ages

Viking Line's involvement in the Stockholm – Turku service began in 1973, although the company had linked Mariehamn with a number of different mainland Swedish and Finnish ports since their early years in the late 1950s (notably Kapellskär on the edge of the Stockholm archipelago and Naantali near Turku). The company was founded by two Åland captains, Gunnar Eklund and Henning Rundberg, who purchased the former Southern Railways steamer *Dinard* to operate their new Vikinglinjen car ferry services out of Mariehamn. Simultaneously, Rederi AB Slite, a separate outfit founded by Carl Bertil Myrsten, established a rival operation. Eventually, the two operators – along with Rederi AB Sally, an existing company – established Viking Line as a marketing organization and the stage set for the development of the modern service that we see today. The role of Åland Islands as the hub of the trans-Baltic ferry system is, of course, driven by their unique tax-exempt status within the European Union, acting as one of the last outposts of duty free sales and which has fuelled the ferry industry in the region over the years.

Arguably, the birth of the modern, successful Viking Line network that we see today began on 2 May 1970 when Slite's *Apollo* entered service between Kapellskär, Mariehamn and Naantali. She wasn't Viking Line's first purpose-built car ferry, but she was the first of the 'Papenburg' series that not only set new standards on the cross-Baltic routes, but were so legion that they prompted their owners to establish new routes in order to drive utilization. Thus, not only were Viking Line services between Stockholm, Turku and Helsinki commenced, but the fuse was lit for the ferry war between them and Silja that lasted the best part of three decades.

In 1979, further major investment arrived in the form of the *Turella* and the following year, the *Rosella* and the *Viking Sally* which maintained the link until the arrival of the *Amorella* in 1988 and the *Kalypso* in 1990. During subsequent years, a series of economic woes, the bankruptcy of Slite and the calamitous sinking of the *Viking Sally* (as the *Estonia*) in 1994 put the entire ferry industry into recession. Viking soldiered on with the *Amorella* and her sister *Isabella* for most of this time, but Silja retained the edge on both routes. By the late 'noughties' the Viking Line pair were visibly ageing and when the *Galaxy* was cascaded onto Silja's Turku route by their new Estonian owners, it was clearly time for Viking Line to act.

The three-deck atrium on the starboard side of the vessel with striking modern illuminated lanterns

Seamore Champagne Lounge (*Viking Line*)

Looking out from the atrium (*Viking Line*)

Wellness Spa, deck 11 (*Viking Line*)

Reception desk and Conference facilities, deck 9 (*Viking Line*)

Building the *Viking Grace*

The Stockholm – Mariehamn – Turku route is possibly one of the most demanding ferry services in the world with the two ships at sea for twenty-four hours and operating the entire year, with a brief interlude for Christmas and annual docking. The ships serve four separate ports (including Långnäs on the night-time sailing). Not only that, but the route needs to accommodate a wide range of different passenger groups including overnighting minicruisers, day-only picnic-cruisers, regular port-to-port ferry passengers, plus a modicum of freight. The geography of the service is challenging, with the only open sea being a small stretch between Kapellskär and the approaches to Mariehamn; the remainder comprises a tortuous route through the archipelago between Sweden and Finland. On board, the ships feature the entirety of the Baltic cruiseferry offering including vast shopping complexes, increasingly spectacular show-lounges plus a variety of catering facilities to suit every palette and wallet.

The letter of intent for the *Viking Grace* was signed between Viking Line and STX in October 2010 and the order confirmed on 22 December. Right from the outset, the aim was to have the ship powered by LNG, although the order was dependent on European Union environmental grants being awarded. Although protracted, these were eventually forthcoming and therefore construction of "NB 1376" began at Turku on 28 September 2011 and her keel was laid on 6 March 2012. An option for a second vessel was initially negotiated, although this eventually expired and the contract became that of a single ship. The final design was heavily influenced by Mikael Backman, the new Viking Line CEO, who forced through a complete redesign from the prototype prior to construction commencing in order to ensure his company's new vessel was paradigm shifting in every way.

Wärtsilä were chosen to provide the revolutionary new gas engines. These would enable significant gains to be made in environmental credentials with greenhouse gases reduced by 15% and particle emissions virtually eliminated. Fuel for the new vessel was contracted to AGA which necessitated an entirely new infrastructure: the fuel itself is stored at Nynäshamn (south of Stockholm) and brought to the capital by road tanker where it is transferred to local storage at Värtahamnen. From there, it is bunkered onto the *Viking Grace* using the *Seagas*, a small tanker especially converted for the purpose. The gas tanks are situated at the stern of the vessel on deck 6 and are fairly prominent, particularly when viewed from the stern. The tanks are accompanied by a small, yet striking, slender, funnel which rakes to the stern.

The Finnish design agency dSign Vertti Kivi & Co were selected to create her public spaces and later in 2011 a competition was announced which eventually resulted in the name *Viking Grace* being selected, a break with tradition for Viking Line, but one which the *Viking XPRS* of 2008 had heralded. dSign were tasked with creating a striking new ferry interior unlike any previously seen in the region. The central objective was to move beyond the nautical pastiche that has been the design standard for much of the ferry industry (and in particular Viking Line) over the last few decades and to realise a genuinely contemporary interior space characterized by modern colours, fixtures and spaces.

It would be fair to say that Viking Line have essentially modernized the existing ferry format through design treatment rather than re-inventing it as the previous generation Silja flagships did. The *Viking Grace* concept remains broadly the same: three decks of passenger facilities including bars, restaurants, cafeterias and nightclubs interspersed with comfortable seating plus the mandatory spa and conference centres. Each represents a highly evolved design, yet overall the whole is very recognisable – albeit in a stunning décor that transforms the visual experience onboard. Of particular focus was the relationship between the interior of the vessel and the superlative passing scenery outside; extensive use was made of large windows throughout the passenger decks to ensure that the archipelago provided a continual backdrop. Viking Line and dSign also wanted to attract a younger clientele with the Baltic ferry market becoming over-reliant on the middle aged and middle class. To that extent, the concept represents a radical repositioning away from booze, dancing and buffets towards a more resort-orientated offering with the focus on a more holistic, 'rejuvenating' experience.

The new ship would pose heightened operational challenges both onboard and ashore. With a passenger complement of 2,800 and beds for 2,400, the turnaround in each port is massively tight, particularly at Stockholm at the end of her night crossing when there is just 50 minutes to clean the vessel. An army of 200 staff board at each port to assist with this task. Away from the hotel side of the operation, new loading arrangements had to be constructed at both Mariehamn and Långnäs, the former needing an entirely new berth and gangway across which a thousand 'picnic-cruisers' are shepherded during the 15 minute window

Buffet Aurora, deck 10 (*Viking Line*)

Club Vogue bar, deck 11 (*Viking Line*)

when both westbound and eastbound ships are in port and passengers transfer between the two to return to their port of embarkation.

On 10 August 2012, after less than a year of construction, the *Viking Grace* was launched at Turku. Several months of fit-out followed before the ship's fully-booked maiden voyage from Turku on 13 January 2013. The next Baltic revolution had arrived.

Onboard the amazing *Viking Grace*

The unique nature of the service was amply illustrated in early April whilst waiting to board the *Viking Grace* at Turku. It was a freezing cold Friday evening, shortly after the Easter weekend on a night that most British ferry services would struggle to command a load worth leaving port for. Yet in the ferry terminal, 2,800 Finns and Swedes, of all ages and demographics waited excitedly to board the new flagship. Boarding at night, one is immediately struck by dSign's *pièce de résistance*: the spectacular use of onboard lighting that creates a visually stunning effect across many of the public spaces.

The lower of the ship's three passenger decks (deck 9) hosts the reception area and conference facilities, both of which overlook a wide arcade at the lower of a large three-deck window down the port side with lanterns elevating up and down the void and changing colour over time. The majority of deck 9 is given over to a vast, U-shaped shopping centre offering a wide variety of products, including a well-appointed whisky concession. A teen zone is situated on this deck also.

Up a deck, on deck 10, the main 'Buffet Aurora' overlooks the bow, offering wonderful daytime views over the passing scenery through large floor-to-ceiling windows. This area is incredibly striking, with much use of backlit white panels and navy colouring. The server area in the centre is surrounded by seating nearer the windows which introduce a splash of yellow and purple colouring to the palette. The buffet serves breakfast, lunch and dinner *smörgåsbord* with the latter in particular being very well patronized over two sittings. The decidedly modern setting and very tightly apportioned food on offer somewhat detracted from the overall food credentials, but nonetheless, the range and ambience were second to none. Adjacent to the entrance, bottles (and boxes) of the high quality house wine could be purchased.

Moving astern through the port-side arcade, the next space is another teen zone, somewhat incongruously (and raucously) situated at the entrance to the Aurora. Beyond this, the 'Sweet & Salty' café is situated, offering a good range of daytime coffee and snacks and adjacent to a children's play area. Continuing astern, the vessel divides into two areas with the starboard comprising 'Retro Bar & Dancing', a somewhat bland area décor-wise that comes alive with all day karaoke and a night-time troubadour. The port side features the 'Rockmore' bar, another striking space making extensive use of black, metallic-effect, animal print seating and red backlighting. This segues into the 'Club Vogue', a split-level nightclub at the stern with large panoramic windows over the LNG tanks but with the focus on a large stage and dance area. The dominantly black colour scheme throughout is once again offset with lighting panels around the dance floor and on the ceilings. Club Vogue features two bars, one on each level.

Ascending to deck eleven and moving forward this time, the deck is broken by a large spa area with only a narrow passageway connecting Vogue to the forward spaces. The spa itself is arranged around two large semi-circular Jacuzzis that overlook a panoramic starboard window. In addition to the usual sauna and steam rooms, the centre also features a snow cave where hardy Scandinavians can shiver away their cares before plunging back into the more welcoming hot tub.

Health and wellness sated, it is time to continue forward where a second children's play area is found adjacent to 'Frank's', a casual restaurant, part diner, part food court. This venue, attractively decorated in beech effect, greys and lime, offers a range of affordable world cuisine including pizza, burgers and Asian although it is waiter-served rather than self-serve, the effect being somewhat undermined by the ketchup bottles on each table.

At the forward end of this deck is the superb 'Seamore' champagne lounge to port and the 'Oscar' à la carte overlooking the bow and to starboard. Seamore is decorated in muted greys and blues with the focal point being a grand piano, daintily played as we departed Stockholm at dawn. Oscar continues the theme, but reliant more on greys and blacks for its exceedingly elegant design.

Overall, the *Viking Grace* is a truly stunning vessel, but the daytime return crossing from Stockholm perhaps showed up her main (albeit minor) flaw: the visual experience is far better by night than by day, when she

Frank's Casual Dining, deck 11 (*Viking Line*)

Oscar a la carte, deck 11 (*Viking Line*)

Seamore Cocktail Bar, deck 11 (*Viking Line*)

Viking Grace sundeck (*Viking Line*)

Suite Romantic (*Viking Line*)

Stairwell (*Viking Line*)

can come across as slightly insipid, with heavy use of mid grey for many of the connecting public spaces. Indeed, during the day, there is a major contrast between the still-attractive key areas (notably the à la carte and the buffet) and the comparatively uninspiring thoroughfares and stairwells. And this criticism of the visual design is possibly symptomatic of broader layout issues also as the ship is really a collection of disparate spaces with no real flow or linkage between them. The *Viking Grace* lacks the feature space of the Silja and Color atria (perhaps quite rightly so, as there is little to be done to take these further). Yet she doesn't really hang together as a unified whole, other than at night when the use of striking illuminations creates a cohesive effect that vanishes during the day. The flow of the ship is disrupted in several surprising ways: the spa is a massive interruption to deck 11; there are video games in odd places; a walkway crosses a small dance floor in the Rockmore; the conference facility lacks any natural light. Perhaps this is the fundamental difficulty in trying to design a ship which is simultaneously facing in as well as out; unlike the Helsinki routes where the emphasis is on the destination, on the Turku services, the ships themselves are the big attraction; yet the vessels need to showcase not just their facilities (which the atria do well) but the passing scenery using large windows. Much of the central areas of decks 10 and 11 are taken up by the galleys with the passenger spaces wrapping around these to maximize window seating. When even the Jacuzzis need an outside window, it is unsurprising that something has to give.

The Future

Still, these are minor issues: what matters is that the *Viking Grace* attracts more passengers. And more passengers she is indeed attracting, reportedly doubling the old *Isabella*'s numbers on the same roster compared to 2012 although admittedly some of these will be cannibalised from other Viking ships. The introduction of the ship has been supported by a very high marketing spend to not only announce her arrival but also to reposition Viking Line's product towards the younger, more upmarket clientele. So far, the strategy appears to be working.

Not only have the passengers been coming, but so have the awards, with the *Viking Grace* picking up no fewer than five trophies from the annual Shippax awards, including for her environmental innovations and interior design.

Finally, it is evident that the *Viking Grace* story doesn't – cannot - end here. The current pairing of the stylish newcomer with the elderly *Amorella* is now one of the oddest couplings in Northern Europe and an order for "VG2" is presumably being actively considered, once the new arrival has settled down operationally. What impact a pair of trend-setting ships on the once secondary service has on the wider regional industry remains a question for the future, but it is clear that the latest chapter in this fascinating Viking saga has only just begun.

Matthew Punter

Loading via the stern doors, with the LNG tanks clearly visible (*Viking Line*)

Seagas refuels during a Stockholm layover (*Viking Line*)

REVIEW OF 2012 - BRITISH ISLES
EAST COAST & THAMES

Sea-Cargo's new *Sea-Cargo Express* entered service in October on the service from Aberdeen to the Norwegian West Coast. She was one of two vessels ordered in 2005 from Bharati Ratnagiri Ltd, Mumbai, India and was originally due to be delivered in 2006. A con-ro vessel with a side door for palletised loads, she replaced the 1979 built *SC Aberdeen*, the last 1970s built ro-ro operating on the North Sea.

In late April, DFDS Seaways reshuffled their North Sea Freight fleet, with the *Anglia Seaways* moving to the Zeebrugge – Rosyth service, replacing *Tor Finlandia* which moved to the Immingham – Cuxhaven route. However, her time on the twice weekly Scottish route was short lived as her slower speed made time-keeping difficult. The following month she was replaced by the chartered *Clipper Point* as part of a swap arrangement, with the *Anglia Seaways* going to Seatruck Ferries. In July, the *Tor Finlandia* returned to the route. During the year other Seatruck vessels were also chartered.

In June DFDS Seaways switched the three stretched Flensburg built ro-ros - *Tor Begonia*, *Freesia Seaways* and *Ficaria Seaways* - which were used on the Immingham - Gothenburg route - with the three un-stretched versions - *Tor Magnolia*, *Tor Petunia* and *Primula Seaways* used on the Gothenburg - Ghent service. Due to the recession and competition from new operator North Sea RoRo (which ceased operations in March 2013), traffic on the Immingham route had declined whilst traffic on the Ghent route was booming. Earlier in the year, trials proved that the longer vessels could navigate the lock at Terneuzen, used to access the canal which leads up to Ghent. In May 2013 the vessels reverted to their previous roles.

During the year there was talk of the Newcastle - Bergen and Stavanger service, withdrawn by DFDS Seaways in 2008, being revived. However, nothing materialised.

In April, P&O reduced the Middlesbrough - Zeebrugge service to a single ship operation, three times per week, operated by the chartered *Bore Song*. The 35 year old *European Trader*, which had shared the route with the much newer vessel, was withdrawn and sold to Turkish breakers. This followed the reduction of the Middlesbrough - Rotterdam service to a single ship operation the previous year.

Cobelfret Ferries second newbuild, the *Severine*, entered service in March and inaugurated a two ship overnight service on the Ipswich - Rotterdam route. However, in August the service was ended. Shortly afterwards, she was, along with her 2011 built sister *Capucine*, chartered to Stena Line, and placed on their Rotterdam - Harwich route, replacing the larger *Stena Freighter* and *Stena Carrier*, which were transferred to Stena RoRo. In January the two Stena vessels were chartered to Transfennica to operate between Zeebrugge and Bilbao.

The third newbuild the *Wilhelmine*, which had been retrofitted with an extra deck and sponsons, arrived in July and was placed on the Zeebrugge - Purfleet service, enabling the *Melusine* to be moved to the Vlissingen - Dagenham service operated for the Ford Motor Company and allowing the *Eglantine* and *Symphorine* to be laid up. The *Symphorine* was later sold to Sunlink Maritime of Turkey for further use but the *Eglantine* remained laid up at Tilbury until sold in March 2013 to Saudi interests. At the beginning of December the *Wilhelmine* was laid up and in January 2013 went on charter to P&O Ferries, initially for their Tilbury - Zeebrugge service but after three weeks switched to the Middlesbrough - Rotterdam service, swapping roles with the *Norsky*.

The final newbuild, the *Adeline*, arrived in September. She saw little use but in October made a trip to Purfleet and then proceeded through Tower Bridge for a christening ceremony moored alongside City Hall. In November she was chartered to RMR Shipping to operate from Northern Europe to West Africa. After one round trip she was sub-chartered to Castor Shipping of Italy but later returned to RMR Shipping.

In September, CLdN purchased the three Epic Shipping owned Odense built ro-ros *Maas Viking*, *Mercia* and *Wessex*. The first vessel, chartered initially to Norfolkline and then taken over by DFDS Seaways, ended her charter to the Danish company and was renamed the *Kent*. She undertook a short charter to the Mediterranean and also operated on the Rotterdam - Purfleet route before, in January 2013 going, with her two sisters (which had been laid up in Greece), to inaugurate a new

Stena Transit (*Cees de Bijl*)

Spirit of Britain (*Brian Smith*

Berlioz (*Darren Holdaway*)

Cote D'Albatre (*John Bryant*)

Condor Express *(Andrew Cooke)*

Barfleur *(Kevin Mitchell)*

service between Turkey and Italy for Ekol Lojistik of Turkey. Meanwhile, DFDS chartered a replacement vessel in the form of the *Cragside*, a sister vessel, owned by Maersk Tankers of Denmark.

EASTERN CHANNEL

For much of the year, TransEuropa Ferries continued their fairly low key operation between Ramsgate and Ostend with the elderly *Larkspur* and *Gardenia*. Although passengers in cars continued to be conveyed, little attempt was made to develop this side of the business. However, in December it was announced that the company had taken on a three year charter with a purchase option P&O's *Pride of Calais*. Renamed the *Ostend Spirit*, the ship left Tilbury just before Christmas and entered service at the end of January 2013. However, in April 2013 the operator went into liquidation and the *Ostend Spirit* was repossessed and returned to lay up.

Most significant event in the Eastern Channel was the final demise of SeaFrance, which was formally liquidated in January. The three owned ships were put up for sale and the chartered *SeaFrance Moliere* returned to her owners and renamed the *Moliere*. Although both DFDS and Stena Line bid for the vessels, the eventual purchaser was *Eurotransmanche*, a subsidiary of *Eurotunnel SA*, operators of the Channel Tunnel. The vessels were chartered to SCOP, a co-operative formed primarily of former SeaFrance employees and the service launched as My Ferry Link in late August with the *Berlioz* and *Rodin*. The *Nord Pas-de-Calais* joined the operation later in the year.

The ending of SeaFrance services had implications for other operators. In February DFDS and LD Lines launched a Dover - Calais service using the LD Lines owned *Norman Spirit*, which had been brought back to Dover in December 2011 to provide additional capacity on the Dover-Dunkerque route. In November, this operation later became a joint venture between the two companies, incorporating additionally the Newhaven - Dieppe and Portsmouth - Le Havre routes, 82% owned by DFDS and 12% by LD Lines.

A running mate for the *Norman Spirit* was acquired in April in the form of the *Barfleur* of Brittany Ferries, laid up since the previous autumn following the ending of the Poole - Cherbourg passenger service. Renamed the *Deal Seaways* and with minimal livery changes, she provided much needed additional capacity for the summer season but her slow speed and the need to sometimes adjust the trim to match the berths at Dover and Calais meant that her timekeeping was poor. In October she was replaced by the *Dieppe Seaways*, the former *SeaFrance Moliere*. Initial plans to place her on the Dunkerque route and move one of the Dunkerque vessels were postponed.

P&O's second newbuild the *Spirit of France* entered service in January, much later than expected owing to her initial rejection from the builders as a result of unacceptable vibration levels. The *Spirit of Britain* returned to Rauma in Finland for modifications to be made to rectify the same problems. In July the *European Seaway* was chartered to GLID, a joint venture between Centrica Renewable Energy Limited and EIG, for use by technicians working on the North Sea Lynn and Inner Dowsing wind farm array, four miles off Skegness. In October she returned to the Dover - Calais service.

Because of all these factors and the withdrawal of the SeaFrance vessels from the Dover - Calais route until late August, the *Pride of Calais* was retained in service much longer than originally planned, albeit in freight only mode for much of the year. She was eventually withdrawn in October and laid up at Tilbury alongside her sister. During the year it was necessary to take some parts from the laid up *Pride of Dover* to keep her going and this meant that the slightly older vessel was no longer in working order by the end of the year. Sold to German interests, she left under tow in early December and although initially heading for a Turkish port with repair facilities, her orders were changed en route and she ended up with breakers at Aliaga - a sad end for a vessel built as recently as 1987.

The Newhaven - Dieppe route continued much as before with the *Cote D'Albatre* providing the twice daily service and the *Seven Sisters* laid up most of the year.

WESTERN CHANNEL & SOLENT

During the year, Brittany Ferries announced a series of economy measures. Although no routes were to close or vessels be disposed of, the measured provoked a series of sporadic strikes which then led to a ten day 'lock-out' by the company at the end of September during which no service operated. The conflict was eventually resolved.

LD lines (and later the DFDS Seaways/LD Lines joint venture) continued to operate the *Norman Voyager* on Portsmouth - Le Havre service. In April she was sold to Stena RoRo but the charter continued.

Despite the completion of much delayed work at the Lymington terminal to provide a new passenger gangway to avoid passengers having to use the car ramp, Wightlink were unable to reinstate the half hourly summer frequency previously operated by the 'C Class' vessels on the service to Yarmouth in the Isle of Wight. This was due to speed restrictions and the longer time needed to load and unload the larger ferries.

Following a directive from the MCA that passengers should not be allowed to stay in cars when hazardous loads were carried, the company decided to insist on passengers leaving their cars on all sailings to avoid confusion. Allowing passengers to stay with their cars dates from the time that the service was operated by open vessels with limited accommodation.

In November Wightlink announced cuts in services for 2013, particularly affecting late night and early morning services and the total elimination of through the night sailings on the Lymington-Yarmouth route.

On the Poole - Cherbourg route only the daily fast ferry service operated by Condor Ferries provided passenger services during 2013, the *Barfleur* being on charter to DFDS at Dover. However, at the end of the year, Brittany Ferries announced that in 2013 the *Barfleur* would return and it would be the freighter *Cotentin* which would no longer serve the French port. It was later announced that, from March, she would operate mainly from Poole to Spain, with twice weekly sailings to Cherbourg. The fast ferry service would cease.

Condor Ferries were unable to operate from Weymouth for the most of 2012 owing to problems experienced with the berth, needing extensive repairs which could not be completed until summer 2013. Services were expected to resume at the end of July.

IRISH SEA

On the Holyhead - Dun Laoghaire route the HSS *Stena Explorer* made a summer return, operating a single round trip from April to September.

Seatruck Ferries' final Flensburg built newbuild, the *Seatruck Power* arrived in February and was placed on the Liverpool - Dublin service. Having a total fleet of ten vessels (plus two on long-term charter to NorthLink Ferries) with a requirement of only seven to operate all services, posed something of a dilemma for the company. From May one vessel was on charter to DFDS Seaways in the North Sea although, as part of the charter arrangement, the *Anglia Seaways* was taken on charter in return. For parts of the year, a second vessel was chartered to them to cover the absence of their own vessels. Other charters were also arranged but some vessels, particularly the oldest two - the *Clipper Ranger* and *Arrow* - spent a considerable part of the year laid up. In January 2013 the *Clipper Pennant* was chartered to Stena Ro-Ro for two years for sub charter out and the *Seatruck Pace* was chartered to Bluewater Shipping for up to a year to move wind turbines between Esbjerg and Mostyn.

In May Seatruck transferred their Heysham - Larne service to Belfast but in August, the service was withdrawn and two of the company's newest vessels, the *Seatruck Performance* and *Seatruck Precision* were chartered to Stena Line and replaced the ex Norfolkline *Stena Hibernia* and *Stena Scotia* on their Heysham - Belfast route. They were renamed the *Stena Performer* (there already being a tanker called *Stena Performance*) and *Stena Precision* . The two older Stena Line vessels were transferred to Stena RoRo for charter work.

During the earlier part of the year, Stena Line embarked on a £4m refurbishment of the *Stena Mersey* and *Stena Lagan* to bring the vessels' rather spartan Visentini interiors up to the company's standards. Further improvements took place in early 2013.

On the North Channel route, Stena Line's 'Superfast' vessels on the Cairnryan - Belfast route took market share from P&O Ferries Cairnryan - Larne operation. In June the *Stena Caledonia*, last of the

European Highlander (*Gordon Hislip*)

'Sealink Saints' to operate in British waters, was sold to PT ASDP Indonesia Ferry and renamed the *Port Link*. However, the HSS *Stena Voyager* remained laid up in Belfast. Prospects that she might follow her sister, the former *Stena Discovery*, to Venezuela, faded when the operators of that vessel ran into financial difficulties. In May 2013 she was towed to breakers in Sweden.

SCOTLAND

Services in Western Scotland continued much as in 2011. A new vessel was ordered for the Stornoway - Ullapool service, to replace both the *Isle of Lewis* and freight vessel *Muirneag* (the only 1970s ro-ro freighter now operating regularly in British waters). To be delivered in 2014 she is being built, not in Poland as might have been expected but by Flensburger Schiffbau-Gesellschaft, Flensburg, Germany, the first passenger vessel the yard will have built for a European operator for many years, although four ships were built for Canada between 2007 and 2009. The first of two diesel/battery ferries was launched in December by Ferguson Shipbuilders, Port Glasgow. Named the *Hallaig*, she entered service in summer 2013 on the Sconser - Raasay service. A sister vessel, the *Lochinvar*, will enter service in the autumn on the Tarbert - Portavadie route.

A review sponsored by the Scottish Government of ferry services in Scotland provoked mixed reactions. Whilst some routes - such as Oban - Craignure were recommended for improved service, reduction in some services, particularly to some of the smaller islands, were also part of the package.

From 1st April, the Gourock - Kilcreggan passenger service was taken over by Yoker - Renfrew ferry operator Clydelink from traditional operator Clyde Marine. This controversial move, which also involved the ending of the long-standing Gourock - Helensburgh route, meant that the five year old *Seabus*, which was built for the service, was replaced by the 1996-built former Lymington harbour tour boat *Island Princess*. A second vessel, the Limerick based *Cailin Oir* was brought in as a relief vessel.

In June, Western Ferries ordered two new ferries for their Gourock to Dunoon route. Again the contract went to an unexpected shipyard, Cammell Laird in Birkenhead. To be named the *Sound of Seil* and *Sound of Soay*, they will enter service during 2013 and replace the elderly *Sound of Sanda* and *Sound of Scalpay*.

David MacBrayne subsidiary Argyll Ferries had a somewhat turbulent year, having replaced the car ferries with smaller passenger ferries in 2011. The level of weather and technical based cancellations was deemed unacceptable by many passengers. A suggestion that the reserve car ferry, the *Coruisk*, be used during the winter period was rejected as impractical but it was agreed that replacement of the smaller *Ali Cat* by a more suitable vessel would be considered.

The contract to operate services to Orkney and Shetland was transferred from David MacBrayne subsidiary NorthLink Ferries Ltd to the services company Serco Northlink Ferries. Inevitably the private sector company proposed staff cuts and a reduction in staff terms and conditions and, perhaps equally inevitably, this resulted in strike action from crews in mid-December. Further action, was due to take place over the festive season but, in the end, it was called off. As part of the economies, the two ship freight service was reduced to a single ship operation with occasional extra livestock sailings during the first five months of the year. Northlink's three passenger vessels were surveyed 'in water – in service' at Lerwick and Stromness thus avoiding reducing the Aberdeen – Lerwick service to a single passenger ship.

During winter 2012/13 the Orkney Ferries Houton - Lyness - Flotta vessel *Hoy Head* was stretched at Cammell Laird, Birkenhead to 52 metres overall thus increasing car capacity from 18 to 24.

Smyril Line chartered *Clipper Pennant* to cover the Torshavn – Hirtshals route during survey period of the *Norröna* and she (*Norröna*) then covered the Torshavn – Tvoroyri (Suduroy) route for Strandfaraskip Landsins while *Smyril* was dry-docked.

Nick Widdows

Finlaggan *(Stuart Mackillop)*

Raasay *(Stuart Mackillop)*

BRITTANY FERRIES

THE COMPANY *Brittany Ferries* is the trading name of *BAI SA*, a French private sector company and the operating arm of the *Brittany Ferries Group*. The UK operations are run by *BAI (UK) Ltd*, a UK private sector company, wholly owned by the *Brittany Ferries Group*.

MANAGEMENT Group Managing Director Martine Jourdren, Commercial Director, Passengers Mike Bevens, Commercial Director, Freight Jon Clarke.

ADDRESS Millbay Docks, Plymouth, Devon PL1 3EW.

TELEPHONE Passenger - Administration *Plymouth* + 44 (0)871 244 0500, *Portsmouth* + 44 (0)871 244 0600, Reservations *All Services* + 44 (0)871 244 1400, Freight - Administration & Enquiries + 44 (0)871 244 0411, Reservations + 44 (0)871 244 0912.

FAX Freight - Administration & Reservations + 44 (0)871 244 0912.

INTERNET Passenger - Website www.brittanyferries.com *(English, French, Spanish, German)*, Freight Website www.brittanyferriesfreight.co.uk *(English)*

ROUTES OPERATED Conventional Ferries *All year* Plymouth - Roscoff (6 hrs (day), 7 hrs - 9 hrs (night); *ARMORIQUE, PONT-AVEN*; up to 2 per day (Summer), 1 per day (Winter)), Poole - Cherbourg (4 hrs 15 mins; *BARFLEUR*; 1 per day), Portsmouth - St Malo (8 hrs 45 mins (day), 10 hrs 45 mins (night); *BRETAGNE*; (1 per day), Portsmouth - Caen (Ouistreham) (6 hrs (day), 6 hrs - 8 hrs (night); *NORMANDIE, MONT ST MICHEL;* (3 per day), Portsmouth - Santander (Spain) (24 hrs; *CAP FINISTERE, PONT-AVEN*; up to 2 per week, Portsmouth - Bilbao (Spain) (24/32 hrs; *CAP FINISTERE*; 2 per week. *Summer only* Plymouth - Santander (Spain) (19 hrs 30 mins; *PONT-AVEN;* 1 per week (April - October)), Cork - Roscoff (14 hrs; *PONT-AVEN;* 1 per week (March - November)). Fast Ferries *Summer only* Portsmouth – Cherbourg (3 hrs; *NORMANDIE EXPRESS*; 1 per day (May-September)), Portsmouth - Le Havre (3 hrs 45 mins; *NORMANDIE EXPRESS*; Thu-Sun (May - September); 1 per day), Freight only services Poole - Bilbao (26 hrs; *COTENTIN*; 1 per week), Poole - Santander (26 hrs; *COTENTIN*; 1 per week).

1	ARMORIQUE	29468 t	09	23.0k	167.0m	1500P	470C	65L	BA2	FR	9364980
2	BARFLEUR	20133t	92	19.0k	158.0m	1212P	590C	112T	BA2	FR	9007130
3	BRETAGNE	24534t	89	19.5k	151.0m	1926P	580C	84T	BA	FR	8707329
4	CAP FINISTERE	32728t	01	28.0k	203.9m	1608P	1000C	140T	BA	FR	9198927
5F+	COTENTIN	22542t	07	23.0k	167.0m	160P	-	140L	BA2	FR	9364978
6	MONT ST MICHEL	35592t	02	21.2k	173.0m	2200P	880C	166T	BA2	FR	9238337
7	NORMANDIE	27541t	92	20.5k	161.0m	2120P	600C	126T	BA2	FR	9006253
8»	NORMANDIE EXPRESS	6581t	00	40.0k	97.2m	900P	260C	-	A	FR	8814134
9	PONT-AVEN	41748t	04	26.0k	184.3m	2400P	650C	85L	BA	FR	9268708

ARMORIQUE Built by STX Europe, Helsinki, Finland for *Brittany Ferries* to operate between Plymouth and Roscoff.

BARFLEUR Built as the BARFLEUR by Kvaerner Masa-Yards, Helsinki for the *Truckline* (freight division of *Brittany Ferries*) Poole - Cherbourg service to replace two passenger vessels and to inaugurate a year-round passenger service. In 1999 the *Truckline* branding was dropped for passenger services and she was repainted into full *Brittany Ferries* livery. In 2005 operated partly Cherbourg - Poole and partly Cherbourg - Portsmouth but in 2006 returned to operating mainly to Poole. In February 2010, she was laid up. The conventional car ferry service ended the following month. In February 2011 she resumed service on the Poole - Cherbourg route. In September 2011 she was withdrawn again. In April 2012 chartered to *DFDS Seaways* to operate between Dover and Calais and renamed the DEAL SEAWAYS. In November 2012 returned to *Brittany Ferries* and renamed the BARFLEUR. Resumed the Poole - Cherbourg service in March 2013, replacing the COTENTIN but offering a service for both freight and passengers.

BRETAGNE Built by Chantiers de l'Atlantique, St Nazaire for the Plymouth - Santander and Cork - Roscoff services (with two sailings per week between Plymouth and Roscoff). In 1993 she was transferred to the Portsmouth - St Malo service. In 2004 also operated between Portsmouth and

Cherbourg. In 2005 operated between Plymouth and Roscoff. In 2006 returned to the Portsmouth - St Malo route.

CAP FINISTERE Built as the SUPERFAST V by Howaldtswerke Deutsche Werft AG, Kiel, Germany for *Attica Enterprises* (now *Attica Group*) for use by *Superfast Ferries* of Greece. Initially operated between Patras and Ancona and in January 2007 switched to the Patras - Igoumenitsa - Bari route. In 2008 the route became Patras - Igoumenitsa - Ancona. In 2010 sold to *Brittany Ferries*, renamed the CAP FINISTERE and in March placed on the Portsmouth - Santander service, also operating some sailings between Portsmouth and Cherbourg. In 2011 began operating also between Portsmouth and Bilbao and only operated between Portsmouth and Cherbourg during the winter period.

COTENTIN Built by STX Finland, Helsinki, Finland for *Brittany Ferries*. Used on freight service from Poole to Cherbourg and Santander. In March 2013 replaced by the BARFLEUR (operating to Cherbourg only). Now operates twice weekly from Poole to Bilbao and Santander.

MONT ST MICHEL Built by Van der Giessen-de Noord, Krimpen aan den IJssel, Rotterdam for *Brittany Ferries*.

NORMANDIE Built by Kvaerner Masa-Yards, Turku, Finland for *Brittany Ferries*. Used the Portsmouth - Caen route.

NORMANDIE EXPRESS Incat Evolution 10 catamaran built as the INCAT TASMANIA. In November 2000 chartered to *TranzRail* of New Zealand and renamed THE LYNX. Placed on the Wellington – Picton service. In July 2003 replaced by 1997-built Incat 86m craft INCAT 046, given the marketing name 'The Lynx' and laid up. In Spring 2005 chartered to *Brittany Ferries* to operate on their Cherbourg – Portsmouth and Caen – Portsmouth services and renamed the NORMANDIE EXPRESS. In 2007 purchased by *Brittany Ferries*. In 2013 operates to Cherbourg and Le Havre.

PONT-AVEN Built by Jos L Meyer Werft, Papenburg, Germany for *Brittany Ferries* to operate on the Plymouth - Roscoff, Plymouth - Santander and Cork - Roscoff routes.

CELTIC LINK FERRIES

THE COMPANY *Celtic Link Ferries IRL Ltd* is an Irish Republic private sector company.

MANAGEMENT **Marketing Manager** Catriona Rossiter, **Operations Manager** Will O'Flaherty.

ADDRESS Rosslare Europort, Co Wexford, Irish Republic.

TELEPHONE **Administration** + 353 (0)402 38091, **Reservations** *Passenger* + 353 (0)53 9162688, **Freight** + 353 (0)53 9178790, **Ship Management** + 353 (0)53 917 8789.

FAX **Administration & Reservations** + 353 (0)402 38086, **Ship Management** + 35 (0)53 917 8798.

INTERNET **Website** www.celticlinkferries.com *(English)*

ROUTE OPERATED Rosslare - Cherbourg (20 hrs; *CELTIC HORIZON*; 3 per week).

1	CELTIC HORIZON	26500t	06	23.5k	186.5m	1000P	200C	120L	A	IT	9332559

CELTIC HORIZON Built as the CARTOUR BETA by CN Visentini, Porto Viro, Italy for Levantina Trasporti of Italy. Chartered to *Caronte & Tourist*, of Italy and operated between Messina and Salerno (Sicily). In October 2011 chartered to *Celtic Link Ferries*, renamed the CELTIC HORIZON and placed on the Rosslare - Cherbourg route.

Is there *any* better way to discover France or Spain?

For more information visit brittanyferries.com or call 0871 244 0404

Brittany Ferries

Cap Finistere (*John Bryant*)

Mont St Michel (*Matthew Punter*)

Celtic Horizon (*Darren Holdaway*)

Commodore Clipper (*Miles Cowsill*)

CONDOR FERRIES

THE COMPANY *Condor Ferries Ltd* is a Channel Islands private sector company owned by the *Condor Group*, Guernsey which is owned by *Macquarie European Infrastructure*.

MANAGEMENT **Managing Director** Simon Edsall, **Sales and Marketing Director** Alicia Andrews, **Marketing Manager** Justin Amey, **Sales Manager** Jonathan Godson.

ADDRESS **Head Office** PO Box 10, New Jetty Offices, White Rock, St Peter Port, Guernsey GY1 3AF, **Sales and Marketing** Condor House, New Harbour Road South, Hamworthy, Poole BH15 4AJ.

TELEPHONE **Administration** *Guernsey* + 44 (0)1481 728620, *Poole* + 44 (0)1202 207207, **Passenger Reservations** + 44 (0)845 609 1024, Freight Reservations + 44 (0)1481 728521.

FAX **Administration** *Guernsey* + 44 (0)1481 728521, *Poole* + 44 (0)1202 685184, **Reservations** + 44(0)1305 760776.

INTERNET   Email   *Passenger*   reservations@condorferries.co.uk   Freight len.lepage@condorferries.co.uk **Website** www.condorferries.com *(English, French, German)*

ROUTES OPERATED *Conventional Passenger Ferry* Portsmouth to Guernsey (from 7 hrs) and Jersey (from 9 hrs) (*COMMODORE CLIPPER*; daily except Sun). *Fast Ferries* Poole - Guernsey (from 2 hrs 40 mins) and Jersey (from 4 hrs) (*CONDOR EXPRESS, CONDOR VITESSE, CONDOR RAPIDE*; April to October), Poole - St Malo (5 hrs 45 mins) (*CONDOR EXPRESS, CONDOR VITESSE; CONDOR RAPIDE*) May to September), Guernsey - Jersey (from 1 hr) and St Malo* (from 2 hrs), Jersey - Guernsey (from 1 hr) and St Malo (from 1 hr 20 mins) (*CONDOR EXPRESS, CONDOR RAPIDE, CONDOR VITESSE;*). *Some services connect in the Channel Islands. **Freight Ferry** Portsmouth - Guernsey - Jersey (10 hrs 30 min; *COMMODORE GOODWILL*; 1 per day), Guernsey - Jersey - St Malo (13 hrs; *COMMODORE GOODWILL*; 1 per week).

1	COMMODORE CLIPPER	14000t	99	18.0k	129.1m	500P	100C	92T	A	BS	9201750
2F	COMMODORE GOODWILL	11166t	96	17.3k	126.4m	12P	-	92T	A	BS	9117985
3»	CONDOR EXPRESS	5005t	96	39.0k	86.6m	741P	185C	-	A2	BS	9135896
4»	CONDOR RAPIDE	5007t	97	40.5k	86.6m	870P	200C	-	A	BS	9161560
5»	CONDOR VITESSE	5005t	97	40.0k	86.6m	741P	185C	-	A2	BS	9151008

COMMODORE CLIPPER Ro-pax vessel built by Van der Giessen-de Noord, Krimpen aan den IJssel, Rotterdam for *Commodore Ferries* to operate between Portsmouth and the Channel Islands. She replaced the ISLAND COMMODORE, a freight-only vessel. Her passenger capacity is normally restricted to 300 but is increased to 500 when the fast ferries are unable to operate.

COMMODORE GOODWILL Built by Koninklijke Scheldegroep BV, Vlissingen, The Netherlands for *Commodore Ferries*.

CONDOR EXPRESS Incat 86m catamaran built at Hobart, Tasmania, Australia. She was delivered in December 1996 and entered service in 1997.

CONDOR RAPIDE Incat 86m catamaran built at Hobart, Tasmania, Australia as the INCAT 045. Chartered to *Transport Tasmania* of Australia and operated between Melbourne (Victoria) and Devonport (Tasmania). In 1999 she was chartered to the *Royal Australian Navy*, renamed the HMAS JERVIS BAY and took part in moving Australian troops from Darwin to Dili (East Timor) as part of the United Nations operation. She operated over 75 trips between the two points carrying personnel and equipment for the United Nations Transitional Administration in East Timor (UNTAET). The charter ended in May 2001 and she was renamed the INCAT 045 and laid up. In Spring 2003 she was chartered to *Traghetti Isole Sarde (TRIS)* of Italy, renamed the WINNER and operated between Genoa and Palau (Sardinia). In Autumn 2003 the charter ended, she resumed the name INCAT 045 and was laid up at Portland, Dorset. In 2004 chartered to *SpeedFerries* and renamed the SPEED ONE. In May 2008 purchased by *SpeedFerries*. In November 2008 the services ceased and the company went into administration. She was laid up at Tilbury. In May she was sold at auction to *Epic Shipping* of the UK and renamed the SEA LEOPARD. In April 2010 sold to *Condor Ferries* and renamed the CONDOR RAPIDE. Entered service in May 2010.

CONDOR VITESSE Incat 86m catamaran built at Hobart. Built speculatively and launched as the INCAT 044. Moved to Europe in Summer 1997 and spent time in both the UK and Denmark but was not used. In 1998 she was chartered to *Condor Ferries* and renamed the CONDOR VITESSE. During Winter 1999/2000 she was chartered to *TranzRail* of New Zealand. Returned to UK in Spring 2000.

DAVID MACBRAYNE GROUP

THE COMPANY *David MacBrayne Limited* is a Scottish registered company, wholly owned by the Scottish Ministers. Its ferry operations are conducted through two subsidiary companies - *Argyll Ferries Ltd* and *CalMac Ferries Ltd* (trading as *Caledonian MacBrayne*). The majority of *CalMac Ferries* vessels are owned by *Caledonian Maritime Assets Limited*, a separate company which is also owned by the Scottish Ministers.

ARGYLL FERRIES

MANAGEMENT **Managing Director** Martin Dorchester, **Public Affairs Manager** David Cannon.

ADDRESS Ferry Terminal, Gourock PA19 1QP.

TELEPHONE **Administration** +44 (0)1475 650100, **Customer services** +66 (0)1475 650 338

FAX **Administration** +44 (0)1475 650336,

INTERNET Email enquiries@ argyllferries.co.uk **Website** www.argyllferries.co.uk *(English)*

ROUTE OPERATED All-year passenger-only ferry Gourock - Dunoon (20 mins; *ALI CAT, ARGYLL FLYER*; 1 or 2 per hour.

1p	ALI CAT	74t	99	-	19.8m	250P	0C	0L	-	UK
2p	ARGYLL FLYER	300t	01	19.5k	29.9m	227P	0C	0L	-	UK 9231016

ALI CAT Catamaran built for *Solent & Wight Line Cruises* of Ryde, Isle of Wight. She operated a passenger service from Cowes to Hamble and Warsash and cruises from Cowes. At times chartered to *Wightlink* to cover for the fast catamarans. In 2002 chartered to *Red Funnel Ferries* who had contracted with *Caledonian MacBrayne* to operate passenger-only services between Gourock and Dunoon in the morning and evening peaks. In June 2011 purchased by and operated by *Argyll Ferries*.

ARGYLL FLYER Built as the QUEEN OF ARAN II by OCEA, Les Sables d'Olonne, France for *Inis Mór Ferries*. In 2007 sold to *Aran Island Ferries* and renamed the BANRION CHONAMARA. In June 2011 sold to *Argyll Ferries*, renamed the ARGYLL FLYER and replaced the car ferry SATURN on the Gourock - Dunoon service.

CALEDONIAN MACBRAYNE

MANAGEMENT **Managing Director** Martin Dorchester, **Marketing Manager and e. Commerce Manager** Cathy Craig, **Public Affairs Manager** David Cannon.

ADDRESS Ferry Terminal, Gourock PA19 1QP.

TELEPHONE **Administration** +44 (0)1475 650100, **Vehicle Reservations** +44 (0)800 066 5000.

FAX **Administration** +44 (0)1475 650336, **Vehicle Reservations** +44 (0)1475 635235.

INTERNET Email enquiries@calmac.co.uk **Website** www.calmac.co.uk *(English)*

ROUTES OPERATED All-year vehicle ferries (frequencies are for Summer – services are listed alphabetically, by mainland port or larger island port where service is between two islands), Ardmhor (Barra) - Eriskay (40 mins; *LOCH ALAINN*; up to 5 per day), Ardrossan - Brodick (Arran) (55 mins; *CALEDONIAN ISLES, ISLE OF ARRAN*; up to 6 per day), Colintraive - Rhubodach (Bute) (5 mins; *LOCH DUNVEGAN*; frequent service), Kennacraig - Port Askaig (Islay) (2 hrs 5 mins; *FINLAGGAN, HEBRIDEAN ISLES*; up to 4 per day), Kennacraig - Port Ellen (Islay) (2 hrs 20 mins; *FINLAGGAN, HEBRIDEAN ISLES*; service currently suspended due to harbour works), Largs - Cumbrae Slip (Cumbrae) (10 mins; *LOCH SHIRA, LOCH RIDDON*; every 30 or 15 mins), Leverburgh (Harris) - Berneray (1 hr 10 mins; *LOCH PORTAIN*; 3-4 per day), Lochaline - Fishnish (Mull) (15 mins; *LOCH*

Hebrides *(Stuart Mackillop)*

Isle of Mull *(Stuart Mackillop)*

FYNE; up to 14 per day), Mallaig - Armadale (Skye) (23 mins; *CORUISK* (Summer), *LOCHNEVIS* (Winter); up to 9 per day (2 in Winter)), Oban - Castlebay (Barra) (5 hrs (direct); *CLANSMAN, LORD OF THE ISLES*; 1 per day), Oban - Lochboisdale (South Uist) (5 hrs (if direct), 7 hrs (via Barra); *CLANSMAN, LORD OF THE ISLES*; 4 per week), Oban - Coll - Tiree (2 hrs 45 min to Coll, 3 hrs 50 min to Tiree via Coll; *CLANSMAN, LORD OF THE ISLES*; 1 per day), Oban - Colonsay (2 hrs 15 mins; *CLANSMAN, LORD OF THE ISLES*; 5 per week), Oban - Craignure (Mull) (45 mins; *ISLE OF MULL*; up to 7 per day), Oban - Lismore (50 mins; *EIGG*; up to 4 per day), Sconser (Skye) - Raasay (15 mins; *HALLAIG*; up to 11 per day), Tarbert (Loch Fyne) - Portavadie (25 mins; *ISLE OF CUMBRAE (from Autumn 2013 LOCHINVAR)*; up to 12 per day), Tayinloan - Gigha (20 mins; *LOCH RANZA*; up to 10 per day), Tobermory (Mull) - Kilchoan (35 mins; *LOCH LINNHE*; up to 7 per day), Uig (Skye) - Lochmaddy (North Uist) (1 hr 45 mins; *HEBRIDES*; 1 or 2 per day), Uig (Skye) - Tarbert (Harris) (1 hr 40 mins; *HEBRIDES*; 1 or 2 per day), Ullapool - Stornoway (Lewis) (2 hrs 45 mins; *ISLE OF LEWIS*; up to 3 per day), Wemyss Bay - Rothesay (Bute) (35 mins; *ARGYLE, BUTE*; hourly), All-year **passenger and restricted vehicle ferries** (frequencies are for Summer) Fionnphort (Mull) - Iona (5 mins; *LOCH BUIE*; frequent), Mallaig - Eigg - Muck - Rum - Canna - Mallaig (round trip 7 hrs (all islands); *LOCHNEVIS*; at least 1 sailing per day - most islands visited daily). **Note** Although these services are operated by vehicle ferries, special permission is required to take a vehicle and tourist cars are not normally conveyed, **Summer-only vehicle ferries** Ardrossan - Campbeltown (2 hrs 30 mins; *ISLE OF ARRAN*; 3 per week), Claonaig - Lochranza (Arran) (30 mins; *LOCH TARBERT*; up to 9 per day), Kennacraig - Port Askaig - Colonsay - Oban (3 hrs 35 mins; *HEBRIDEAN ISLES*; 1 per week), **Winter-only vehicle ferry** Tarbert (Loch Fyne) - Lochranza (Arran) (1 hr; *varies*; 1 per day), **Freight-only ferry** Ullapool - Stornoway (Lewis) (3 hrs 45 mins; *MUIRNEAG*; 1 per day).

1	ARGYLE	2643t	07	14.0k	69.0m	450P	60C	-	BAS	UK	9365178
2	BUTE	2612t	05	14.0k	69.0m	450P	60C	-	AS	UK	9319741
3	CALEDONIAN ISLES	5221t	93	15.0k	94.3m	1000P	120C	10L	BA	UK	9051284
4	CLANSMAN	5499t	98	16.5k	99.0m	638P	90C	6L	BA	UK	9158953
5	CORUISK	1599t	03	14.0k	65.0m	250P	40C	-	BA	UK	9274836
6	EIGG	69t	75	8.0k	24.3m	75P	6C	-	B	UK	
7	FINLAGGAN	5626t	11	16.5k	89.9m	550P	88C	-	BA	UK	9482902
8	HALLAIG	523t	13	9.0k	43.5m	150P	23C	2L	BA	UK	9652832
9	HEBRIDEAN ISLES	3040t	85	15.0k	85.1m	494P	68C	10L	BAS	UK	8404812
10	HEBRIDES	5506t	00	16.5k	99.0m	612P	110C	6L	BA	UK	9211975
11	ISLE OF ARRAN	3296t	84	15.0k	85.0m	446P	68C	8L	BA	UK	8219554
12	ISLE OF CUMBRAE	201t	77	8.5k	37.7m	139P	18C	-	BA	UK	8219554
13	ISLE OF LEWIS	6753t	95	18.0k	101.2m	680P	123C	10L	BA	UK	9085974
14	ISLE OF MULL	4719t	88	15.0k	90.1m	962P	80C	20L	BA	UK	8608339
15	LOCH ALAINN	396t	98	10.0k	43.0m	150P	24C	-	BA	UK	9147722
16	LOCH BHRUSDA	246t	96	8.0k	35.4m	150P	18C	-	BA	UK	9129483
17	LOCH BUIE	295t	92	9.0k	35.5m	250P	9C	-	BA	UK	9031375
18	LOCH DUNVEGAN	549t	91	9.0k	54.2m	200P	36C	-	BA	UK	9006409
19	LOCH FYNE	549t	91	9.0k	54.2m	200P	36C	-	BA	UK	9006411
20	LOCH LINNHE	206t	86	9.0k	35.5m	199P	12C	-	BA	UK	8512308
21	LOCH PORTAIN	950t	03	10.5k	50.0m	200P	32C	-	BA	UK	9274824
22	LOCH RANZA	206t	87	9.0k	35.7m	199P	12C	-	BA	UK	8519887
23	LOCH RIDDON	206t	86	9.0k	35.5m	199P	12C	-	BA	UK	8519875
24	LOCH SHIRA	1024t	07	13.0k	43.0m	250P	24C	-	BA	UK	9376919
25	LOCH STRIVEN	206t	86	9.0k	35.7m	199P	12C	-	BA	UK	8512293
26	LOCH TARBERT	211t	92	9.0k	34.5m	149P	18C	-	BA	UK	9039389
27	LOCHNEVIS	941t	00	13.0k	49.1m	190P	14C	-	A	UK	9209063
28	LORD OF THE ISLES	3504t	89	16.0k	84.6m	506P	56C	16L	BAS	UK	8710869
29F	MUIRNEAG	5801t	79	15.5k	105.6m	0P	-	54T	AS	UK	7725362
30	RAASAY	69t	76	8.0k	24.3m	75P	6C	-	B	UK	
31•	SATURN	899t	78	13.0k	69.5m	381P	40C	-	AS	UK	7615490

Loch Fyne (*Stuart Mackillop*)

Coruisk (*John Hendy*)

Note In the following list, Gaelic names are shown in parenthesis.

ARGYLE (EARRA-GHÀIDHEAL), BUTE (EILEAN BHÒID) Built by Stocznia Remontowa, Gdansk, Poland to operate on the Wemyss Bay - Rothesay route.

CALEDONIAN ISLES (EILEANAN CHALEDONIA) Built by Richards Shipyard, Lowestoft, UK for the Ardrossan - Brodick (Arran) service.

CLANSMAN (FEAR-CINNIDH) Built by Appledore Shipbuilders Ltd, Appledore, UK to replace the LORD OF THE ISLES on the Oban - Coll and Tiree and Oban - Castlebay and Lochboisdale services in the summer. She also serves as winter relief vessel on the Stornoway, Tarbert, Lochmaddy, Mull/Colonsay and Brodick routes.

CORUISK (COIR' UISG') Built by Appledore Shipbuilders Ltd, Appledore, UK to operate on the Mallaig - Armadale route during the summer. She operates on the Upper Clyde as a relief vessel during the winter.

EIGG (EILEAN EIGE) Built by James Lamont & Co, Port Glasgow, UK. Since 1976 she has been employed mainly on the Oban - Lismore service. In 1996 she was transferred to the Tobermory (Mull) - Kilchoan route, very occasionally making sailings to the Small Isles (Canna, Eigg, Muck and Rum) for special cargoes. In 1999 her wheelhouse was raised to make it easier to see over taller lorries and she returned to the Oban - Lismore route.

FINLAGGAN (FIONN LAGAN) Built by Stocznia Remontowa, Gdansk, Poland for the Kennacraig - Islay service.

HALLAIG (HALLAIG) Built by Ferguson Shipbuilders, Port Glasgow, UK to replace the LOCH STRIVEN on the Sconser - Raasay service. The vessel has both diesel and battery electric propulsion and can be 'plugged in' to a land supply on Raasay overnight.

HEBRIDEAN ISLES (EILEANAN INNSE GALL) Built by Cochrane Shipbuilders, Selby UK for the Uig - Tarbert/Lochmaddy service. She was used initially on the Ullapool - Stornoway and Oban - Craignure/Colonsay services pending installation of link-span facilities at Uig, Tarbert and Lochmaddy. She took up her regular role in May 1986. From May 1996 she no longer operated direct services in summer between Tarbert and Lochmaddy, this role being taken on by the new Harris - North Uist services of the LOCH BHRUSDA. In 2001 she was replaced by the HEBRIDES and transferred to the Islay service. In Autumn 2002 she operated between Scrabster and Stromness for NorthLink Orkney and Shetland Ferries before port modifications at Scrabster enabled the HAMNAVOE to enter service in Spring 2003. She then returned to the Islay service. She also relieved on the NorthLink Pentland Firth service between 2004 and 2007.

HEBRIDES (INNSE GALL) Built by Ferguson Shipbuilders Ltd, Port Glasgow, UK for the Uig - Tarbert and Uig - Lochmaddy services.

ISLE OF ARRAN (EILEAN ARAINN) Built by Ferguson Ailsa, Port Glasgow, UK for the Ardrossan - Brodick service. In 1993 transferred to the Kennacraig - Port Ellen/Port Askaig service, also undertaking the weekly Port Askaig - Colonsay - Oban summer service. From then until 1997/98 she also relieved on the Brodick, Coll/Tiree, Castlebay/Lochboisdale, Craignure and Tarbert/Lochmaddy routes in winter. In 2001 she was replaced by the HEBRIDEAN ISLES and became a reserve for the larger vessels. She has operated on the two-ship Islay service in summer since 2003; this service is now all-year-round. Following the delivery of the FINLAGGAN in May 2011 she became a spare vessel, and operates extra services between Ardrossan and Brodick and Ardrossan and Campbeltown during the peak summer period.

ISLE OF CUMBRAE (EILEAN CHUMRAIGH) Built by Ailsa Shipbuilding Ltd, Troon, UK for the Largs - Cumbrae Slip (Cumbrae) service. In 1986 she was replaced by the LOCH LINNHE and the LOCH STRIVEN and transferred to the Lochaline - Fishnish (Mull) service. She used to spend most of the winter as secondary vessel on the Kyle of Lochalsh - Kyleakin service; however, this ceased following the opening of the Skye Bridge in 1995. In 1997 she was transferred to the Colintraive - Rhubodach service. In Summer 1999 she was transferred to the Tarbert - Portavadie service. In Autumn 2013 to be replaced by the new LOCHINVAR.

ISLE OF LEWIS *(EILEAN LEÒDHAIS)* Built by Ferguson Shipbuilders Ltd, Port Glasgow, UK for the Ullapool - Stornoway service.

ISLE OF MULL *(AN T-EILEAN MUILEACH)* Built by Appledore Ferguson, Port Glasgow, UK for the Oban - Craignure (Mull) service. She also operates some Oban - Colonsay sailings and until 1997/98 was the usual winter relief vessel on the Ullapool - Stornoway service. She has also deputised on the Oban - Castlebay/Lochboisdale and Oban - Coll/Tiree routes.

LOCH ALAINN *(LOCH ÀLAINN)* Built by Buckie Shipbuilders Ltd, Buckie, UK for the Lochaline - Fishnish service. Launched as the LOCH ALINE but renamed the LOCH ALAINN before entering service. After a brief period on the service for which she was built, she was transferred to the Colintraive - Rhubodach route. In 1998 she was transferred to the Largs - Cumbrae Slip service. In 2007 moved to the Ardmhor (Barra) - Eriskay service. She relieves the larger 'Loch' class vessels in the winter, with her own service covered by the LOCH BHRUSDA.

LOCH BHRUSDA *(LOCH BHRÙSTA)* Built by McTay Marine, Bromborough, Wirral, UK to inaugurate a new Otternish (North Uist) - Leverburgh (Harris) service. In 2001 the service became Berneray - Leverburgh. In 2003 she moved to the Eriskay - Barra service, previously operated by *Comhairle Nan Eilean Siar* vessels. In 2007 she became a spare vessel on the Clyde. Note 'Bhrusda' is pronounced "Vroosta".

LOCH BUIE *(LOCH BUIDHE)* Built by J W Miller & Sons Ltd, St Monans, Fife, UK for the Fionnphort (Mull) - Iona service to replace the MORVERN (see *Arranmore Island Ferry Services*) and obviate the need for a relief vessel in the summer. Due to height restrictions, loading arrangements for vehicles taller than private cars are stern-only. Only islanders' cars and service vehicles (eg. mail vans, police) are carried; no tourist vehicles are conveyed.

LOCH DUNVEGAN *(LOCH DÙNBHEAGAN)* Built by Ferguson Shipbuilders Ltd, Port Glasgow, UK for the Kyle of Lochalsh - Kyleakin service. On the opening of the Skye Bridge in October 1995 she was withdrawn from service and offered for sale. In Autumn 1997, she returned to service on the Lochaline - Fishnish route. In 1998 she was due to be transferred to the Colintraive - Rhubodach route but this was delayed because of problems in providing terminal facilities. She operated on the Clyde and between Mallaig and Armadale during the early summer and spent the rest of that summer laid up. In 1999 she was transferred to the Colintraive - Rhubodach route.

LOCH FYNE *(LOCH FINE)* Built by Ferguson Shipbuilders Ltd, Port Glasgow, UK for the Kyle of Lochalsh - Kyleakin service (see the LOCH DUNVEGAN). In Autumn 1997, she also served on the Lochaline - Fishnish route and was transferred to this route as regular vessel in 1998.

LOCH LINNHE *(AN LINNE DHUBH)* Built by Richard Dunston (Hessle) Ltd, Hessle, UK. Until 1997 she was used mainly on the Largs - Cumbrae Slip (Cumbrae) service and until Winter 1994/95 she was usually used on the Lochaline - Fishnish service during the winter. Since then she has relieved on various routes in winter. In Summer 1998 she operated mainly on the Tarbert - Portavadie route. In 1999 she was transferred to the Tobermory - Kilchoan service in summer.

LOCH PORTAIN *(LOCH PORTAIN)* Built by McTay Marine, Bromborough, Wirral, UK (hull constructed in Poland) to replace the LOCH BHRUSDA on the Berneray - Leverburgh service.

LOCH RANZA *(LOCH RAONASA)* Built by Richard Dunston (Hessle) Ltd, Hessle, UK for the Claonaig - Lochranza (Arran) seasonal service and used a relief vessel in the winter. In 1992 she was replaced by the LOCH TARBERT and transferred to the Tayinloan - Gigha service.

LOCH RIDDON *(LOCH RAODAIN)* Built by Richard Dunston (Hessle) Ltd, Hessle, UK. Until 1997 she was used almost exclusively on the Colintraive - Rhubodach service. In 1997, she was transferred to the Largs - Cumbrae Slip service. Now a spare vessel in the winter and second vessel on the Largs - Cumbrae Slip service in the summer.

LOCH SHIRA *(LOCH SIORA)* Built by Ferguson Shipbuilders, Port Glasgow, UK for the Largs – Cumbrae Slip route.

LOCH STRIVEN *(LOCH SROIGHEANN)* Built by Richard Dunston (Hessle) Ltd, Hessle, UK. Used mainly on the Largs - Cumbrae Slip service until 1997. In Winter 1995/96 and 1996/97 she was used

Lochinvar (*Stuart Mackillop*)

Argyle (*Stuart Mackillop*)

on the Tarbert - Portavadie and Claonaig - Lochranza routes. In 1997 she took over the Sconser - Raasay service. In spring 2013 replaced by the HALLAIG.

LOCH TARBERT *(LOCH AN TAIRBEIRT)* Built by J W Miller & Sons Ltd, St Monans, Fife, UK for the Claonaig - Lochranza service. She was the winter relief vessel on the Largs - Cumbrae Slip route between 1994/95 and 2007/08.

LOCHNEVIS *(LOCH NIBHEIS)* Built by Ailsa Shipbuilding, Troon, UK to replace the LOCHMOR on the Mallaig - Small Isles service and the winter Mallaig - Armadale service. Although a vehicle ferry, cars are not normally carried to the Small Isles; the ro-ro facility is used for the carriage of agricultural machinery and livestock and it is possible to convey a vehicle on the ferry from which goods can be unloaded directly onto local transport rather than transhipping at Mallaig.

LORD OF THE ISLES *(RIGH NAN EILEAN)* Built by Appledore Ferguson, Port Glasgow, UK to replace the CLAYMORE on the Oban - Castlebay and Lochboisdale services and also the COLUMBA (1420t, 1964) on the Oban - Coll and Tiree service. She took over the Mallaig - Armadale and Mallaig - Outer Isles services in July 1998 but returned to her previous routes during the winter period. In Spring 2003 the Mallaig – Armadale service was taken over by the PIONEER standing in for the new CORUISK and she operated services from Oban to South Uist and Barra. She now serves Colonsay, Coll, Tiree, Barra, Craignure and Lochboisdale from Oban.

MUIRNEAG Built as the MERCANDIAN CARRIER II by Frederikshavn Værft A/S, Frederikshavn, Denmark for *Mercandia* of Denmark and used on a variety of services. In 1983 she was briefly renamed ALIANZA and between 1984 and 1985 she carried the name CARRIER II. In 1985 sold to P&O, renamed the BELARD and used by *Northern Ireland Trailers* on a service between Ardrossan and Belfast (later Larne), subsequently becoming part of *Pandoro*. In 1993 she was chartered to IOMSP subsidiary *Mannin Line* to inaugurate a new service between Great Yarmouth and IJmuiden. In 1994 she was purchased by IOMSP; however, in 1995 the *Mannin Line* service ceased and she was chartered back to *Pandoro*. At the end of 1995 she was returned to IOMSP. In 1996, after deputising for the PEVERIL, she was briefly chartered to *Exxtor Ferries* (operating between Immingham and Rotterdam) and then laid up. In 1997, she again deputised for the PEVERIL, followed by a short period of charter to *P&O European Ferries*. In 1997 she returned to IOMSP and replaced the PEVERIL as the main freight vessel. In 1998 she was sold to *Aabrenaa Rederi* and operated between Åbenrå (Denmark) and Klaipėda (Lithuania). This service ended in 1999 and she was used on a number of short-term charters. In Spring 2002 chartered to *Ferryways* and operated between Ipswich and Ostend. In Autumn 2002 she was chartered to *Caledonian MacBrayne*, renamed the MUIRNEAG and placed on the Ullapool - Stornoway service, replacing the HASCOSAY. She was subsequently sold to *Harrisons (2002) Ltd* and chartered back. To be replaced temporarily by another freighter in October 2013. When the LOCH SEAFORTH is delivered in 2014, the separate freighter service will end.

RAASAY *(EILEAN RATHARSAIR)* Built by James Lamont & Co Ltd, Port Glasgow, UK for and used primarily on the Sconser (Skye) - Raasay service. In 1997 she was replaced by the LOCH STRIVEN, became a spare/relief vessel and inaugurated in October 2003 the winter service between Tobermory (Mull) and Kilchoan (Ardnamurchan).

SATURN *(SATHARN)* Built by Ailsa Shipbuilding, Troon for the Wemyss Bay - Rothesay services. Between 1986 and 2005 she usually rotated on this services and services from Gourock; until 2000 this, in summer, included Clyde cruising but this was not repeated in 2001. In the summers 2005 - 2010, she operated additional peak summer sailings between Ardrossan and Brodick with a maximum capacity of 250 passengers. In October 2010 she took over the Gourock - Dunoon service. In June 2011 replaced by *Argyll Ferries* passenger ferries. During Summer 2011 she operated additional sailings between Ardrossan and Brodick. In September returned to the Gourock - Dunoon route to provide additional capacity for the Cowal Games. She was then laid up.

Under construction

32	LOCHINVAR	523t	13	9.0k	43.5m	150P	23C	2L	BA	UK	9652844
33	LOCH SEAFORTH	8478t	14	19.2k	116.0m	700P	143C	20L	BA	UK	-

LOCHINVAR As the HALLAIG. To be delivered in Autumn 2013. To operate on the Tarbert - Portavadie route.

Sirena Seaways *(Peter Therkildsen)*

Princess Seaways *(Miles Cowsill)*

LOCH SEAFORTH On order from Flensburger Schiffbau-Gesellschaft, Flensburg, Germany for the Stornoway - Ullapool service, replacing the ISLE OF LEWIS and freight vessel MUIRNEAG.

DFDS SEAWAYS

THE COMPANY *DFDS Seaways* is a business unit within *DFDS A/S*, a Danish private sector company.

MANAGEMENT President and CEO DFDS A/S Niels Smedegaard, Head of Shipping Division Peder Gellert Pedersen, Managing Director, DFDS Seaways PLC Sean Potter, Head of North Sea Business Area Kell Robdrup, Head of English Channel Business Area Carsten Jensen, Head of Passenger Business Area Brian Thorsted Hansen.

ADDRESS A/S Sundkrogsgade 11 DK-2100 Copenhagen.

TELEPHONE Administration +45 3342 3342, Passenger Reservations 0871 522 9955, Freight Reservations +44 (0)1469 552 644.

FAX Freight Reservations +44 (0)1469 551180.

INTERNET Websites www.dfds.com *(Chinese, Danish, Dutch, English, German, Italian, Japanese, Norwegian, Polish, Swedish)*

ROUTES OPERATED *Passenger ferries* Harwich - Esbjerg (Denmark) (17 hrs; *SIRENA SEAWAYS*; 3 per week), Newcastle (North Shields) - IJmuiden (near Amsterdam, The Netherlands) (15 hrs; *KING SEAWAYS, PRINCESS SEAWAYS*; daily). *Freight only ferries* Zeebrugge (Belgium) - Rosyth (Scotland) (20 hrs; *LONGSTONE*; 3 per week), Esbjerg - Immingham (18 hrs; *FIONIA SEAWAYS, JUTLANDIA SEAWAYS*; 6 per week), Cuxhaven - Immingham (19 hrs; *FINLANDIA SEAWAYS, SELANDIA SEAWAYS*; 4/5 per week, Immingham - Antwerp (21 hrs; *CRAGSIDE, HAFNIA SEAWAYS*; 3-4 times per month), Gothenburg - Tilbury (37 hrs; *TRANSPULP*; 2 per week), Gothenburg - Immingham (26 hrs (direct), *45 hrs (via Brevik (Fri)); *BEGONIA SEAWAYS, FREESIA SEAWAYS, FICARIA SEAWAYS*; 7 per week), Brevik - Immingham (25 hrs (direct), 42 hrs (via Gothenburg); *BEGONIA SEAWAYS, FREESIA SEAWAYS, FICARIA SEAWAYS*; 2 per week), Gothenburg - Brevik (Norway) - Ghent (Belgium) (Gothenburg 32 hrs, Brevik 32 hrs; *MAGNOLIA SEAWAYS, PETUNIA SEAWAYS, PRIMULA SEAWAYS*; 5 per week), Vlaardingen - Immingham (14 hrs; *CRAGSIDE, HAFNIA SEAWAYS*; 6 per week), Vlaardingen - Felixstowe (7 hrs; *FLANDRIA SEAWAYS, BRITANNIA SEAWAYS, SUECIA SEAWAYS*; 3 per day). **Note** Freight vessels are often moved between routes.

1F	ARK FUTURA	18725t	96	19.7k	183.3m	12P	-	164T	AS	DK	9129598
2F	BEGONIA SEAWAYS	37722t	04	22.5k	230.0m	12P	-	340T	AS	DK	9262089
3F	BRITANNIA SEAWAYS	24196t	00	21.1k	197.5m	12P	-	200T	AS	DK	9153032
4F	CRAGSIDE	29429t	11	21.5k	193.0m	12P	-	270T	A	UK	9457218
5F	FICARIA SEAWAYS	37939t	04	22.5k	230.0m	12P	-	340T	AS	DK	9320568
6F	FINLANDIA SEAWAYS	11530t	00	20.0k	162.2m	12P	-	140T	A	LT	9198721
7F	FIONIA SEAWAYS	25609t	09	20.0k	184.8m	12P	-	250T	AS	UK	9395343
8F	FLANDRIA SEAWAYS	13073t	00	18.6k	142.5m	12P	-	114T	A	DK	9186637
9F	FREESIA SEAWAYS	37722t	04	22.5k	230.0m	12P	-	340T	AS	DK	9274848
10F	HAFNIA SEAWAYS	25609t	08	20.0k	184.8m	12P	-	250T	AS	UK	9357602
11F	JUTLANDIA SEAWAYS	25609t	10	20.0k	184.8m	12P	-	250T	AS	UK	9395355
12	KING SEAWAYS	31788t	87	20.0k	161.6m	2140P	600C	104T	BA	DK	8502406
13F	LONGSTONE	23235t	03	21.0k	193.0m	12P	-	180T	A	UK	9234082
14F	MAGNOLIA SEAWAYS	32289t	03	22.5k	199.8m	12P	-	280T	AS	DK	9259496
15F	PETUNIA SEAWAYS	32289t	04	22.5k	199.8m	12P	-	280T	AS	DK	9259501
16F	PRIMULA SEAWAYS	32289t	04	22.5k	199.8m	12P	-	280T	AS	DK	9259513
17	PRINCESS SEAWAYS	31356t	86	18.5k	161.0m	1600P	600C	100T	BA	DK	8502391
18F	SELANDIA SEAWAYS	24196t	98	21.0k	197.5m	12P	-	206T	A	DK	9157284
19	SIRENA SEAWAYS	22382t	03	22.0k	199.4m	596P	316C	154T	A	DK	9212163
20F	SUECIA SEAWAYS	24196t	99	21.0k	197.5m	12P	-	206T	AS	DK	9153020
21F	TRANSPULP	23128t	06	16.0k	190.7m	12P	-	200T	A	SE	9343261

A to B by SEA

Northern Europe's Leading Liner Shipping Network

63 Daily Crossings

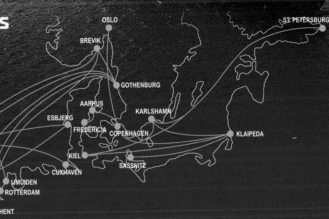

OSLO
BREVIK
ST PETERSBURG
ROSYTH
NEWCASTLE
GOTHENBURG
AARHUS
KARLSHAMN
ESBJERG
FREDERICIA
COPENHAGEN
KLAIPEDA
IMMINGHAM
KIEL
FELIXSTOWE
HARWICH
CUXHAVEN
SASSNITZ
TILBURY
IJMUIDEN
DOVER
ROTTERDAM
DUNKERQUE
ZEEBRÜGGE
GHENT

SAVE
'000s of road miles a year

ENJOY
a good nights sleep,
food & refreshments

ARRIVE
refreshed for the day ahead

Calais Seaways *(John Hendy)*

Flandria Seaways *(Cees de Bijl)*

ARK FUTURA Built as the DANA FUTURA by C N Visentini di Visentini Francesco & C, Donada, Italy for *DFDS*. In 2001 she was renamed the TOR FUTURA. Initially operated mainly between Esbjerg and Harwich, but latterly operated mainly between Esbjerg and Immingham. In 2004 chartered to *Toll Shipping* of Australia. Later time-chartered to the *Danish MoD* for 5.5 years. However, when not required for military service she has been chartered to other operators such as *P&O Ferries*, *Cobelfret Ferries* and *Van Uden Ro-Ro* and used on *DFDS Tor Line* services. In 2006 sold to *DFDS Lys Line Rederi A/S* of Norway, a *DFDS* subsidiary and chartered back. In April 2011 renamed the ARK FUTURA.

BEGONIA SEAWAYS Built as the TOR BEGONIA by Flensburger Schiffbau-Gesellschaft, Flensburg, Germany for *DFDS Tor Line*. Operates on the Gothenburg - Immingham/Brevik route. In Summer 2009 lengthened by 30m by MWB Motorenwerke Bremerhaven AG, Germany. In July 2012 renamed the BEGONIA SEAWAYS.

BRITANNIA SEAWAYS Built as the TOR BRITANNIA by Fincantieri-Cantieri Navali Italiani SpA, Ancona, Italy for *DFDS Tor Line*. Operated on the Gothenburg - Immingham route until 2004 when she was transferred to the Esbjerg - Immingham route. In January 2010 chartered to *Norfolkline* to operate between Vlaardingen and Felixstowe. In May 2011 renamed the BRITANNIA SEAWAYS.

CRAGSIDE Built speculatively by Odense Staalskibsværft A/S, Odense, Denmark. On completion sold to *Maersk Tankers A/S* of Denmark. Initially chartered to *Grimaldi Line* of Italy. In September 2012, chartered to *DFDS Seaways* and placed on the Vlaardingen - Immingham service.

FICARIA SEAWAYS Built as the TOR FICARIA by Flensburger Schiffbau-Gesellschaft, Flensburg, Germany for *DFDS Tor Line*. Operates on the Gothenburg - Immingham/Brevik service. In Summer 2009 lengthened by 30m by MWB Motorenwerke Bremerhaven AG, Germany. In July 2011 renamed the FICARIA SEAWAYS.

FINLANDIA SEAWAYS Launched as the FINNMAID but renamed the FINNREEL before delivery. Built by Jinling Shipyard, Nanjing, China for the *Macoma Shipping Group* and chartered to *Finnlines*. In 2008 sold to *DFDS Lisco* and in January 2009 delivered, chartered to *DFDS Tor Line* and renamed the TOR FINLANDIA. Operated on the Immingham - Rotterdam route until January 2011 when she was transferred to the Rosyth - Zeebrugge route. In May 2012 moved to the Cuxhaven - Immingham service but returned in July. In December 2012 renamed the FINLANDIA SEAWAYS.

FIONIA SEAWAYS Built as the TOR FIONIA by Jinling Shipyard, Nanjing, China for *Macoma Shipping Ltd* of the UK. Launched as the JINGLING 3. She was time-chartered to *DFDS Tor Line* for ten years (with an option on a further three). Delivered in May 2009 and initially replaced the TOR BEGONIA, TOR FICARIA and TOR FREESIA while they were being lengthened. In October 2011 renamed the FIONIA SEAWAYS. Currently operates on the Esbjerg - Immingham route.

FLANDRIA SEAWAYS Built as the MAERSK FLANDERS by Guangzhou Shipyard International, Guangzhou, China for *Norfolkline*. Used on the Scheveningen (from 2007 Vlaardingen) - Felixstowe service. In July 2010 renamed the FLANDRIA SEAWAYS.

FREESIA SEAWAYS Built as the TOR FREESIA by Flensburger Schiffbau-Gesellschaft, Flensburg, Germany for *DFDS Tor Line*. Operates on the Gothenburg - Immingham/Brevik service. In Summer 2009 lengthened by 30m by MWB Motorenwerke Bremerhaven AG, Germany. In August 2012 renamed the FREESIA SEAWAYS.

HAFNIA SEAWAYS Built as the TOR HAFNIA by Jinling Shipyard, Nanjing, China for *Macoma Shipping Ltd* of the UK and time-chartered to *DFDS Tor Line* for ten years. Until 2013, mainly operated on the Immingham - Esbjerg route. In March 2011 renamed the HAFNIA SEAWAYS. In February 2013 transferred to the Vlaardingen - Immingham route.

JUTLANDIA SEAWAYS Built as the TOR JUTLANDIA by Jinling Shipyard, Nanjing, China for *Macoma Shipping Ltd* of the UK and time-chartered to *DFDS Tor Line* for ten years. Operates on the Immingham - Esbjerg route. In July 2011 renamed the JUTLANDIA SEAWAYS.

KING SEAWAYS Built as the NILS HOLGERSSON by Schichau Seebeckwerft AG, Bremerhaven, Germany for *Rederi AB Swedcarrier* of Sweden for their service between Trelleborg and Travemünde, joint with *TT-Line* of Germany (trading as *TT-Line*). In 1992 purchased by *Brittany Ferries* for entry into service in Spring 1993. After a major rebuild, she was renamed the VAL DE LOIRE and introduced onto the Plymouth - Roscoff, Plymouth - Santander and Cork - Roscoff routes. In 2004 transferred to the Portsmouth - St Malo and Portsmouth - Cherbourg services. In 2005 operated mainly Portsmouth - St Malo. In 2006 sold to *DFDS*, renamed the KING OF SCANDINAVIA and placed on the Newcastle - IJmuiden route. In January 2011 renamed the KING SEAWAYS.

LONGSTONE Built by Flensburger Schiffbau-Gesellschaft, Flensburg, Germany for *AWSR Shipping*. Chartered to *Transfennica* and operated between Hanko (Finland) and Lübeck (Germany). In January 2009 chartered to *Finnlines* and placed on the Helsinki - Aarhus route. In January 2012 chartered to *North Sea RoRo*. In March 2013 the operation ceased and the charter was taken over by *DFDS Seaways* and she was placed on the Immingham - Cuxhaven route. In May took over the Zeebrugge - Rosyth route.

MAGNOLIA SEAWAYS Built as the TOR MAGNOLIA by Flensburger Schiffbau-Gesellschaft, Flensburg, Germany for *DFDS Tor Line*. In July 2011 renamed the MAGNOLIA SEAWAYS. Currently operates on the Gothenburg - Ghent route.

PETUNIA SEAWAYS Built as the TOR PETUNIA by Flensburger Schiffbau-Gesellschaft, Flensburg, Germany for *DFDS Tor Line*. In July 2011 renamed the PETUNIA SEAWAYS. Currently operates on the Gothenburg - Ghent route.

PRIMULA SEAWAYS Built as the TOR PRIMULA by Flensburger Schiffbau-Gesellschaft, Flensburg, Germany for *DFDS Tor Line*.. In July 2010 renamed the PRIMULA SEAWAYS. Currently operates on the Gothenburg - Ghent route.

PRINCESS SEAWAYS Built by Schichau Seebeckwerft AG, Bremerhaven, Germany as the PETER PAN for *TT-Line* for the service between Travemünde and Trelleborg. In 1992 sold to *TT Line* of Australia (no connection) for use on their service between Port Melbourne (Victoria) and Devonport (Tasmania) and renamed the SPIRIT OF TASMANIA. In 2002 sold to *Nordsjøferger K/S* of Norway and renamed the SPIR. After modification work she was, in 2003, renamed the FJORD NORWAY and chartered to *Fjord Line*. Placed on the Bergen - Egersund - Hanstholm route. In 2005 placed on the Bergen - Stavanger - Newcastle route, but operated once a week to Hanstholm. In October 2006 sold to *DFDS* and renamed the PRINCESS OF NORWAY, remaining on the Newcastle - Norway service but no longer serving Hanstholm. In May 2007 moved to the Newcastle - IJmuiden route. In February 2011 renamed the PRINCESS SEAWAYS.

SELANDIA SEAWAYS Built as the TOR SELANDIA by Fincantieri-Cantieri Navali Italiani SpA, Ancona, Italy for *DFDS Tor Line*. Operated on the Gothenburg - Immingham route until 2004 when she was moved to the Gothenburg - Ghent route. In 2005 she moved to the Gothenburg - Harwich route. In July the UK terminal moved to Tilbury. In August 2010 renamed the SELANDIA SEAWAYS. Currently operates on the Cuxhaven - Immingham route.

SIRENA SEAWAYS Built as the GOLFO DEI DELFINI by Stocznia Szczecinska, Szczecin, Poland for *Lloyd Sardegna* of Italy for service between Italy and Sardinia. However, due to late delivery the order was cancelled. In 2002 purchased by *DFDS Seaways*, and, during Winter 2002/03, passenger accommodation was enlarged and refitted, increasing passenger capacity from 308 to 596. In June 2003, renamed the DANA SIRENA, she replaced unmodified sister vessel, the DANA GLORIA on the Esbjerg - Harwich service. In February 2013 she was renamed the SIRENA SEAWAYS.

SUECIA SEAWAYS Built as the TOR SUECIA by Fincantieri-Cantieri Navali Italiani SpA, Ancona, Italy for *DFDS Tor Line*. Operated on the Gothenburg - Immingham route until 2004 when she was transferred to the Esbjerg - Immingham route. Later transferred to the Danish flag. In March 2010 chartered to *Norfolkline* to operate between Vlaardingen and Felixstowe and continued on the route when it was taken over by *DFDS*. In June 2011 renamed the SUECIA SEAWAYS.

TRANSPULP Built by Aker Finnyards, Rauma, Finland for *Baltic Container Shipping* of the UK and chartered to *Rederi AB Transatlantic* of Sweden. Operated on service operated for Stora Enso Paper Group, mainly in the Baltic. In early 2011 transferred to the Gothenburg - Tilbury (once weekly) and Gothenburg - Zeebrugge (*CLdN* service) (once weekly) services. In January 2013 began operating twice weekly to Tilbury, replacing the SELANDIA SEAWAYS of *DFDS Seaways*.

Under Construction

22F	ARK DANIA	- 13	20.0k 195.2m	12P	-	206T	A	DK	-
23F	ARK GERMANIA	- 14	20.0k 195.2m	12P	-	206T	A	DK	-

ARK DANIA, ARK GERMANIA Under construction by GmbH, Stralsund, Germany. They will be used for the German/Danish joint ARK Project providing NATO transport but will be available for *DFDS* use and charter when not required. They will have a crane for loading containers on the weather deck. In December 2012 the order for these vessels was cancelled due to late delivery. Following negotiations with the shipyard it was agreed that they would be completed under a new contract which was signed in February 2013. The first vessel will now be delivered in Autumn 2013 and the second in Winter 2014.

DFDS Seaways also owns the ANGLIA SEAWAYS, currently on charter to *Seatruck Ferries*.

DFDS SEAWAYS FRANCE

THE COMPANY *DFDS Seaways France* was inaugurated in March 2013 following the establishment of a *DFDS Seaways/LD Lines* joint venture in November 2012. It is 82% owned by *DFDS* and 12% by *LD Lines*. (see sections 6). The Newhaven - Dieppe route is branded as *Transmanche Ferries*, operating under a franchise awarded by *Syndicat Mixte de L'Activité Transmanche* in Dieppe.

MANAGEMENT Director General Jean-Claude Charlo.

ADDRESS A/S Sundkrogsgade 11 DK-2100 Copenhagen.

TELEPHONE Administration +45 3342 3342, **Passenger Reservations** *Dover* 0871 574 7235, *Newhaven and Portsmouth* 0844 576 8836. **Freight Reservations** *Dover* +44 (0) 1304 874001, *Newhaven and Portsmouth* +33 2 32 145 205.

FAX Freight Reservations *Dover* +44 (0)1304 874040.

INTERNET Website www.dfds.com *(Chinese, Danish, Dutch, English, German, Italian, Japanese, Norwegian, Polish, Swedish)*

ROUTES OPERATED *DFDS Seaways France)* Dover - Dunkerque (2 hrs; *DELFT SEAWAYS, DOVER SEAWAYS, DUNKERQUE SEAWAYS*, 12 per day), Dover Calais (1 hr 30 mins; *CALAIS SEAWAYS, DIEPPE SEAWAYS*; 10 per day), Newhaven - Dieppe (4 hrs; *COTE D'ALBATRE*; 2 per day (ships continue to be branded *Transmanche Ferries*), Le Havre - Portsmouth (5 hrs 30 mins (day), 7 hrs 30 mins (night); *NORMAN VOYAGER*; 1 per day, Marseilles – Tunis (currently freight only) *(BEACHY HEAD*; 3 per week), **Note** the Marseilles - Tunis route is outside the scope of this book but is included for completeness.

1F	BEACHY HEAD	23235t	03	17.1k	193.0m	12P	-	180T	A	UK	9234094
2	CALAIS SEAWAYS	28833t	91	21.0k	163.6m	1850P	600C	100L	BA2	FR	8908466
3	COTE D'ALBATRE	18425t	06	22.0k	112.0m	600P	300C	62L	BA	FR	9320128
4	DELFT SEAWAYS	35923t	06	25.5k	187.0m	780P	200C	120L	BA2	UK	9293088
5	DIEPPE SEAWAYS	30285t	02	22.0k	203.3m	1200P	480C	110L	BA2	FR	9211511
6	DOVER SEAWAYS	35923t	06	25.8k	187.0m	780P	200C	120L	BA2	UK	9318345
7	DUNKERQUE SEAWAYS	35923t	05	25.8k	187.0m	780P	200C	120L	BA2	UK	9293076
8	NORMAN VOYAGER	26500t	08	23.5k	186.5	800P	185C	120L	A	FR	9420423
9	SEVEN SISTERS	18425t	06	22.0k	112.0m	600P	300C	62L	BA	FR	9320130

BEACHY HEAD Built by Flensburger Schiffbau-Gesellschaft, Flensburg, Germany for *AWSR Shipping*. On delivery, chartered to *Transfennica* and operated between Hanko (Finland) and Lübeck (Germany). In July 2006 chartered to *Stora Enso* and placed on the Kotka - Gothenburg route. In late August transferred to the Antwerp - Gothenburg service. In 2007 chartered to *Transfennica*. In January 2009 chartered to *Finnlines*. Normally used on the Helsinki - Aarhus route. In January 2012 chartered to *North Sea RoRo*. In March 2013 the service ceased and she was chartered to *DFDS Seaways*.

CALAIS SEAWAYS Built as the PRINS FILIP by NV Boelwerf SA, Temse, Belgium for *Regie voor Maritiem Transport (RMT)* of Belgium for the Ostend - Dover service. Although completed in 1991, she did not

Dunkerque Seaways (*John Hendy*)

enter service until May 1992. In 1994 the British port became Ramsgate. Withdrawn in 1997 and laid up for sale. In 1998 she was sold to *Stena RoRo* and renamed the STENA ROYAL. In November 1998 she was chartered to *P&O Ferries* to operate as a freight-only vessel on the Dover - Zeebrugge route. In Spring 1999 it was decided to charter the vessel on a long-term basis and she was repainted into *P&O Stena Line* (later *P&O Ferries*) colours and renamed the P&OSL AQUITAINE. In Autumn 1999 she was modified to make her suitable to operate between Dover and Calais and was transferred to that route, becoming a passenger vessel again. In 2002 renamed the PO AQUITAINE and in 2003 the PRIDE OF AQUITAINE. In September 2005 sold to *LD Lines* and renamed the NORMAN SPIRIT. In October, inaugurated a Le Havre - Portsmouth service, replacing that previously operated by *P&O Ferries*. In November 2009 moved to the Dover - Boulogne route. In March 2010 chartered to *TransEuropa Ferries*, placed on the Ostend - Ramsgate service (as part of a joint venture) and renamed the OSTEND SPIRIT. In May 2011 returned to the Portsmouth - Le Havre route and renamed the NORMAN SPIRIT. In November 2011 chartered to *DFDS Seaways* to add extra capacity to their Dover - Dunkerque route. In February 2012 transferred to the new Dover - Calais route, joint with *DFDS Seaways*. In March 2013 refurbished, repainted into *DFDS Seaways* colours and renamed the CALAIS SEAWAYS.

COTE D'ALBATRE Built by Astilleros Barreras SA, Vigo, Spain for *Transmanche Ferries* to operate between Newhaven and Dieppe. In February 2009 she was moved to the Boulogne - Dover and Dieppe - Dover routes. In September 2009 moved to the Le Havre - Portsmouth route. In April 2011 replaced by the NORMAN SPIRIT. Laid up most of the time except when required to replace the SEVEN SISTERS.

DELFT SEAWAYS, DOVER SEAWAYS, DUNKERQUE SEAWAYS Built as the MAERSK DELFT, DOVER SEAWAYS and MAERSK DUNKERQUE by Samsung Heavy Industries, Koje (Geoje) Island, South Korea for *Norfolkline* to operate between Dover and Dunkerque. In July and August 2010 renamed the DELFT SEAWAYS, DOVER SEAWAYS and DUNKERQUE SEAWAYS. In November 2012 the DOVER SEAWAYS was moved to the Dover - Calais route.

DIEPPE SEAWAYS Built as the SUPERFAST X by Howaldtswerke Deutsche Werft AG, Kiel, Germany for *Attica Enterprises* (now *Attica Group*) for use by *Superfast Ferries*. In May 2002 she and the SUPERFAST IX (see ATLANTIC VISION, *Tallink*, Section 6) began operating between Rosyth (Scotland) and Zeebrugge. In 2004 fitted with additional cabins and conference/seating areas. In 2007 sold to *Veolia Transportation* and renamed the JEAN NICOLI. Chartered to *CoTuNav* of Tunisia and operated between France/Italy and Tunisia. Later chartered to *ANEK Lines* of Greece and operated on the Patras - Corfu - Igoumenitsa - Venice route. In July 2008 chartered to *SeaFrance* and renamed the SEAFRANCE MOLIERE. After modifications she was placed on the Dover - Calais route. In November 2011 laid up. In January 2012 offered for sale or charter. In July 2012 sold to *Scapino Shipping Ltd* of Monaco and renamed the MOLIERE. In October 2012 chartered to *DFDS/LD Lines* joint venture and, in November, renamed the DIEPPE SEAWAYS and introduced onto the Dover - Calais service.

NORMAN VOYAGER Built by CN Visentini, Porto Viro, Italy for *Epic Shipping* of the UK and chartered to *LD Lines*. Operated between Le Havre and Portsmouth and Le Havre and Rosslare. In September 2009 sub-chartered to *Celtic Link Ferries*. Initially operated between Cherbourg and Portsmouth and Cherbourg and Rosslare but the Portsmouth service was abandoned in November 2009. In October 2011 returned to *LD Lines* and placed on the St Nazaire - Gijon route. In November moved to the Portsmouth - Le Havre service. In April 2012 sold to *Stena RoRo*; she continues to be chartered to *LD Lines*.

SEVEN SISTERS Built by Astilleros Barreras SA, Vigo, Spain for *Transmanche Ferries* to operate between Newhaven and Dieppe.

IRISH FERRIES

THE COMPANY *Irish Ferries* is an Irish Republic private sector company, part of the *Irish Continental Group*. It was originally mainly owned by the state-owned *Irish Shipping* and partly by *Lion Ferry AB* of Sweden. *Lion Ferry* participation ceased in 1977 and the company was sold into the private sector in 1987. Formerly state-owned *B&I Line* was taken over in 1991 and from 1995 all operations were marketed as *Irish Ferries*.

MANAGEMENT **Group Managing Director** Eamonn Rothwell, **Group Marketing Director** Tony Kelly.

ADDRESS PO Box 19, Ferryport, Alexandra Road, Dublin 1, Irish Republic.

TELEPHONE **Administration** + 353 (0)1 607 5700, **Reservations** *Ireland* + 353 (0)818300 400, *Rosslare Harbour* + 353 (0)53 913 3158, *Holyhead* + 44 (0)8717 300200, *Pembroke Dock* + 44 (0)8717 300500, *National* 44 (0)8717 300400, *24 hour information* + 353 (0)818300 400 (Ireland) or 44 (0)8717 300400 (UK).

FAX **Administration & Reservations** *Dublin* + 353 (0)1 607 5660, *Rosslare* + 353 (0)53 913 3544.

INTERNET **Email** info@irishferries.com **Website** www.irishferries.com *(English, French, German, Italian)*

ROUTES OPERATED **Conventional Ferries** Dublin - Holyhead (3 hrs 15 mins; *ULYSSES*; 2 per day), Rosslare - Pembroke Dock (4 hrs; *ISLE OF INISHMORE*; 2 per day), Rosslare - Cherbourg (France) (17 hrs 30 mins; *OSCAR WILDE*; 1 or 2 per week), Rosslare - Roscoff (France) (16 hrs; *OSCAR WILDE*; 1 or 2 per week). **Fast Ferry** Dublin - Holyhead (1 hr 49 min; *JONATHAN SWIFT*; 2 per day) marketed as 'DUBLINSwift'.

1	ISLE OF INISHMORE	34031t	97	21.3k	182.5m	2200P	802C	152T	BA2	CY	9142605
2»	JONATHAN SWIFT	5989t	99	37.0k	86.6m	800P	200C	-	BA	CY	9188881
3	KAITAKI	22365t	95	19.0k	181.6m	1650P	600C	130T	BA	UK	9107942
4	OSCAR WILDE	31914t	87	22.0k	166.3m	1458P	730C	90T	BA	BS	8506311
5	ULYSSES	50938t	01	22.0k	209.0m	1875P	1342C	300T	BA2	CY	9214991

ISLE OF INISHMORE Built by Van der Giessen-de Noord, Krimpen aan den IJssel, Rotterdam for *Irish Ferries* to operate on the Holyhead - Dublin service. In 2001 replaced by the ULYSSES and moved to the Rosslare - Pembroke Dock route. She also relieves on the Dublin – Holyhead route when the ULYSSES receives her annual overhaul. In 2006 transferred to Cypriot registry.

JONATHAN SWIFT Austal Auto-Express 86 catamaran built by Austal Ships Pty, Fremantle, Australia for *Irish Ferries* for the Dublin - Holyhead route. In 2006 transferred to Cypriot registry.

KAITAKI Built as the ISLE OF INNISFREE by Van der Giessen-de Noord, Krimpen aan den IJssel, Rotterdam for *Irish Ferries* to operate on the Holyhead - Dublin route. In 1997 transferred to the Rosslare - Pembroke Dock service; for a short period, before modifications at Pembroke Dock were completed, she operated between Rosslare and Fishguard. In Spring 2001 she was replaced by the ISLE OF INISHMORE and laid up. In July 2002 she was chartered to *P&O Portsmouth* for 5 years and renamed the PRIDE OF CHERBOURG. Entered service in October 2002. Withdrawn in October 2004. In January 2005, sub-chartered by *P&O* to *Stena RoRo*, renamed the STENA CHALLENGER and operated on the Karlskrona - Gdynia route. In June 2006 sub-chartered by *Stena RoRo* to *Toll Shipping* of New Zealand and renamed the CHALLENGER. In August 2006 she arrived in New Zealand and was placed on the Wellington - Picton route. In 2007 renamed the KAITAKI. In 2009 charter extended until 2013 and in 2013 charter extended until June 2017.

OSCAR WILDE Built as the KRONPRINS HARALD by Oy Wärtsilä AB, Turku, Finland for *Jahre Line* of Norway for the Oslo - Kiel service. In 1991 ownership was transferred to *Color Line*. In early 2007 sold to *Irish Ferries* for delivery in September 2007. Chartered back to *Color Line* until that date. When delivered, renamed the OSCAR WILDE and in November placed on the Rosslare - Roscoff/Cherbourg routes.

Leading the way.

The finest ships, the highest standards and the best value fares. It's little wonder that Irish Ferries is Ireland's leading ferry company.

Irishferries.com

Jonathan Swift (*Miles Cowsill*)

Ben-my-Chree (*Miles Cowsill*)

ULYSSES Built by Aker Finnyards, Rauma, Finland for *Irish Ferries* for the Dublin - Holyhead service. In 2006 transferred to Cypriot registry.

ISLE OF MAN STEAM PACKET COMPANY

THE COMPANY *The Isle of Man Steam Packet Company Limited* is an Isle of Man-registered company.

MANAGEMENT **Chief Executive Officer** Mark Woodward.

ADDRESS Imperial Buildings, Douglas, Isle of Man IM1 2BY.

TELEPHONE **Administration** + 44 (0)1624 645645, **Reservations** *From UK* 08722 992992, *From elsewhere* + 44 (0)1624 661661, **Freight Bookings** + 44 (0)1624 645620.

FAX **Administration** + 44 (0)1624 645609.

INTERNET **Email** iom.reservations@steam-packet.com **Website** www.steam-packet.com *(English)*

ROUTES OPERATED **Conventional Ferries** *All year* Douglas (Isle of Man) - Heysham (3 hrs 30 mins; *BEN-MY-CHREE*; up to 2 per day), *November-March* Douglas (Isle of Man) - Liverpool (Birkenhead) (4 hrs 15 mins; *BEN-MY-CHREE*; 2 per week). **Fast Ferries** *March-October* Douglas (Isle of Man) - Liverpool (2 hrs 40 mins; *MANANNAN*; up to 2 per day), Douglas - Belfast (2 hrs 55 mins; *MANANNAN*; up to 2 per week), Douglas - Dublin (2 hrs 55 mins; *MANANNAN*; up to 2 per week), Douglas - Heysham (2 hrs; *MANANNAN*; occasional).

1	BEN-MY-CHREE	12747t	98	18.0k	124.9m	630P	-	90T	A	IM	9170705
2»	MANANNAN	5743t	98	43.0k	96.0m	820P	200C	-	A	IM	9176072

BEN-MY-CHREE Built by Van der Giessen-de Noord, Krimpen aan den IJssel, Rotterdam for the *IOMSP Co* and operates between Douglas and Heysham. Additional passenger accommodation was added at her Spring 2004 refit. In 2005 her passenger certificate was increased from 500 to 630. She operates some sailings between Douglas and Liverpool (Birkenhead) in the winter.

MANANNAN Incat 96m catamaran built at Hobart, Tasmania. Initially chartered to *Transport Tasmania* of Australia and operated between Port Melbourne (Victoria) and Georgetown (Tasmania). In 1999 chartered to *Fast Cat Ferries* of New Zealand and operated between Wellington (North Island) and Picton (South Island) under the marketing name 'Top Cat'. In 2000 she was laid up. In 2001 she was chartered to the *US Navy* and renamed the USS JOINT VENTURE (HSV-X1). In 2008 the charter was terminated and she was renamed the INCAT 050. Later purchased by *IOMSP*. Following conversion back to civilian use she was renamed the MANANNAN and entered service in May 2009.

MYFERRYLINK

THE COMPANY *MyFerryLink* is a French private sector company owned by *Groupe Eurotunnel* and operated by a *SCOP*, a co-operative formed primarily of former *SeaFrance* employees. Operations stared in August 2012.

MANAGEMENT **Managing Director (UK)** Robin Wilkins.

ADDRESS *France* 60 Boulevard de Turin, Tour de Lille, Euralille, 59777 Lille, France, *UK* Whitfield Court, Honeywood Close, Whitfield, Dover, Kent CT16 3PX.

TELEPHONE *Passenger reservations and information* 0844 2482 100 (from UK); 0811 654 765 (from Continental Europe), *Freight* + 33(0)3 21 46 80 40.

FAX *UK - Passenger* + 44 (0)1304 828379, *Freight* + 33(0)3 21 46 80 39.

INTERNET **Email** clientservices@myferrylink.com (**Freight** freightsales@myferrylink.com) **Website** www.myferrylink.com *(English, French)*

1	BERLIOZ	33940t	05	25.0k	186.0m	1900P	700C	120L	BA2	FR	9305843
2F +	NORD PAS-DE-CALAIS	7264t	87	21.5k	160.1m	100P	-	85L	BA2	FR	8512152
3	RODIN	33796t	01	25.0k	186.0m	1900P	700C	120L	BA2	FR	9232527

BERLIOZ Built as the SEAFRANCE BERLIOZ by Chantiers de l'Atlantique, St Nazaire for *SeaFrance*. Launched in March 2005. In November 2011 laid up. In June 2012 sold to *Eurotransmanche, a Groupe Eurotunnel* company. In July 2012 renamed the BERLIOZ. In August 2012 chartered to *MyFerryLink* and resumed operation between Calais and Dover.

NORD PAS-DE-CALAIS Built by Chantiers du Nord et de la Mediterranée, Dunkerque, France as the NORD PAS-DE-CALAIS at Dunkerque, France for *SNCF* for the Dunkerque (Ouest) - Dover train ferry service. Before being used on this service (which required the construction of a new berth at Dover (Western Docks)) in May 1988, she operated road freight services from Calais to Dover Eastern Docks. The train ferry service continued to operate following the opening of the Channel Tunnel in 1994, to convey road vehicles and dangerous loads which were banned from the Tunnel. However, it ceased in December 1995 and, after a refit, in February 1996 she was renamed the SEAFRANCE NORD PAS-DE-CALAIS and switched to the Calais - Dover service, primarily for road freight vehicles and drivers but also advertised as carrying up to 50 car passengers. Since the entry into service of a third multi-purpose ferry, she operated on a freight-only basis. In November 2011 laid up. In June 2012 sold to *Eurotransmanche*. In July renamed the NORD PAS-DE-CALAIS. In November 2012 chartered to *MyFerryLink* and resumed operation between Calais and Dover.

RODIN Built as the SEAFRANCE RODIN by Aker Finnyards, Rauma, Finland for *SeaFrance*. Launched in November 2001. In November 2011 laid up. In June 2012 sold to *Eurotransmanche*. In July 2012 renamed the RODIN. In August 2012 chartered to *MyFerryLink* and resumed operation between Calais and Dover.

NORTHLINK FERRIES

THE COMPANY *NorthLink Ferries Ltd* is a UK based company, wholly owned by the *David MacBrayne Group*, which is owned by the Scottish Ministers. During summer 2012 the services was transferred to *Serco Group plc*. The trading name was unaffected.

MANAGEMENT **Managing Director** Bill Davidson, **Commercial Director** Cynthia Spencer.

ADDRESS Ferry Terminal, Ferry Road, Stromness, Orkney KW16 3BH.

TELEPHONE **Administration** +44 (0)1856 885500, **Passenger Reservations** +44 (0)845 6000 449, **Freight Reservations** +44 (0)845 6060 449.

FAX **Administration** +44 (0)1856 879588.

INTERNET **Email** info@northlinkferries.co.uk **Website** www.northlinkferries.co.uk *(English)*

www.northlinkferries.co.uk/freight-timetables.html *(English)*

ROUTES OPERATED *Passenger Ferries* Scrabster - Stromness (Orkney) (1 hr 30 min; *HAMNAVOE*; up to 3 per day), Aberdeen - Lerwick (Shetland) (direct) (12 hrs; *HJALTLAND, HROSSEY*; 3 northbound/4 southbound per week), Aberdeen - Kirkwall, Hatston New Pier (Orkney) (5 hrs 45 mins) - Lerwick (14 hrs; *HJALTLAND, HROSSEY*; 4 northbound/3 southbound per week). *Freight Ferries* Aberdeen - Kirkwall (Orkney) (12 hrs; *HELLIAR, HILDASAY*; 4 per week), Aberdeen - Lerwick (Shetland). (*HELLIAR, HILDASAY*; 4 per week).

1	HAMNAVOE	8780t	02	19.3k	112.0m	600P	95C	20L	BA	UK	9246061
2F	HELLIAR	7800t	98	17.0k	122.3m	12P	-	86T	A	IM	9119397
3F	HILDASAY	7606t	99	17.0k	122.3m	12P	-	84T	A	IM	9119426
4	HJALTLAND	11720t	02	24.0k	125.0m	600P	150C	30L	BA	UK	9244958
5	HROSSEY	11720t	02	24.0k	125.0m	600P	150C	30L	BA	UK	9244960

HAMNAVOE Built by Aker Finnyards, Rauma, Finland for *NorthLink Orkney and Shetland Ferries Ltd* to operate on the Scrabster - Stromness route. Did not enter service until Spring 2003 due to late completion of work at Scrabster to accommodate the ship. *Caledonian MacBrayne's* HEBRIDEAN ISLES covered between October 2002 and Spring 2003.

HELLIAR Built as the LEHOLA by Astilleros de Huelva SA, Huelva, Spain for the *Estonian Shipping Company*. Initially used on *ESCO* Baltic services. In 1998 chartered to *Czar Peter Line* to operate

Rodin (*Andrew Cooke*)

Nord Pas-de-Calais (*Darren Holdaway*)

between Moerdijk (The Netherlands) and Kronstadt (Russia). In 1999 chartered to *Delom* of France to operate between Marseilles and Sete and Tunis. In 2000 she returned to *ESCO*, operating between Kiel and Tallinn. In 2003 chartered to *Scandlines AG* and transferred to subsidiary *Scandlines Estonia AS*. Operated Rostock - Helsinki – Muuga initially and later Rostock – Helsinki. Service finished at the end of 2004 and in 2005 she was chartered to *P&O Ferries* to operate between Hull and Rotterdam and Hull and Zeebrugge. In 2005 sold to *Elmira Shipping* of Greece. Later renamed the RR TRIUMPH. In 2006 transferred to *P&O Irish Sea* to operate between Liverpool and Dublin. In 2007 chartered to *Balearia* of Spain and operated from Barcelona. In December 2007 purchased by *Seatruck Ferries* and renamed the TRIUMPH. In Spring 2008 she was sub-chartered to *Condor Ferries* to cover for the refit period of the COMMODORE GOODWILL. In June 2008 placed on the Liverpool - Dublin route and in July renamed the CLIPPER RACER. In February 2009 replaced by the new CLIPPER PACE. In April 2009 again chartered to *Balearia*. In January 2011 chartered to *NorthLink Ferries* and renamed the HELLIAR.

HILDASAY Built as the LEILI by Astilleros de Huelva SA, Huelva, Spain for the *Estonian Shipping Company*. Used on Baltic services. In 2002 chartered to *Crowley Maritime* of the USA and renamed the PORT EVERGLADES EXPRESS. In 2004 resumed the name LEILI and chartered to *NorseMerchant Ferries* to operate between Birkenhead and Dublin. In July 2005 moved to the Heysham - Belfast route and at the same time sold to *Elmira Shipping* of Greece and renamed the RR SHIELD. In 2007 sold to *Attica Group* of Greece and renamed the SHIELD. In January 2008 sold to *Seatruck Ferries* but continued to be chartered to *Norfolkline*. In June 2009 returned to *Seatruck Ferries*. In January 2009 chartered to *NorthLink Orkney and Shetland Ferries* and renamed the HILDASAY.

HJALTLAND, HROSSEY Built by Aker Finnyards, Rauma, Finland for *NorthLink Orkney and Shetland Ferries* to operate on the Aberdeen - Kirkwall - Lerwick route when services started in 2002.

ORKNEY FERRIES

THE COMPANY *Orkney Ferries Ltd* (previously the *Orkney Islands Shipping Company*) is a British company, owned by *Orkney Islands Council*.

MANAGEMENT **Operations Director** Capt N H Mills, **Ferry Services Manager** D I Sawkins.

ADDRESS Shore Street, Kirkwall, Orkney KW15 1LG.

TELEPHONE **Administration** + 44 (0)1856 872044, **Reservations** + 44 (0)1856 872044.

FAX **Administration & Reservations** + 44 (0)1856 872921.

INTERNET **Email** info@orkneyferries.co.uk **Website** www.orkneyferries.co.uk *(English)*

ROUTES OPERATED Kirkwall (Mainland) to Eday (1 hr 15 mins), Rapness (Westray) (1 hr 25 mins), Sanday (1 hr 25 mins), Stronsay (1 hr 35 mins), Papa Westray (1 hr 50 mins), North Ronaldsay (2 hrs 30 mins) ('North Isles service') (timings are direct from Kirkwall - sailings via other islands take longer; *EARL SIGURD, EARL THORFINN, VARAGEN*; 1/2 per day except Papa Westray which is twice weekly and North Ronaldsay which is weekly), Pierowall (Westray) - Papa Westray (25 mins; *GOLDEN MARIANA*; up to six per day (Summer service - passenger-only)), Kirkwall - Shapinsay (25 mins; *SHAPINSAY*; 6 per day), Houton (Mainland) to Lyness (Hoy) (35 mins; *HOY HEAD*; 5 per day), and Flotta (35 mins; *HOY HEAD*; 4 per day) ('South Isles service') (timings are direct from Houton - sailings via other islands take longer), Tingwall (Mainland) to Rousay (20 mins; *EYNHALLOW*; 6 per day), Egilsay (30 mins; *EYNHALLOW*; 5 per day) and Wyre (20 mins; *EYNHALLOW*; 5 per day) (timings are direct from Tingwall - sailings via other islands take longer), Stromness (Mainland) to Moaness (Hoy) (25 mins; *GRAEMSAY*; 2/3 per day) and Graemsay (25 mins; *GRAEMSAY*; 2/3 per day) (passenger/cargo service - cars not normally conveyed).

1	EARL SIGURD	771t	90	12.5k	45.0m	190P	26C	-	BA	UK	8902711
2	EARL THORFINN	771t	90	12.5k	45.0m	190P	26C	-	BA	UK	8902723
3	EYNHALLOW	104t	87	10.5k	28.8m	95P	11C	-	BA	UK	8960880
4p	GOLDEN MARIANA	33t	73	9.5k	15.2m	40P	0C	-	-	UK	
5	GRAEMSAY	90t	96	10.0k	20.6m	73P	2C	-	C	UK	
6	HOY HEAD	482t	94	11.0k	53.5m	125P	24C	3L	BA	UK	9081722

Hrossey (*Miles Cowsill*)

Graemsay (*Miles Cowsill*)

Pride of Burgundy *(John Hendy)*

Pride of Hull *(Cees de Bijl)*

7	SHAPINSAY	199t	89	10.0k	32.6m	91P	16C	-	BA	UK	8814184
8	THORSVOE	385t	91	10.6k	35.0m	122P	16C	-	BA	UK	9014743
9	VARAGEN	928t	88	14.5k	49.9m	144P	33C	5L	BA	UK	8818154

EARL SIGURD, EARL THORFINN Built by McTay Marine, Bromborough, Wirral, UK to inaugurate ro-ro working on the 'North Isles service'.

EYNHALLOW Built by David Abels Boat Builders, Bristol, UK to inaugurate ro-ro services from Tingwall (Mainland) to Rousay, Egilsay and Wyre. In 1991 she was lengthened by 5 metres, to increase car capacity.

GOLDEN MARIANA Built by Bideford Shipyard Ltd, Bideford, UK for A J G England of Padstow as a dual-purpose passenger and fishing vessel. In 1975 sold to M MacKenzie of Ullapool, then to Pentland Ferries, Wide Firth Ferry in 1982, and Orkney Islands Council in 1986. Passenger-only vessel. Generally operates summer-only feeder service between Pierowall (Westray) and Papa Westray.

GRAEMSAY Built by Ailsa Shipbuilding, Troon UK to operate between Stromness (Mainland), Moaness (Hoy) and Graemsay. Designed to offer an all-year-round service to these islands, primarily for passengers and cargo. Between October 2009 and January 2010 lengthened by 4.4 metres.

HOY HEAD Built by Appledore Shipbuilders Ltd, Appledore, UK to replace the THORSVOE on the 'South Isles service'. During winter 2012/13 extended by 14 metres at Cammell Laird Shiprepairers & Shipbuilders, Birkenhead, England.

SHAPINSAY Built by Yorkshire Drydock Ltd, Hull, UK for the service from Kirkwall (Mainland) to Shapinsay. In April 2011 lengthened by 6 metres at the Macduff Shipyards, Macduff, Scotland to increase car capacity from 12 to 16 and re-engined.

THORSVOE Built by Campbeltown Shipyard, Campbeltown, UK for the 'South Isles service'. In 1994 replaced by the new HOY HEAD and became the main reserve vessel for the fleet.

VARAGEN Built by Cochrane Shipbuilders, Selby, UK for Orkney Ferries, a private company established to start a new route between Gills Bay (Caithness, Scotland) and Burwick (South Ronaldsay, Orkney). However, due to problems with the terminals it was not possible to maintain regular services. In 1991, the company was taken over by Orkney Islands Shipping Company and the VARAGEN became part of their fleet, sharing the 'North Isles service' with the EARL SIGURD and the EARL THORFINN and replacing the freight vessel ISLANDER (494t, 1969).

P&O FERRIES

THE COMPANY P&O Ferries Holdings Ltd is a private sector company, a subsidiary of Dubai World, owned by the Government of Dubai. In Autumn 2002 P&O North Sea Ferries, P&O Irish Sea, P&O Portsmouth and P&O Stena Line (Stena Line involvement having ceased) were merged into a single operation.

MANAGEMENT Chief Executive Officer Helen Deeble, Fleet Director John Garner, Communications Director Chris Laming, Freight Director Ronald Daelman, Human Resources Director Lesley Cotton, Ports Director Sue Mackenzie, Passenger Services Director Simon Johnson, Company Secretary Susan Kitchin.

ADDRESSES Head Office and Dover Services Channel House, Channel View Road, Dover, Kent CT17 9TJ, Hull King George Dock, Hedon Road, Hull HU9 5QA, Larne P&O Irish Sea, Larne Harbour, Larne, Co Antrim BT40 1AW Rotterdam Beneluxhaven, Rotterdam (Europoort), Postbus 1123, 3180 Rozenburg, Netherlands, Zeebrugge Leopold II Dam 13, Havendam, 8380 Zeebrugge, Belgium.

TELEPHONE Administration UK +44 (0)1304 863000, Passenger Reservations UK 08716 64 64 64, France +33 (0)825 12 01 56, Belgium +32 (0)70 70 77 71, The Netherlands +31 (0)20 20 08333, Spain +34 (0)902 02 04 61, Luxembourg +34 (0)20 80 82 94. Freight Reservations UK 0870 6000 868, Irish Republic +353 (0)1 855 0522.

FAX Passenger Reservations *UK East and South Coast* +44 (0)1304 863464, *West Coast* 44 (0)02828 872195, *The Netherlands* +31 (0)118 1225 5215, *Belgium* +32 (0)50 54 71 12, Freight Reservations *Cairnryan* +44 (0)1581 200282, *Larne* +44 (0)28 2827 2477.

INTERNET Email customer.services@poferries.com Website www.poferries.com *(English, French, Dutch, German)* www.poirishsea.com *(English)* www.poferriesfreight.com *(English, French, German)*

ROUTES OPERATED Passenger - conventional ferries Dover - Calais (1 hr 15 mins - 1 hr 30 mins; *PRIDE OF BURGUNDY, PRIDE OF CANTERBURY, PRIDE OF KENT, SPIRIT OF BRITAIN, SPIRIT OF FRANCE*; up to 25 per day), Hull - Zeebrugge (Belgium) (from 12 hrs 30 mins; *PRIDE OF BRUGES, PRIDE OF YORK*; 1 per day), Hull - Rotterdam (Beneluxhaven, Europoort) (The Netherlands) (from 10 hrs; *PRIDE OF HULL, PRIDE OF ROTTERDAM*; 1 per day), Cairnryan - Larne (1 hr 45 min; *EUROPEAN CAUSEWAY, EUROPEAN HIGHLANDER*; 7 per day), Liverpool - Dublin (8 hrs; *EUROPEAN ENDEAVOUR, NORBANK, NORBAY*; up to 3 per day (some sailings are freight only). Fast Ferry (March-October) Cairnryan - Larne (1 hr; *EXPRESS*; 1 per day), Troon – Larne (1 hr 49 min; *EXPRESS* 2 per day). Freight-only Tilbury - Zeebrugge (8 hrs; *NORSKY, NORSTREAM* ; 10 per week), Middlesbrough (Teesport) - Rotterdam (Beneluxhaven, Europoort) (16 hrs; *WILHELMINE* ; 3 per week), Middlesbrough (Teesport) - Zeebrugge (15 hrs 30 mins; *BORE SONG*; 3 per week).

1	BORE SONG	25235t	11	18.5k	195.0m	12P	-	210T	A2	FI	9443566
2	EUROPEAN CAUSEWAY	20646t	00	22.7k	159.5m	410P	315C	84T	BA2	BS	9208394
3	EUROPEAN ENDEAVOUR	22152t	00	22.5k	180.0m	366P	-	120L	BA2	UK	9181106
4	EUROPEAN HIGHLANDER	21128t	02	22.6k	162.7m	410P	315C	84T	BA2	BS	9244116
5F+•	EUROPEAN SEAWAY	22986t	91	21.0k	179.7m	200P	-	120L	BA2	UK	9007283
6»	EXPRESS	5902t	98	43.0k	91.3m	868P	195C	-	A	BS	9176046
7	NORBANK	17464t	93	22.5k	166.7m	114P	-	125T	A	NL	9056583
8	NORBAY	17464t	92	21.5k	166.7m	114P	-	125T	A	BM	9056595
9 F	NORSKY	19992t	99	20.0k	180.0m	12P	-	194T	A	NL	9186182
10F	NORSTREAM	19992t	99	20.0k	180.0m	12P	-	194T	A	NL	9186194
11•	OSTEND SPIRIT	26433t	87	22.0k	169.6m	2290P	585C	85L	BA2	UK	8517748
12	PRIDE OF BRUGES	31598t	87	18.5k	179.0m	1050P	310C	185T	A	NL	8503797
13	PRIDE OF BURGUNDY	28138t	92	21.0k	179.7m	1420P	465C	120L	BA2	UK	9015254
14	PRIDE OF CANTERBURY	30635t	91	21.0k	179.7m	2000P	537C	120L	BA2	UK	9007295
15	PRIDE OF HULL	59925t	01	22.0k	215.4m	1360P	205C	263T	AS	BS	9208629
16	PRIDE OF KENT	30635t	92	21.0k	179.7m	2000P	537C	120L	BA2	UK	9015266
17	PRIDE OF ROTTERDAM	59925t	00	22.0k	215.4m	1360P	205C	263T	AS	NL	9208617
18	PRIDE OF YORK	31785t	87	18.5k	179.0m	1050P	310C	185T	A	BS	8501957
19	SPIRIT OF BRITAIN	47592t	11	22.0k-	212.0m	2000P	194C	180L	BA2	UK	9524231
20	SPIRIT OF FRANCE	47592t	12	22.0k-	212.0m	2000P	194C	180L	BA2	UK	9533816
21F	WILHELMINE	21020t	12	15.8k	150.0m	12P	-	170T	A	LU	9539080

BORE SONG Built by Flensburger Schiffbau-Gesellschaft, Flensburg, Germany for *Bore Shipowners (Rettig Group Bore)* of Finland. In July 2011 chartered to *Mann Lines* to cover for the ESTRADEN'S refit. In September 2011 chartered to *P&O Ferries* and placed on the Middlesbrough - Zeebrugge route.

EUROPEAN CAUSEWAY Built by Mitsubishi Heavy Industries, Shimonoseki, Japan for *P&O Irish Sea* for the Cairnryan - Larne service.

EUROPEAN ENDEAVOUR Built as the MIDNIGHT MERCHANT by Astilleros Españoles SA, Seville, Spain for *Cenargo* (then owners of *NorseMerchant Ferries*). On delivery, chartered to *Norfolkline* to operate as second vessel on the Dover - Dunkerque (Ouest) service. In 2002 modified to allow two-deck loading. In 2006 chartered to *Acciona Trasmediterranea* of Spain and renamed the EL GRECO. Used on Mediterranean and Canary Island services. In 2007 sold to *P&O Ferries* and renamed the EUROPEAN ENDEAVOUR. Operated on the Dover - Calais route and as a re-fit relief vessel on Irish Sea routes. In May 2010 laid up. In February 2011 moved to the Liverpool - Dublin route.

EUROPEAN HIGHLANDER Built by Mitsubishi Heavy Industries, Shimonoseki, Japan for *P&O Irish Sea* for the Cairnryan - Larne service.

EUROPEAN SEAWAY Built by Schichau Seebeckwerft AG, Bremerhaven, Germany for *P&O European Ferries* for the Dover - Zeebrugge freight service. In 2000 a regular twice-daily freight-only Dover-Calais service was established, using this vessel which continued to operate to Zeebrugge at night. In 2001 car passengers (not foot or coach passengers) began to be conveyed on the Dover - Zeebrugge service. In 2003 the Zeebrugge service ended and she operated only between Dover and Calais in a freight-only mode. In 2004 withdrawn and laid up. In January 2005 returned to the Dover – Calais route. In July 2012 chartered to GLID, a joint venture between Centrica Renewable Energy Limited and EIG, for use by technicians working on the North Sea Lynn and Inner Dowsing wind farm array four miles off Skegness. In October 2012 returned to the Dover - Calais service. In April 2013 laid up at Tilbury.

EXPRESS Incat 91m catamaran built at Hobart, Tasmania, Australia for *Buquebus* of Argentina as the CATALONIA I and used by *Buquebus España* on their service between Barcelona (Spain) and Mallorca. In April 2000 chartered to *P&O Portsmouth* and renamed the PORTSMOUTH EXPRESS. During Winter 2000/01 she operated for *Buquebus* between Buenos Aires (Argentina) and Piriapolis (Uruguay) and was renamed the CATALONIA. Returned to *P&O Portsmouth* in Spring 2001 and was renamed the PORTSMOUTH EXPRESS. Returned to *Buquebus* in Autumn 2001 and then returned to *P&O Portsmouth* in Spring 2002. Laid up in Europe during Winter 2002/03 and renamed the CATALONIA. She returned to *P&O Ferries* in Spring 2003 trading under the marketing name 'Express'. In November she was renamed the EXPRESS. In 2004 she operated as the 'Cherbourg Express'. In 2005 transferred to *P&O Irish Sea* and operated on the Larne - Cairnryan/Troon service.

NORBANK Built by Van der Giessen-de Noord, Krimpen aan den IJssel, Rotterdam, The Netherlands for *North Sea Ferries* for the Hull - Rotterdam service. She was originally built for and chartered to *Nedlloyd* but the charter was taken over by *P&O* in 1996 and she was bought by *P&O* in 2003. She retains Dutch crew and registry. In May 2001 moved to the Felixstowe - Europoort route. In January 2002 transferred to *P&O Irish Sea* and operated on the Liverpool – Dublin route.

NORBAY Built by Van der Giessen-de Noord, Krimpen aan den IJssel, Rotterdam, The Netherlands for *North Sea Ferries* for the Hull - Rotterdam service. Owned by *P&O*. In January 2002 transferred to *P&O Irish Sea* and operated on the Liverpool – Dublin route.

NORSKY, NORSTREAM Built by Aker Finnyards, Rauma, Finland for *Bore Line* of Finland and chartered to *P&O North Sea Ferries*. They generally operated on the Teesport - Zeebrugge service. In September 2011, the NORSTREAM was moved to the Tilbury - Zeebrugge route. In January 2013, the NORSKY was also moved to the Tilbury - Zeebrugge route.

OSTEND SPIRIT Built by Schichau Seebeckwerft AG, Bremerhaven, Germany for *European Ferries* as the PRIDE OF CALAIS for the Dover - Calais service. In 1998 transferred to *P&O Stena Line*. In 1999 renamed the P&OSL CALAIS. In 2003 renamed PO CALAIS and in 2003 renamed the PRIDE OF CALAIS. In October 2012 laid up. In December 2012 demise chartered to TEF for three years and renamed the OSTEND SPIRIT. In late January 2013 introduced onto the Ramsgate - Ostend service. In April 2013 re-possessed and returned to lay-up at Tilbury.

PRIDE OF BRUGES Built as the NORSUN by NKK, Tsurumi, Japan for the Hull - Rotterdam service of *North Sea Ferries*. She was owned by *Nedlloyd* and was sold to *P&O* in 1996 but retains Dutch crew and registry. In May 2001 replaced by the PRIDE OF ROTTERDAM and in July 2001, after a major refurbishment, she was transferred to the Hull - Zeebrugge service, replacing the NORSTAR (26919t, 1974). In 2003 renamed the PRIDE OF BRUGES.

PRIDE OF BURGUNDY Built by Schichau Seebeckwerft AG, Bremerhaven, Germany for *P&O European Ferries* for the Dover - Calais service. When construction started she was due to be a sister vessel to the EUROPEAN SEAWAY (see Section 3) called the EUROPEAN CAUSEWAY and operate on the Zeebrugge freight route. However, it was decided that she should be completed as a passenger/freight vessel (the design allowed for conversion) and she was launched as the PRIDE OF BURGUNDY. In 1998, transferred to *P&O Stena Line* and renamed the P&OSL BURGUNDY. In 2002 renamed the PO BURGUNDY and in 2003 renamed the PRIDE OF BURGUNDY. In 2004 she operated mainly in freight-only mode. In 2005 returned to full passenger service.

PRIDE OF CANTERBURY Built as the EUROPEAN PATHWAY by Schichau Seebeckwerft AG, Bremerhaven, Germany for *P&O European Ferries* for the Dover - Zeebrugge freight service. In 1998

European Highlander (*Gordon Hislip*)

Pride of Canterbury (*Matthew Punter*)

Spirit of Britain (*Darren Holdaway*)

European Endeavour (*Gordon Hislip*)

transferred to *P&O Stena Line*. In 2001 car/foot passengers were again conveyed on the route. In 2002/03 rebuilt as a full passenger vessel and renamed the PRIDE OF CANTERBURY; now operates between Dover and Calais.

PRIDE OF HULL Built by Fincantieri-Cantieri Navali Italiani SpA, Venice, Italy for *P&O North Sea Ferries* to replace (with the PRIDE OF ROTTERDAM) the NORSEA and NORSUN plus the freight vessels NORBAY and NORBANK on the Hull - Rotterdam service.

PRIDE OF KENT Built as the EUROPEAN HIGHWAY by Schichau Seebeckwerft AG, Bremerhaven, Germany for *P&O European Ferries* for the Dover - Zeebrugge freight service. In 1998 transferred to *P&O Stena Line*. In Summer 1999 she operated full-time between Dover and Calais. She returned to the Dover - Zeebrugge route in the autumn when the P&OSL AQUITAINE was transferred to the Dover - Calais service. In 2001 car/foot passengers were again conveyed on the route. In 2002/03 rebuilt as a full passenger vessel and renamed the PRIDE OF KENT; now operates between Dover and Calais.

PRIDE OF ROTTERDAM Built by Fincantieri-Cantieri Navali Italiani SpA, Venice, Italy. Keel laid as the PRIDE OF HULL but launched as the PRIDE OF ROTTERDAM. Owned by Dutch interests until 2006 when she was sold to *P&O Ferries*. Further details as the PRIDE OF HULL.

PRIDE OF YORK Built as the NORSEA by Govan Shipbuilders Ltd, Glasgow, UK for the Hull - Rotterdam service of *North Sea Ferries* (jointly owned by *P&O* and *The Royal Nedlloyd Group* of The Netherlands until 1996). In December 2001 she was replaced by the new PRIDE OF HULL and, after a two-month refurbishment, in 2002 transferred to the Hull - Zeebrugge service, replacing the NORLAND (26290t, 1974). In 2003 renamed the PRIDE OF YORK.

SPIRIT OF BRITAIN, SPIRIT OF FRANCE Built by STX Europe, Rauma, Finland for the Dover - Calais service. Car capacity relates to dedicated car deck only; additional cars can be accommodated on the freight decks as necessary.

WILHELMINE Built by the Kyokuyo Shipyard, Shimonoseki, Japan for *CLdN*. After completion, a additional deck and sponsons were retro-fitted at the Chengxi Shipyard, Jiangyin, China. Initially used on the Zeebrugge - Purfleet service. In January 2013 chartered to *P&O Ferries* to operate between Tilbury and Zeebrugge. After three weeks moved to the Middlesbrough - Rotterdam service.

PENTLAND FERRIES

THE COMPANY *Pentland Ferries* is a UK private sector company.

MANAGEMENT **Managing Director** Andrew Banks, **Office Manager** Kathryn Banks.

ADDRESS Pier Road, St Margaret's Hope, South Ronaldsay, Orkney KW17 2SW.

TELEPHONE **Administration & Reservations** +44 (0)1856 831226.

FAX **Administration & Reservations** +44 (0)1856 831697.

INTERNET **Email** sales@pentlandferries.co.uk **Website** www.pentlandferries.co.uk *(English)*

ROUTE OPERATED Gills Bay (Caithness) - St Margaret's Hope (South Ronaldsay, Orkney) (1 hour; *PENTALINA*; up to 4 per day).

1	PENTALINA	2382t	08	17.1k	59.0m	345P	70C	9L	A	UK	9437969

PENTALINA Built by FBMA Marine, Cebu, Philippines for *Pentland Ferries*.

RED FUNNEL FERRIES

THE COMPANY Red Funnel Ferries is the trading name of the Southampton, Isle of Wight and South of England Royal Mail Steam Packet Company Limited, a British private sector company. The company was acquired by JP Morgan International Capital Corporation in 2000; it was purchased by the management in 2004 and in 2007 it was sold to Infracapital Partners LP – the infrastructure fund of the Prudential Group.

MANAGEMENT Managing Director Tom Docherty, **Commercial Director** Colin Hetherington.

ADDRESS 12 Bugle Street, Southampton SO14 2JY.

TELEPHONE Administration UK 0844 844 2699, **Passenger Reservations** UK 0844 844 9988, Elsewhere + 44 (0) 845 155 2442, **Freight Reservations** UK 0844 844 2666.

FAX Administration & Reservations UK 0844 844 2698.

INTERNET Email post@redfunnel.co.uk **Website** www.redfunnel.co.uk (English)

ROUTES OPERATED Conventional Ferries Southampton - East Cowes (55 mins; RED EAGLE, RED FALCON, RED OSPREY; hourly). **Fast Passenger Ferries** Southampton - West Cowes (22 mins; RED JET 3, RED JET 4, RED JET 5; every hour or half hour).

1	RED EAGLE	3953t	96	13.0k	93.2m	895P	200C	18L	BA	UK	9117337
2	RED FALCON	3953t	94	13.0k	93.2m	895P	200C	18L	BA	UK	9064047
3»p	RED JET 3	213t	98	33.0k	32.9m	190P	0C	0L	-	UK	9182758
4»p	RED JET 4	342t	03	35.0k	39.8m	277P	0C	0L	-	UK	9295854
5»p	RED JET 5	209t	99	35.0k	35.0m	177P	0L	0L	-	UK	8954415
6	RED OSPREY	3953t	94	13.0k	93.2m	895P	200C	18L	BA	UK	9064059

RED EAGLE Built by Ferguson Shipbuilders, Port Glasgow, UK for the Southampton - East Cowes service. During Winter 2004/05 stretched by 10 metres and height raised by 3 metres at Gdansk, Poland.

RED FALCON Built by Ferguson Shipbuilders, Port Glasgow, UK for the Southampton - East Cowes service. In 2004 stretched by 10 metres and height raised by 3 metres at Gdansk, Poland.

RED JET 3 FBM Marine catamaran built at Cowes, UK for the Southampton - West Cowes service.

RED JET 4 North West Bay Ships Pty Ltd catamaran built in Hobart, Tasmania, Australia for the Southampton - West Cowes service.

RED JET 5 Built by Pequot River Shipworks, New London, Connecticut, USA to FBM Marine design as the BO HENGY for Bahamas Fast Ferries of The Bahamas. In May 2009 sold to Red Funnel Ferries and renamed the RED JET 5.

RED OSPREY Built by Ferguson Shipbuilders, Port Glasgow, UK for the Southampton - East Cowes service. In 2003 stretched by 10 metres and height raised by 3 metres at Gdansk, Poland.

SHETLAND ISLANDS COUNCIL

THE COMPANY Shetland Islands Council is a British local government authority.

MANAGEMENT Ferry Services Manager Ken Duerden, Acting **Marine Superintendent** Kevin Main.

ADDRESS Port Administration Building, Sella Ness, Mossbank, Shetland ZE2 9QR.

TELEPHONE Administration + 44 (0)1806 244234, 244266, **Reservations** Yell Sound & Bluemull + 44 (0)1595 745804, Fair Isle + 44 (0)1595 760222, **Whalsay** + 44(0)1806 566259, **Skerries** + 44 (0)1806 515266,

Papa Stour + 44 (0)1595 745804.

Red Falcon (*John Hendy*)

Red Jet 4 (*Andrew Cooke*)

Daggri (*Miles Cowsill*)

Stena Adventurer (*Miles Cowsill*)

VOICEBANK *Bluemull Sound* +44 (0)1595 743971, *Bressay* +44 (0)1595 743974, *Fair Isle* +44 (0)1595 743978, *Papa Stour* +44 (0)1595 743977, *Skerries* +44 (0)1595 743975, *Whalsay* +44 (0)1595 743973, *Yell Sound* +44 (0)1595 743972.

FAX +44 (0)1806 244232.

INTERNET Email ferries@sic.shetland.gov.uk Website: www.shetland.gov.uk/ferries *(English)*

ROUTES OPERATED Yell Sound Service Toft (Mainland) - Ulsta (Yell) (20 mins; *DAGALIEN*, *DAGGRI*; up to 26 per day), Bluemull Sound Service (Gutcher (Yell) - Belmont (Unst) (10 mins; *BIGGA*, *FIVLA*, *GEIRA*; up to 28 per day), Gutcher – Hamars Ness (Fetlar) (25 mins; *BIGGA*, *FIVLA*, *GEIRA*; up to 8 per day), Bressay Lerwick (Mainland) - Maryfield (Bressay) (5 mins; *LEIRNA*; up to 23 per day), Whalsay Laxo/Vidlin (Mainland) - Symbister (Whalsay) (30-45 mins; *HENDRA*, *LINGA*; up to 18 per day), Skerries Vidlin (Mainland) – Out Skerries (1 hr 30 mins; *FILLA*; up to 10 per week), Out Skerries – Lerwick (3 hours; *FILLA*; 2 per week), Fair Isle (Grutness (Mainland) - Fair Isle (3 hrs; *GOOD SHEPHERD IV*; 2 per week), Papa Stour West Burrafirth (Mainland) – Papa Stour (40 mins; *SNOLDA*; up to 7 per week).

1	BIGGA	274t	91	11.0k	33.5m	96P	21C	4L	BA	UK	9000821
2	DAGALIEN	1861t	04	12.0k	61m	145P	30C	4L	BA	UK	9291626
3	DAGGRI	1861t	04	12.0k	61m	145P	30C	4L	BA	UK	9291614
4	FILLA	356t	03	12.0k	35.5m	30P	10C	2L	BA	UK	9269192
5	FIVLA	230t	85	11.0k	29.9m	95P	15C	4L	BA	UK	8410237
6	GEIRA	226t	88	10.8k	29.9m	95P	15C	4L	BA	UK	8712489
7	GOOD SHEPHERD IV	76t	86	10.0k	18.3m	12P	1C	0L	C	UK	
8	HENDRA	248	82	11.0k	33.8m	100P	18C	4L	BA	UK	8200254
9	LEIRNA	420t	92	9.0k	35.1m	100P	20C	4L	BA	UK	9050199
10	LINGA	658t	01	11.0k	35.8m	100P	16C	2L	BA	UK	9242170
11	SNOLDA	130t	83	9.0k	24.4m	12P	6C	1L	A	UK	8302090
12	THORA	147t	75	8.5k	25.3m	93P	10C	2L	BA	UK	7347354

BIGGA Built by JW Miller & Sons Ltd, St Monans, Fife, UK. Used on the Toft - Ulsta service. In 2005 moved to the Bluemull Sound service.

DAGALIEN, DAGGRI Built by Stocznia Polnócna, Gdansk, Poland to replace the BIGGA and HENDRA on Toft - Ulsta service.

FILLA Built by Stocznia Polnócna, Gdansk, Poland for the Lerwick /Vidlin - Out Skerries service. She looks like an oil rig supply vessel and is capable of transporting fresh water for replenishing the tanks on the Skerries in case of drought.

FIVLA Built by Ailsa Shipbuilding, Troon, UK. Now a spare vessel, though often used on the Bluemull service.

GEIRA Built by Richard Dunston (Hessle), Hessle, UK. Formerly used on the Laxo - Symbister route. Replaced by the HENDRA in 2005 and moved to the Bluemull Sound service.

GOOD SHEPHERD IV Built by JW Miller & Sons Ltd, St Monans, Fife, UK. Used on the service between Grutness (Mainland) and Fair Isle. Vehicles conveyed by special arrangement and generally consist of agricultural vehicles. She is pulled up on the marine slip on Fair Isle at the conclusion of each voyage.

HENDRA Built by McTay Marine, Bromborough, Wirral, UK for the Laxo - Symbister service. In 2002 transferred to the Toft - Ulsta service. In 2004 replaced by new vessels DAGGRI and DAGALIEN and moved to the Bluemull Sound service. In May 2005 returned to the Laxo - Symbister service as second vessel.

LEIRNA Built by Ferguson Shipbuilders, Port Glasgow, UK. Used on the Lerwick - Maryfield (Bressay) service.

LINGA Built by Stocznia Polnócna, Gdansk, Poland. Used on the Laxo - Symbister service.

SNOLDA Built as the FILLA by Sigbjorn Iversen, Flekkefjord, Norway. Used on the Lerwick (Mainland) - Out Skerries and Vidlin (Mainland) - Out Skerries services. At other times she operated freight and charter services around the Shetland Archipelago. She resembles a miniature oil rig supply vessel. Passenger capacity was originally 20 from 1st April to 31st October inclusive but is now 12 all year. In 2003 renamed the SNOLDA; replaced by the new FILLA and, in 2004, transferred to the West Burrafirth - Papa Stour route.

THORA Built by Tórshavnor Skipasmidja, Tórshavn, Faroe Islands. After a period as a spare vessel, in 1998 she took over the Laxo - Symbister service from the withdrawn KJELLA (158t, 1957). Withdrawn again in 2001 and became a spare vessel.

STENA LINE

THE COMPANY *Stena Line Limited* is incorporated in Great Britain and registered in England and Wales. *Stena Line BV* is a Dutch company. The ultimate parent undertaking is *Stena AB* of Sweden.

MANAGEMENT Area Director, North Sea Pim de Lange, Area Director, Irish Sea Michael McGrath.

ADDRESS *UK* 1 Suffolk Way, Sevenoaks, Kent TN13 1YL, *The Netherlands* PO Box 2, 3150 AA, Hook of Holland, The Netherlands.

TELEPHONE Administration *UK* +44 (0)1732 585858, *The Netherlands* +31 (0)174 389333, Reservations *UK* 08075 707070 (from UK only), *The Netherlands* +31 (0)174 315811.

FAX Administration & Reservations *UK* +44 (0)1407 606811, *The Netherlands* +31 (0)174 387045, Telex 31272.

INTERNET Email info@stenaline.com Website www.stenaline.com *(English, Danish, Dutch, German, Norwegian, Polish, Swedish)*

ROUTES OPERATED Conventional Ferries Cairnryan - Belfast (2 hrs 15 mins; *STENA SUPERFAST VII, STENA SUPERFAST VIII*; up to 6 per day, Port of Liverpool (Twelve Quays River Terminal, Birkenhead) - Belfast (8 hrs; *STENA LAGAN, STENA MERSEY*; 1 per day (Mon), 2 per day (Sun, Tue-Sat)), Holyhead - Dublin (3 hrs 15 mins; *STENA ADVENTURER, STENA NORDICA*; 4 per day), Fishguard - Rosslare (3 hrs 30 mins; *STENA EUROPE*; 2 per day), Harwich - Hook of Holland (The Netherlands) (7 hrs 30 mins; *STENA BRITANNICA, STENA HOLLANDICA*; 2 per day), Fast Ferry Holyhead - Dún Laoghaire (2 hrs; *STENA EXPLORER (April - September only)*; 1 per day), Freight Ferries Heysham - Belfast (7 hrs; *STENA PERFORMER, STENA PRECISION*; 2 per day), Harwich - Rotterdam (8 hrs; *CAPUCINE, SEVERINE*; 11 per week), Killingholme - Hook of Holland (11 hrs; *STENA TRANSIT, STENA TRANSPORTER*; 1 per day).

1F	CAPUCINE	16342t	11	16.0k	150.0m	12P	-	140T	A	UK	9539066
2F	SEVERINE	16342t	12	16.0k	150.0m	12P	-	140T	A	NL	9539078
3	STENA ADVENTURER	43532t	03	22.0k	210.8m	1500P	-	210L	BA2	UK	9235529
4	STENA BRITANNICA	63600t	10	22.0k	240.0m	1200P	-	300T	BA2	UK	9419175
5	STENA EUROPE	24828t	81	20.5k	149.0m	2076P	456C	60T	BA	UK	7901760
6»	STENA EXPLORER	19638t	96	40.0k	126.6m	1500P	375C	50L	A	UK	9080194
7	STENA HOLLANDICA	63600t	10	22.5k	240.0m	1200P	-	300T	BA2	NL	9419163
8	STENA LAGAN	27510t	05	23.5k	186.5m	980P	160C	135T	A	UK	9329849
9	STENA MERSEY	27510t	05	23.5k	186.5m	980P	160C	135T	A	UK	9329851
10	STENA NORDICA	24206t	01	25.7k	169.8m	405P	375C	122T	BA2	UK	9215505
11F	STENA PERFORMER	19722t	12	21.0k	142.0m	12P	-	151T	A	IM	9506227
12F	STENA PRECISION	19722t	12	21.0k	142.0m	12P	-	151T	A	IM	9506239
13	STENA SUPERFAST VII	30285t	01	26.6k	203.3m	717P	695C	110L	BA2	UK	9198941
14	STENA SUPERFAST VIII	30285t	01	26.6k	203.3m	717P	695C	110L	BA2	UK	9198953
15F+	STENA TRANSIT	34700t	11	22.2k	212.0m	300P	-	290T	A2	NL	9469388
16F+	STENA TRANSPORTER	34700t	11	22.2k	212.0m	300P	-	290T	A2	NL	9469376

Stena Precision (*Matt Davies*)

Stena Britannica (*Cees de Bijl*)

CAPUCINE, SEVERINE Built by the Kyokuyo Shipyard, Shimonoseki, Japan for *Cobelfret Ferries*. Initially operated on the *CLdN* Ipswich - Rotterdam service. This service was suspended in August 2012. In September, they were chartered to *Stena Line* and placed on the Harwich - Rotterdam service.

STENA ADVENTURER Ro-pax vessel built by Hyundai Heavy Industries, Ulsan, South Korea, for *Stena RoRo* and chartered to *Stena Line* to operate between Holyhead and Dublin.

STENA BRITANNICA Built by Waden Yards in Wismar and Warnemünde, Germany, for *Stena Rederi* (bow sections constructed at Warnemünde and stern and final assembly at Wismar). Replaced the 2003 built STENA BRITANNICA on the Harwich - Hook of Holland service.

STENA EUROPE Built as the KRONPRINSESSAN VICTORIA by Götaverken Arendal AB, Gothenburg, Sweden for *Göteborg-Frederikshavn Linjen* of Sweden (trading as *Sessan Linjen*) for their Gothenburg - Frederikshavn service. Shortly after delivery, the company was taken over by *Stena Line* and services were marketed as *Stena-Sessan Line* for a period. In 1982 she was converted to an overnight ferry by changing one vehicle deck into two additional decks of cabins and she was switched to the Gothenburg - Kiel route (with, during the summer, daytime runs from Gothenburg to Frederikshavn and Kiel to Korsør (Denmark)). In 1989 she was transferred to the Oslo - Frederikshavn route and renamed the STENA SAGA. In 1994, transferred to *Stena Line BV*, renamed the STENA EUROPE and operated between Hook of Holland and Harwich. She was withdrawn in June 1997, transferred to the *Lion Ferry* (a *Stena Line* subsidiary) Karlskrona - Gdynia service and renamed the LION EUROPE. In 1998 she was transferred back to *Stena Line* (remaining on the same route) and renamed the STENA EUROPE. In early 2002 the cabins installed in 1982 were removed and other modifications made and she was transferred to the Fishguard - Rosslare route.

STENA EXPLORER Finnyards HSS1500 built at Rauma, Finland for *Stena RoRo* and chartered to *Stena Line*. Operates on the Holyhead - Dún Laoghaire route.

STENA HOLLANDICA Built by Nordic Yards in Wismar and Warnemünde, Germany, for *Stena Rederi* (bow sections constructed at Warnemünde and stern and final assembly at Wismar) to replace the previous STENA HOLLANDICA on the Harwich - Hook of Holland service. Entered service May 2010.

STENA LAGAN, STENA MERSEY Built as the LAGAN VIKING and MERSEY VIKING by CN Visentini, Donada, Italy for *Levantina Trasporti* of Italy. Chartered to *NorseMerchant Ferries* and placed on the Birkenhead - Belfast route. In 2008 sold to *Norfolkline*, then resold to *Epic Shipping* and chartered back. In August 2010, following *Norfolkline's* purchase by *DFDS Seaways*, they were renamed the LAGAN SEAWAYS and MERSEY SEAWAYS respectively. Between January and July 2011 they were operated by *Stena Line Irish Sea Ferries*, a 'stand-alone' company pending consideration of the take-over by the UK and Irish competition authorities. In July 2011 the take-over was confirmed and in August 2011 they were renamed the STENA LAGAN and STENA MERSEY. In April 2012 they sold to *Stena RoRo*; they continue to be chartered to *Stena Line*.

STENA NORDICA Built as the EUROPEAN AMBASSADOR by Mitsubishi Heavy Industries, Shimonoseki, Japan for *P&O Irish Sea* for the Liverpool - Dublin service. Service transferred to Mostyn in November 2001. Also operated between Dublin and Cherbourg once a week. In 2004 the Mostyn route closed and she was sold to *Stena RoRo*. Chartered to *Stena Line* to operate between Karlskrona and Gdynia and renamed the STENA NORDICA. In 2008 transferred to the Holyhead - Dublin service. In 2009 transferred to UK registry.

STENA PERFORMER Built as the SEATRUCK PERFORMANCE by Flensburger Schiffbau-Gesellschaft, Flensburg, Germany for *Seatruck Ferries*. In September 2012 chartered to *Stena Line* to operate between Heysham and Belfast and renamed the STENA PERFORMER.

STENA PRECISION Built as the SEATRUCK PRECISION by Flensburger Schiffbau-Gesellschaft, Flensburg, Germany for *Seatruck Ferries*. In September 2012 chartered to *Stena Line* to operate between Heysham and Belfast and renamed the STENA PRECISION.

STENA SUPERFAST VII, STENA SUPERFAST VIII Built as the SUPERFAST VII and SUPERFAST VIII by Howaldtswerke Deutsche Werft AG, Kiel, Germany for *Attica Enterprises* (now *Attica Group*) for use by *Superfast Ferries* between Rostock and Hanko. In 2006 sold to *Tallink*. The Finnish terminal was transferred to Helsinki and daily return trips between Helsinki and Tallinn were introduced. These ceased in September 2008. The operation was ceased for the winter season in December 2009 and

Stena Superfast VII (*Gordon Hislip*)

Stena Lagan (*Gordon Hislip*)

Sound of Shuna (Brian Maxted)

St Cecilia (Miles Cowsill)

2010. Service resumed at the end of April 2010 and 2011. In August 2011 chartered to *Stena Line* for three years (with an option to extend by one year) and renamed the STENA SUPERFAST VII, STENA SUPERFAST VIII. In November 2011, after a major refit, they were placed on a service between Cairnryan and Belfast (replacing the Stranraer - Belfast service).

STENA TRANSIT, STENA TRANSPORTER Built by Samsung Heavy Industries, Koje, South Korea. Used on the Hook of Holland - Killingholme service.

WESTERN FERRIES

THE COMPANY *Western Ferries (Clyde) Ltd* is a British private sector company.

MANAGEMENT Managing Director Gordon Ross.

ADDRESS Hunter's Quay, Dunoon, Argyll PA23 8HJ.

TELEPHONE Administration + 44 (0)1369 704452, Reservations Not applicable.

FAX Administration + 44 (0)1369 706020, Reservations Not applicable.

INTERNET Email enquiries@western-ferries.co.uk Website www.western-ferries.co.uk *(English)*

ROUTE OPERATED McInroy's Point (Gourock) - Hunter's Quay (Dunoon) (20 mins; *SOUND OF SANDA, SOUND OF SCALPAY, SOUND OF SCARBA, SOUND OF SHUNA*; every 20 mins (15 mins in peaks)).

1	SOUND OF SANDA	403t	64	10.3k	48.43m	220P	37C	4/5L	BA	UK	8928894
2	SOUND OF SCALPAY	403t	61	10.3k	48.43m	220P	37C	4/5L	BA	UK	8928882
3	SOUND OF SCARBA	489t	01	11.0k	49.95m	220P	40C	4/5L	BA	UK	9237424
4	SOUND OF SHUNA	489t	03	11.0k	49.95m	220P	40C	4/5L	BA	UK	9289441

SOUND OF SANDA Built as the GEMEENTEPONT 24 by Gutehoffnungshulte Sterkrade AG, Rheinwerft, Walsum, Germany for *Amsterdam City Council* and operated from Centraal Station to the other side of the River IJ. In 1996 purchased by *Western Ferries* and renamed the SOUND OF SANDA.

SOUND OF SCALPAY Built as the GEMEENTEPONT 23 by Arnhemsche Scheepsbouw Maatschappij NV, Arnhem, The Netherlands for *Amsterdam City Council*. In 1995 sold to *Western Ferries* and renamed the SOUND OF SCALPAY.

SOUND OF SCARBA, SOUND OF SHUNA Built by Ferguson Shipbuilders, Port Glasgow, UK for *Western Ferries*.

Under Construction

| 5 | SOUND OF SEIL | 489t | 13 | 11.0k | 49.95m | 220P | 40C | 4/5L | BA | UK |
| 6 | SOUND OF SOAY | 489t | 13 | 11.0k | 49.95m | 220P | 40C | 4/5L | BA | UK |

SOUND OF SEIL, SOUND OF SOAY Under construction by Cammell Laird Shiprepairers & Shipbuilders, Birkenhead, UK to replace the SOUND OF SANDA and SOUND OF SCALPAY.

WIGHTLINK

THE COMPANY *Wightlink* is a British private sector company, owned by the *Macquarie Group* of Australia. The routes and vessels were previously part of *Sealink (British Rail)* but were excluded from the purchase of most of the *Sealink* operations by *Stena Line AB* in 1990. They remained in *Sea Containers'* ownership until purchased by *CINVen* Ltd, a venture capital company in 1995. The company was the subject of a management buy-out financed by the *Royal Bank of Scotland* in 2001 and was sold to the *Macquarie Group* in 2005.

MANAGEMENT Chief Executive Russell Kew, Marketing Manager Kerry Jackson, Commercial Director Clive Tilley.

ADDRESS Gunwharf Road, Portsmouth PO1 2LA.

TELEPHONE Administration and Reservations 0871 376 1000 (from UK only), +44 (0)23 9285 5230 (from overseas).

FAX Administration & Reservations +44 (0)23 9285 5257.

INTERNET Email bookings@wightlink.co.uk Website www.wightlink.co.uk (*English, Dutch, French, German*)

ROUTES OPERATED Conventional Ferries Lymington - Yarmouth (Isle of Wight) (approx 35 mins; *WIGHT LIGHT, WIGHT SKY, WIGHT SUN*; every 40 or 60 mins), Portsmouth - Fishbourne (Isle of Wight) (approx 35 mins; *ST. CECILIA, ST. CLARE, ST. FAITH, ST. HELEN*; half-hourly or hourly depending on time of day). **Fast Passenger Ferries** Portsmouth - Ryde (Isle of Wight) (passenger-only) (under 20 mins; *WIGHT RYDER I, WIGHT RYDER II*; 2 per hour).

1	ST. CECILIA	2968t	86	12.0k	77.0m	771P	142C	12L	BA	UK	8518546
2	ST. CLARE	5359t	01	13.0k	86.0m	878P	186C	-	BA	UK	9236949
3	ST. FAITH	3009t	89	12.5k	77.0m	771P	142C	12L	BA	UK	8907228
4	ST. HELEN	2983t	83	12.0k	77.0m	771P	142C	12L	BA	UK	8120569
5	WIGHT LIGHT	1500t	08	11.0k	62.4m	360P	65C	-	BA	UK	9446972
6»p	WIGHT RYDER I	520t	09	20.0k	40.9m	260P	0C	-	-	UK	9512537
7»p	WIGHT RYDER II	520t	09	20.0k	40.9m	260P	0C	-	-	UK	9512549
8	WIGHT SKY	1500t	08	11.0k	62.4m	360P	65C	-	BA	UK	9446984
9	WIGHT SUN	1500t	09	11.0k	62.4m	360P	65C	-	BA	UK	9490416

ST. CECILIA, ST FAITH Built by Cochrane Shipbuilders, Selby, UK for *Sealink British Ferries* for the Portsmouth - Fishbourne service.

ST. CLARE Built by Stocznia Remontowa, Gdansk, Poland for the Portsmouth - Fishbourne service. She is a double-ended ferry with a central bridge.

ST. HELEN Built by Henry Robb Caledon Yard, Leith, UK (part of British Shipbuilders Ltd) for *Sealink UK Ltd* for the Portsmouth - Fishbourne service.

WIGHT LIGHT, WIGHT SKY, WIGHT SUN Built by Brodogradilište Kraljevica, Croatia for the Lymington - Yarmouth route.

WIGHT RYDER I, WIGHT RYDER II Catamarans built by FBMA Marine, Balamban, Cebu, Philippines. Operate on the Portsmouth - Ryde service.

St Clare *(Andrew Cooke)*

Wight Light *(Andrew Cooke)*

SECTION 2 - MINOR FERRY OPERATORS

ARGYLL AND BUTE COUNCIL

THE COMPANY *Argyll and Bute Council* is a British local government authority.

MANAGEMENT Executive Director of Development and Infrastructure Sandy Mactaggart, Head of Economic Development and Strategic Transportation Robert Pollock, Operations Manager Martin Gorringe.

ADDRESS Manse Brae, Lochgilphead, Argyll PA31 8RD.

TELEPHONE Administration + 44 (0)1546 604614.

FAX Administration + 44 (0)1546 606443.

INTERNET Email martin.gorringe@argyll-bute.gov.uk Website www.argyll-bute.gov.uk/transport-and-streets/ferry-travel.

ROUTES OPERATED Vehicle ferries Seil - Luing (5 mins; *BELNAHUA*; approx half-hourly), Port Askaig (Islay) - Feolin (Jura) (5 mins; *EILEAN DHIURA*; approx half-hourly). Passenger-only ferries Port Appin – Lismore (10 mins; *THE LISMORE*; approx hourly), Ellenabeich – Easdale (5 mins; *EASDALE*; approx quarter-hourly).

1	BELNAHUA	35t	72	8.0k	17.1m	40P	5C	1L	BA	UK
2p	EASDALE	-	93	6.5k	6.4m	11P	0C	0L	-	UK
3	EILEAN DHIURA	86t	98	9.0k	25.6m	50P	13C	1L	BA	UK
4p	THE LISMORE	12t	88	8.0k	9.7m	20P	0C	0L	-	UK

BELNAHUA Built by Campbeltown Shipyard, Campbeltown, UK for *Argyll County Council* for the Seil - Luing service. In 1975, following local government reorganisation, transferred to *Strathclyde Regional Council*. In 1996, transferred to *Argyll and Bute Council*.

EASDALE Built for *Strathclyde Regional Council* for the Ellenabeich - Easdale passenger-only service. In 1996, following local government reorganisation, transferred to *Argyll and Bute Council*.

EILEAN DHIURA Built by McTay Marine, Bromborough, Wirral, UK for *Argyll and Bute Council* to replace the *Western Ferries (Argyll)* SOUND OF GIGHA on the Islay - Jura route. *ASP Ship Management* manage and operate this vessel on behalf of *Argyll and Bute Council*.

THE LISMORE Built for *Strathclyde Regional Council* for the Port Appin – Lismore passenger-only service. In 1996, following local government reorganisation, transferred to *Argyll and Bute Council*.

ARRANMORE FAST FERRIES

THE COMPANY *Arranmore Fast Ferries* is the trading name of *Arranmore Charters* is an Irish Republic private sector company.

MANAGEMENT Managing Director Seamus Boyle.

ADDRESS Leabgarrow, Arranmore, County Donegal, Irish Republic.

TELEPHONE Administration & Reservations + 353 (0)87 3171810.

INTERNET Email: seamusboyle4@eircom.net Website www.arranmorefastferry.com *(English)*

ROUTE OPERATED *Summer only* Car Ferry Burtonport (County Donegal) - Leabgarrow (Arranmore Island) (15 mins; *MORVERN*; up to 5 per day). *All Year* Fast Ferry Burtonport - Leabgarrow (5 mins; *REALT NA MAIDNE*; up to 3 per day).

1	GIRL GRAY	-	96	14.0k	13.1m	12P	0C	-	-	IR
2	MORVERN	64t	73	8.0k	23.8m	12P	6C	-	B	IR
3	REALT NA MAIDNE	-	07	30.0k	11.0m	12P	0C	-	-	IR
4	RENFREW ROSE	65t	84	-	21.9m	12P	2C	-	B	IR

Corran (*Brian Maxted*)

Eilean Dhiura (*Miles Cowsill*)

GIRL GRAY AquaStar 43' built by Aqua-Star Ltd, St Sampsons, Guernsey for *Southern Marine Services* of Brighton and used as a charter boat out of Brighton Marina. Later sold to *Arranmore Charters*. Normally used for fishing trips but used as a back-up for the ferries as required.

MORVERN Built by James Lamont & Co Ltd, Port Glasgow, UK for *Caledonian MacBrayne*. After service on a number of routes she was, after 1979, the main vessel on the Fionnphort (Mull) - Iona service. In 1992 she was replaced by the LOCH BUIE and became a spare vessel. In 1995 sold to *Arranmore Island Ferry Services*. In 2001 sold to *Bere Island Ferries*. In February 2010 refurbished by Bere Island Boatyard and sold to *Arranmore Charters*.

REALT NA MAIDNE Stormforce 11 RIB (Rigid Inflatable Boat) built by Redbay Boats Ltd, Cushendall, Co Antrim. As well as the fast ferry service, she is also used on fishing, sight-seeing, photography or other ocean expeditions.

RENFREW ROSE Built by MacCrindle Shipbuilding Ltd, Ardrossan for *Strathclyde PTE* (later *Strathclyde Partnership for Transport*). Operated passenger only between Renfrew and Yoker. In March 2010 laid up. In June 2012 sold to *Arranmore Fast Ferries* and used as a passenger/car ferry.

ARRANMORE ISLAND FERRY SERVICES

THE COMPANY *Arranmore Island Ferry Services* (*Bád Farrantoireacht Arainn Mhór*) is an Irish Republic company, supported by *Roinn na Gaeltachta* (*The Gaeltacht Authority*), a semi-state-owned body responsible for tourism and development in the Irish-speaking areas of The Irish Republic.

MANAGEMENT **Managing Director** Dominic Sweeney.

ADDRESS Cara na nOilean, Burtonport Pier, Letterkenny, Co. Donegal Irish Republic.

TELEPHONE **Administration & Reservations** + 353 (0)7495 20532, + 353 (0)7495 42233,

INTERNET **Email:** arranmoreferry@gmail.com **Website** www.arranmoreferry.com (*English*)

ROUTE OPERATED Burtonport (County Donegal) - Leabgarrow (Arranmore Island) (15 mins; *COLL, RHUM*; up to 10 per day (Summer), 8 per day (Winter)).

1	COLL	69t	74	8.0k	25.3m	96P	6C	-	B	IR
2	RHUM	69t	73	8.0k	25.3m	96P	6C	-	B	IR

COLL Built by James Lamont & Co Ltd, Port Glasgow, UK for *Caledonian MacBrayne*. For several years she was employed mainly in a relief capacity. In 1986 she took over the Tobermory (Mull) - Kilchoan service from a passenger-only vessel; the conveyance of vehicles was not inaugurated until 1991. In 1996 she was transferred to the Oban - Lismore route. In 1998 she was sold to *Arranmore Island Ferry Services*.

RHUM Built by James Lamont & Co Ltd, Port Glasgow, UK for *Caledonian MacBrayne*. Until 1987, she was used primarily on the Claonaig - Lochranza (Arran) service. After that time she served on various routes. In 1994 she inaugurated a new service between Tarbert (Loch Fyne) and Portavadie. In 1997 she operated between Kyles Scalpay and Scalpay until the opening of the new bridge on 16th December 1997. In 1998 she was sold to *Arranmore Island Ferry Services*.

BERE ISLAND FERRIES

THE COMPANY *Bere Island Ferries Ltd* is an Irish Republic private sector company.

MANAGEMENT **Operator** Colum Harrington.

ADDRESS Ferry Lodge, West End, Bere Island, Beara, County Cork, Irish Republic.

TELEPHONE **Administration** + 353 (0)27 75009, **Reservations** Not applicable, **Mobile** + 353 (0)86 2423140.

FAX **Administration** + 353 (0)27 75000, **Reservations** Not applicable.

INTERNET **Email** biferry@eircom.net **Website** www.bereislandferries.com (*English*)

1F	KIRSTY M	109t	66	10.5k	23.7m	0P	-	1L	B	IR
2	OILEAN NA H-OIGE	69t	80	7.0k	18.6m	35P	4C	-	B	IR
3	SANCTA MARIA	67t	83	7.0k	18.6m	35P	4C	-	B	IR

KIRSTY M Landing craft (Klasse 521) built as the LCM 12 SPROTTE by Rheinwerft Walsum, Walsum, Germany for the German Navy. In 1993 withdrawn and sold to a German firm and converted to a civilian ferry. She was later sold to *Mainstream Salmon Farm (Aquascot Seafarms Ltd)*, Orkney, renamed the KIRSTY M and used as a work boat. In December 2009 sold to *Bere Island Ferries* and converted back to ferry operation. She is used in a freight-only mode and doesn't have a licence to carry passengers.

OILEAN NA H-OIGE Built as the EILEAN NA H-OIGE by Lewis Offshore Ltd, Stornoway, UK for *Western Isles Islands Council* (from 1st April 1996 the *Western Isles Council* and from 1st January 1998 *Comhairle Nan Eilean Siar*) for their Ludaig (South Uist) - Eriskay service. From 2000 operated from a temporary slipway at the Eriskay causeway. This route ceased in July 2001 following the full opening of the causeway and she was laid up. In 2002 she was moved to the Eriskay - Barra service. In 2003 replaced by the LOCH BHRUSDA of *Caledonian MacBrayne* and laid up. Later sold to *Bere Island Ferries* and renamed the OILEAN NA H-OIGE (same name in Irish rather than Scots Gaelic).

SANCTA MARIA Built as the EILEAN BHEARNARAIGH by George Brown & Company, Greenock, UK for *Western Isles Islands Council* for their Otternish (North Uist) - Berneray service. From 1996 until 1999 she was operated by *Caledonian MacBrayne* in conjunction with the LOCH BHRUSDA on the service between Otternish and Berneray and during the winter she was laid up. Following the opening of a causeway between North Uist and Berneray in early 1999, the ferry service ceased and she became reserve vessel for the Eriskay route. This route ceased in July 2001 following the opening of a causeway and she was laid up. In 2002 operated between Eriskay and Barra as reserve vessel. In 2003 sold to *Transalpine Redemptorists Inc*, a community of monks who live on Papa Stronsay, Orkney. Used for conveying supplies to the island - not a public service. In 2008 sold to *Bere Island Ferries*. Entered service in May 2009.

BK MARINE

THE COMPANY *BK Marine* is a UK company.

MANAGEMENT **Managing Director** Gordon Williamson.

ADDRESS Herrislea House Hotel, Veensgarth, Tingwall, Shetland ZE2 9SB.

TELEPHONE **Administration & Reservations** +44 (0)1595840208, **Sailing information voice bank** +44 (0)1595 743976.

INTERNET **Website** www.bkmarine.org *(English)*

ROUTE OPERATED *All year* Foula - Walls (Mainland) (2 hours; *NEW ADVANCE*; 2 per week (Winter), 3 per week (Summer)), *Summer only* Foula - Scalloway (3 hrs 30 mins; *NEW ADVANCE*; alternate Thursdays).

1	NEW ADVANCE	25t	96	8.7k	9.8m	12P	1C	0L	C	UK

NEW ADVANCE Built by Richardson's, Stromness, Orkney, UK for *Shetland Islands Council* for the Foula service. Although built at Penryn, Cornwall, she was completed at Stromness. She has a Cygnus Marine GM38 hull and is based on the island where she can be lifted out of the water. Vehicle capacity is to take residents' vehicles to the island - not for tourist vehicles. In 2004 it was announced that the vessel and service would be transferred to the *Foula Community*. However, it was then found that under EU rules the route needed to be offered for competitive tender. In July 2006 the contract was awarded to *Atlantic Ferries Ltd* who began operations in October 2006. In August 2011 replaced by *BK Marine*.

CLARE ISLAND FERRY COMPANY

THE COMPANY *Clare Island Ferry Company* is owned and operated by the O'Grady family, natives of Clare Island, Irish Republic, who have been operating the Clare Island Mail Boat Ferry service since 1880.

MANAGEMENT **Managing Director** Chris O'Grady.

ADDRESS Clare Island Ferry Co Ltd, Clare Island, Co Mayo, Republic Of Ireland.

TELEPHONE/FAX *May-September* +353 (0)98 23737 *Winter* +353 (0)98 25212, +353 (0)86 8515003

INTERNET **Email** clareislandferry@anu.ie **Website** www.clareislandferry.com *(English)*

ROUTE OPERATED Roonagh (Co Mayo) - Clare Island (15 mins; *CLEW BAY QUEEN, PIRATE QUEEN*; *Winter* 1 to 2 trips per day, *Summer* up to 5 per day, Roonagh - Inishturk (50 mins; *CLEW BAY QUEEN, PIRATE QUEEN*; *Winter* 1 per day *Summer* up to 2 per day.

1	CLEW BAY QUEEN	64t	72	10.0k	23.8m	96P	6C	-	B	IR
2p	PIRATE QUEEN	73t	96	10.5k	20.1m	96P	0C	-	-	IR

CLEW BAY QUEEN Built as the KILBRANNAN by James Lamont & Co Ltd, Port Glasgow, UK for *Caledonian MacBrayne*. Used on a variety of routes until 1977, she was then transferred to the Scalpay (Harris) - Kyles Scalpay service. In 1990 she was replaced by the CANNA and, in turn, replaced the CANNA in her reserve/relief role. In 1992 sold to *Arranmore Island Ferry Services* and renamed the ÁRAINN MHÓR. She was subsequently sold to *Údarás na Gaeltachta* and leased back to *Arranmore Island Ferry Services*. In 2008 she was sold to *Clare Island Ferry Company* and renamed the CLEW BAY QUEEN. She operates a passenger and heavy freight service to both Clare Island and Inishturk all year round. In winter passenger capacity is reduced to 47 with 3 crew. Fitted with crane for loading and unloading cargo.

PIRATE QUEEN Built by Arklow Marine Services in 1996 for *Clare Island Ferry Company*. She operates a daily passenger and light cargo service to Clare Island and Inishturk all year round. In winter passenger capacity is reduced to 47 with 3 crew. Fitted with crane for loading and unloading cargo.

CROMARTY FERRY COMPANY

THE COMPANY The *Cromarty Ferry Company* operate under contract to *The Highland Council*.

MANAGEMENT **Managing Director** Tom Henderson.

ADDRESS Udale Farm, Poyntzfield By Dingwall, Ross-Shire IV7 8LY.

TELEPHONE +44 (0)1381 610269, **Mobile** +44 (0)7717 207875.

FAX +44 (0)1381 610408.

INTERNET **Email** info@cromarty-ferry.co.uk **Website** www.cromarty-ferry.co.uk *(English)*

ROUTE OPERATED *June-October* Cromarty - Nigg (Ross-shire) (10 mins; *CROMARTY QUEEN*; half-hourly - 0800 to 1800 ex Cromarty (19.00 in July and August)).

1	CROMARTY QUEEN	68t	10	9.0k	17.3m	50P	4C	-	B	UK

CROMARTY QUEEN Built by Southampton Marine Services for *Cromarty Ferry Company*.

CROSS RIVER FERRIES

THE COMPANY *Cross River Ferries Ltd* is an Irish Republic company, part of the *Doyle Shipping Group*.

MANAGEMENT **Operations Manager** Eoin O'Sullivan.

ADDRESS Westlands House, Rushbrooke, Cobh, County Cork, Irish Republic.

TELEPHONE **Administration** +353 (0)21 42 02 900 **Reservations** Not applicable.

FAX Administration +353 (0)21 481 2645, **Reservations** Not applicable.

INTERNET **Website** www.scottcobh.ie/pages/ferry.html *(English)*

ROUTE OPERATED Carrigaloe (near Cobh, on Great Island) - Glenbrook (Co Cork) (4 mins; *CARRIGALOE, GLENBROOK*; frequent service 07.00 - 00.15 (one or two vessels used according to demand).

| 1 | CARRIGALOE | 225t | 70 | 8.0k | 49.1m | 200P | 27C | - | BA | IR | 7028386 |
| 2 | GLENBROOK | 225t | 71 | 8.0k | 49.1m | 200P | 27C | - | BA | IR | 7101607 |

CARRIGALOE Built as the KYLEAKIN by Newport Shipbuilding and Engineering Company, Newport (Gwent), UK for the *Caledonian Steam Packet Company* (later *Caledonian MacBrayne*) for the Kyle of Lochalsh - Kyleakin service. In 1991 sold to *Marine Transport Services Ltd* and renamed the CARRIGALOE. She entered service in March 1993. In Summer 2002 chartered to the *Lough Foyle Ferry Company*, returning in Spring 2003.

GLENBROOK Built as the LOCHALSH by Newport Shipbuilding and Engineering Company, Newport (Gwent), UK for the *Caledonian Steam Packet Company* (later *Caledonian MacBrayne*) for the Kyle of Lochalsh - Kyleakin service. In 1991 sold to *Marine Transport Services Ltd* and renamed the GLENBROOK. She entered service in March 1993.

THE HIGHLAND COUNCIL

THE COMPANY *The Highland Council* (previously *Highland Regional Council*) is a British local government authority.

MANAGEMENT **Area Transport, Environment & Community Works Services Manager** James Cameron Kemp, **Ferry Foremen** Allan McCowan and Donald Dixon.

ADDRESS *Area Office* Lochybridge Depot, Carr's Corner Industrial Estate, Fort William PH33 6TQ, *Ferry Office* Ferry Cottage, Ardgour, Fort William PH33 7AA.

TELEPHONE Administration *Area Office* +44 (0)1397 709000, *Corran* +44 (0)1855 841243, *Camusnagaul* – Now run by private operator *Highland Ferries* by vessel CAILIN AN AISEAG.

INTERNET Email tecs@highland.gov.uk **Website** www.highland.gov.uk/yourenvironment/roadsandtransport/publictransport/ferries.htm *(English)*

ROUTES OPERATED **Vehicle Ferries** Corran - Ardgour (5 mins; *CORRAN, MAID OF GLENCOUL*; half-hourly), **Passenger-only Ferry** Fort William - Camusnagaul (10 mins; *CAILIN AN AISEAG*; frequent).

1p	CAILIN AN AISEAG	-	80	7.5k	9.8m	26P	0C	0L	-	UK	
2	CORRAN	351t	01	10.0k	42.0m	150P	30C	2L	BA	UK	9225990
3	MAID OF GLENCOUL	166t	75	8.0k	32.0m	116P	16C	1L	BA	UK	7521613

CAILIN AN AISEAG Built by Buckie Shipbuilders Ltd, Buckie, UK for *Highland Regional Council* and used on the Fort William - Camusnagaul passenger-only service. In 2006 the service transferred to *Geoff Ward* under contract with a different vessel. In 2013 resumed service under new operator *Highland Ferries*.

CORRAN Built by George Prior Engineering Ltd, Hull, UK for *The Highland Council* to replace the MAID OF GLENCOUL as main vessel.

MAID OF GLENCOUL Built by William McCrindle Ltd, Shipbuilders, Ardrossan, UK for *Highland Regional Council* for the service between Kylesku and Kylestrome. In 1984 the ferry service was replaced by a bridge and she was transferred to the Corran - Ardgour service. In April 1996, ownership transferred to *The Highland Council*. In 2001 she became the reserve vessel.

ISLES OF SCILLY STEAMSHIP COMPANY

THE COMPANY *Isles of Scilly Steamship Company* is a British private sector company.

MANAGEMENT Chief Executive J Marston, **Marketing Manager** Jackie Hayman.

ADDRESS *Scilly* PO Box 10, Hugh Town, St Mary's, Isles of Scilly TR21 0LJ, *Penzance* Steamship House, Quay Street, Penzance, Cornwall, TR18 4BZ.

TELEPHONE Administration & Reservations + 44 (0)845 710 5555.

FAX Administration & Reservations + 44 (0)1736 334228.

INTERNET Email sales@islesofscilly-travel.co.uk **Website** www.ios-travel.co.uk *(English)*

ROUTES OPERATED *Passenger services:* Penzance - St Mary's (Isles of Scilly) (2 hrs 40 mins; SCILLONIAN III; 1 per day), St Mary's - Tresco/St Martin's/St Agnes/Bryher; *LYONESSE LADY, SWIFT LADY (inter-island boats)*; irregular), *Freight service:* GRY MARITHA; Freight from Penzance Monday, Wednesday and Fridays (weather dependant, all year round).

1F	GRY MARITHA	590t	81	10.5k	40.3m	6P	5C	1L	C	UK	8008462
2	LYONESSE LADY	40t	91	9.0k	15.5m	4P	1C	0L	AC	UK	
3	SCILLONIAN III	1346t	77	15.5k	67.7m	432P	5C	-	C	UK	7527796
4F	SWIFT LADY	-	04	30.0k	8.4m	0P	0C	0L	-	UK	

GRY MARITHA Built by Moen Slip AS, Kolvereid, Norway for *Gjofor* of Norway. In design she is a coaster rather than a ferry. In 1990 she was sold to the *Isles of Scilly Steamship Company*. She operates a freight and passenger service all year (conveying most goods to and from the Islands). During the winter she provides the only sea service to the islands, the SCILLONIAN III being laid up.

LYONESSE LADY Built Lochaber Marine Ltd of Corpach, Fort William, Scotland, for inter-island ferry work.

SCILLONIAN III Built by Appledore Shipbuilders Ltd, Appledore, UK for the Penzance - St Mary's service. She operates from late March to November and is laid up in the winter. She is the last major conventional passenger/cargo ferry built for UK waters and probably Western Europe. Extensively refurbished during Winter 1998/99. She can carry cars in her hold and on deck, as well as general cargo/perishables, boats, trailer tents and passenger luggage.

SWIFT LADY Stormforce 8.4 RIB (Rigid Inflatable Boat) built by Redbay Boats of Cushendall, Co Antrim, Northern Ireland for inter-island ferry work conveying mail and as back-up to the LYONESSE LADY.

KERRERA FERRY

THE COMPANY *Kerrera Ferry Ltd* is a UK company.

MANAGEMENT **Managing Director** Duncan MacEachen.

ADDRESS The Ferry, Isle of Kerrera, by Oban PA34 4SX.

TELEPHONE Administration + 44 (0)1631 563665.

INTERNET Email kerreraferry@hotmail.com **Website** www.kerrera-ferry.co.uk *(English)*

ROUTE OPERATED Gallanach (Argyll) - Kerrera (5 mins; *GYLEN LADY*; on demand 10.30 - 12.30 and 14.00 - 18.00, Easter - October, other times by arrangement).

1	GYLEN LADY	9t	99	8.0k	10.0m	12P	1C	-	B	UK

GYLEN LADY Built by Corpach Boatyard, Corpach, UK to inaugurate a vehicle ferry service to the Isle of Kerrera, replacing an open passenger boat.

KNOYDART SEABRIDGE

THE COMPANY *Knoydart Seabridge* is a British company.

MANAGEMENT **Managin Director** Jon Sellars.

ADDRESS Sandaig, Knoydart Seabridge, Knoydart, Mallaig PH41 4PL.

TELEPHONE **Administration & Reservations** +44 (0)1687 462916.

INTERNET **Email** jon@sandaig.com **Website** www.knoydartferry.com *(English)*

ROUTE OPERATED Mallaig - Inverie (Knoydart).

1	MERI 3	12t	-	-	12.0m	12P	1C	-	B	UK
2p	THE ODYSSEY	5t	-	35.0k	10.5m	12P	-	-	-	UK
3p	VENTURER	12t	-	-	13.0m	12P	-	-	-	UK

MERI 3 Built by Lohi Boats. She is a miniature beach landing craft.

THE ODYSSEY ProCharter 3 built by ProCharter, Wadebridge, Cornwall.

VENTURER Interceptor 41 built by Safehaven Marine, Cobh, Republic of Ireland.

LOUGH FOYLE FERRY COMPANY

THE COMPANY *Lough Foyle Ferry Company Ltd* is an Irish Republic Company.

MANAGEMENT **Managing Director** Jim McClenaghan.

ADDRESS The Pier, Greencastle, Co Donegal, Irish Republic.

TELEPHONE **Administration** +353 (0)74 93 81901.

FAX **Administration** +353 (0)74 93 81903.

INTERNET **Email** info@loughfoyleferry.com **Website** www.loughfoyleferry.com *(English)*

ROUTES OPERATED *Lough Foyle Service* Greencastle (Inishowen, Co Donegal, Irish Republic) - Magilligan (Co Londonderry, Northern Ireland) (10 mins; *FOYLE VENTURE*; about every 20 mins), *Lough Swilly Service (Summer only)* Buncrana (Inishowen, Co Donegal) - Rathmullan (Co Donegal) (20 mins; *FOYLE RAMBLER*; hourly).

1	FOYLE RAMBLER	122t	72	10.0k	35.0m	100P	20C	-	BA	IR	8985531
2	FOYLE VENTURE	324t	78	10.0k	47.9m	300P	44C	-	BA	IR	7800033

FOYLE VENTURE Built as the SHANNON WILLOW by Scott & Sons (Bowling) Ltd, Bowling, Glasgow, UK for *Shannon Ferry Ltd*. In 2000 replaced by the SHANNON BREEZE and laid up for sale. In 2003 sold to the *Lough Foyle Ferry Company Ltd* and renamed the FOYLE VENTURE.

FOYLE RAMBLER Built as the STEDINGEN by Abeking & Rasmussen, Lemwerder, Germany for *Schnellastfähre Berne-Farge GmbH* (later *Fähren Bremen-Stedingen GmbH*) to operate across the River Weser (Vegesack - Lemwerder and Berne - Farge). In 2004 sold to the *Lough Foyle Ferry Company Ltd* and renamed the FOYLE RAMBLER.

MURPHY'S FERRY SERVICE

THE COMPANY *Murphy's Ferry Service* is privately operated.

MANAGEMENT **Operator** Carol Murphy.

ADDRESS Anchorage, Lawrence Cove, Bere Island, Co Cork, Irish Republic.

TELEPHONE **Administration** +353 (0)27 75014 **Mobile** +353 (0)87 2386095.

FAX **Administration** +353 (0)27 75014.

INTERNET **Email** info@murphysferry.com **Website** www.murphysferry.com *(English)*

Gry Maritha (*Matthew Punter*)

Glenachulish (*John Hendy*)

SECTION 2 – Minor Ferry Operators

ROUTE OPERATED Castletownbere (Pontoon - 3 miles to east of town centre) - Bere Island (Lawrence Cove, near Rerrin) (20 mins; *IKOM K*; up to 8 per day).

1	IKOM K	55t	99	10.0k	16.0m	60P	4C	1L	B	IR

IKOM K Built by Arklow Marine Services, Arklow, Irish Republic for *Murphy's Ferry Service*.

PASSAGE EAST FERRY

THE COMPANY *Passage East Ferry Company Ltd* is an Irish Republic private sector company.

MANAGEMENT **Managing Director** Derek Donnelly, **Operations Manager** Gary O Hanlon.

ADDRESS Barrack Street, Passage East, Co Waterford, Irish Republic.

TELEPHONE **Administration** + 353 (0)51 382480, **Reservations** Not applicable.

FAX **Administration** + 353 (0)51 382598, **Reservations** Not applicable.

INTERNET **Email** passageferry@yahoo.ie **Website** www.passageferry.ie *(English)*

ROUTE OPERATED Passage East (County Waterford) - Ballyhack (County Wexford) (7 mins; *FBD TINTERN*; frequent service).

1	FBD TINTERN	236t	71	9.0k	54.8m	130P	30C	-	BA	IR

FBD TINTERN Built as the STADT LINZ by Schiffswerft Oberwinter, Oberwinter/Rhein, Germany for *Rheinfähre Linz - Remagen GmbH* of Germany and operated on the Rhine between Linz and Remagen. In 1990 renamed the ST JOHANNES. In 1997 sold to *Fähren Bremen-Stedingen GmbH*, renamed the VEGESACK and operated across the Weser between Lemwerder and Vegesack. In 2003 she became a reserve vessel and in 2004 was renamed the STEDINGEN (the name previously carried by the ferry sold to *Lough Foyle Ferry Company*). Later sold to *Schraven BV* of The Netherlands and refurbished. In Autumn 2005 sold to *Passage East Ferry* and renamed the FBD TINTERN. Entered service in December 2005.

RATHLIN ISLAND FERRY

THE COMPANY *Rathlin Island Ferry Ltd* is a UK private sector company owned by Ciarán and Mary O'Driscoll of County Cork, Irish Republic.

MANAGEMENT **Managing Director** Ciarán O'Driscoll.

ADDRESS Ballycastle Ferry Terminal, 18 Bayview Road, Ballycastle, County Antrim BT54 6BT.

TELEPHONE **Administration & Reservations** + 44 (0)28 2076 9299.

INTERNET **Email** info@rathlinballycastleferry.com **Website** www.rathlinballycastleferry.com *(English)*

ROUTE OPERATED **Vehicle Ferry** Ballycastle - Rathlin Island (45 min; *CANNA*; up to 4 per day). **Passenger-only Fast Ferry** (20 min; *RATHLIN EXPRESS*; up to 5 per day). The service is operated on behalf of the *Northern Ireland Department of Regional Development*.

1	CANNA	69t	76	8.0k	24.3m	140P	6C	1L	B	UK
2»p	RATHLIN EXPRESS	31t	09	18.0k	17.7m	98P	0C	0L	-	UK
3»p	ST SORNEY	12t	99	17.0k	12.2m	38P	0C	0L	-	IR

CANNA Built by James Lamont & Co Ltd, Port Glasgow, UK for *Caledonian MacBrayne*. She was the regular vessel on the Lochaline - Fishnish (Mull) service. In 1986 she was replaced by the ISLE OF CUMBRAE and until 1990 she served in a relief capacity in the north, often assisting on the Iona service. In 1990 she was placed on the Kyles Scalpay (Harris) - Scalpay service (replaced by a bridge in Autumn 1997). In Spring 1997 *Caledonian MacBrayne* was contracted to operate the Ballycastle - Rathlin Island route and she was transferred to this service. In June 2008 she was chartered by *Caledonian Maritime Assets Limited* to *Rathlin Island Ferry Ltd* who took over the operation of the service.

RATHLIN EXPRESS Built by Arklow Marine Services, Arklow, Irish Republic for *Rathlin Island Ferry Ltd*.

ST SORNEY A Lochin 40 cruiser built by Ryan & Roberts, Limerick, Ireland. In 2008 placed on the Ballycastle - Rathlin Island service. Now reserve vessel.

SHANNON FERRY

THE COMPANY *Shannon Ferry Group Ltd* is an Irish Republic private company owned by six families on both sides of the Shannon Estuary.

MANAGEMENT **Managing Director** Eugene Maher.

ADDRESS Ferry Terminal, Killimer, County Clare, Irish Republic.

TELEPHONE **Administration** +353 (0)65 9053124, **Reservations** Not applicable.

FAX **Administration** +353 (0)65 9053125, **Reservations** Not applicable.

INTERNET **Email** enquiries@shannonferries.com **Website** www.shannonferries.com *(English)*

ROUTE OPERATED Killimer (County Clare) - Tarbert (County Kerry) (20 mins; *SHANNON BREEZE, SHANNON DOLPHIN*; hourly (half-hourly during May, June, July, August and September)).

| 1 | SHANNON BREEZE | 611t | 00 | 10.0k | 80.8m | 350P | 60C | - | BA | IR | 9224910 |
| 2 | SHANNON DOLPHIN | 501t | 95 | 10.0k | 71.9m | 350P | 52C | - | BA | IR | 9114933 |

SHANNON BREEZE, SHANNON DOLPHIN Built by Appledore Shipbuilders, Appledore, UK for *Shannon Ferry Group Ltd*.

SKYE FERRY

THE COMPANY The *Skye Ferry* is owned by the *Isle of Skye Ferry Community Interest Company*, a company limited by guarantee.

ADDRESS 6 Coulindune, Glenelg, Kyle, Ross-shire, IV40 8JU.

TELEPHONE **Administration & Reservations** +44 (0)1599 522236.

INTERNET **Email** info@skyeferry.com **Website** www.skyeferry.com *(English)*

ROUTE OPERATED *Easter - October only* Glenelg - Kylerhea (Skye) (10 mins; *GLENACHULISH*; frequent service).

| 1 | GLENACHULISH | 44t | 69 | 9.0k | 20.0m | 12P | 6C | - | BSt | UK |

GLENACHULISH Built by Ailsa Shipbuilding Company, Troon, UK for the *Ballachulish Ferry Company* for the service between North Ballachulish and South Ballachulish, across the mouth of Loch Leven. In 1975 the ferry was replaced by a bridge and she was sold to *Highland Regional Council* and used on a relief basis on the North Kessock - South Kessock and Kyleku - Kylestrome routes. In 1983 she was sold to *Murdo MacKenzie*, who had operated the Glenelg – Skye route as ferryman since 1959. The vessel was eventually bought by *Roddy MacLeod* and the service resumed in September 1990. The *Isle of Skye Ferry Community Interest Company* reached agreement with *Mr MacLeod* that he would operate the ferry in 2006. In 2007 she was sold to the Company. During winter 2012 she was chartered to *The Highland Council* to operate between North and South Strome following a road closure due to a rock fall. She is the last turntable ferry in operation.

STRANGFORD LOUGH FERRY SERVICE

THE COMPANY The *Strangford Lough Ferry Service* is operated by the DRD *(Department for Regional Development)*, a Northern Ireland Government Department (formerly operated by *Department of the Environment (Northern Ireland)*).

MANAGEMENT **Ferry Manager** Seamus Fitzsimons.

ADDRESS Strangford Lough Ferry Service, The Slip, Strangford, Co Down BT30 7NE.

TELEPHONE Administration +44 (0)28 4488 1637, **Reservations** Not applicable.

FAX Administration +44 (0)28 4488 1044, **Reservations** Not applicable.

INTERNET Website www.strangfordferry.co.uk *(English)*

ROUTE OPERATED Strangford - Portaferry (County Down) (10 mins; *PORTAFERRY II, STRANGFORD FERRY*; half-hourly).

| 1 | PORTAFERRY II | 312t | 01 | 12.0k | 38.2m | 260P | 28C | - | BA | UK | 9237436 |
| 2 | STRANGFORD FERRY | 186t | 69 | 10.0k | 32.9m | 263P | 20C | - | BA | UK | 6926311 |

PORTAFERRY II Built by McTay Marine, Bromborough, Wirral, UK for *DRD (Northern Ireland).*

STRANGFORD FERRY Built by Verolme Dockyard Ltd, Cork, Irish Republic for *Down County Council.* Subsequently transferred to the *DOE (Northern Ireland)* and then the *DRD (Northern Ireland).* Following delivery of the PORTAFERRY II, she became reserve ferry.

C TOMS & SON LTD

THE COMPANY *C Toms & Son Ltd* is a British private sector company.

MANAGEMENT **Managing Director** Allen Toms.

ADDRESS East Street, Polruan, Fowey, Cornwall PL23 1PB.

TELEPHONE Administration +44 (0)1726 870232.

FAX Administration +44 (0)1726 870318.

INTERNET Email enquiries@ctomsandson.co.uk **Website** www.ctomsandson.co.uk *(English)*

ROUTE OPERATED Fowey - Bodinnick (Cornwall) (5 mins; *GELLAN, JENACK*; frequent)

| 1 | GELLAN | 50t | 03 | 4.5k | 36.0m | 50P | 10C | - | BA | UK |
| 2 | JENACK | 60t | 00 | 4.5k | 36.0m | 50P | 15C | - | BA | UK |

GELLAN, JENACK Built by C Toms & Sons Ltd, Fowey, UK.

VALENTIA ISLAND FERRIES

THE COMPANY *Valentia Island Ferries Ltd* is an Irish Republic private sector company.

MANAGEMENT **Manager** Richard Foran.

ADDRESS Valentia Island, County Kerry, Irish Republic.

TELEPHONE Administration +353 (0)66 76141, **Reservations** Not applicable.

FAX Administration +353 (0)66 76377, **Reservations** Not applicable.

INTERNET Email reforan@indigo.ie **Website** indigo.ie/%7ecguiney/ferry.html *(English)*

ROUTE OPERATED Reenard (Co Kerry) - Knightstown (Valentia Island) (5 minutes; *GOD MET ONS III*; frequent service, 1st April - 30th September).

| 1 | GOD MET ONS III | 95t | 63 | - | 43.0m | 95P | 18C | - | BA | IR |

GOD MET ONS III Built by BV Scheepswerven Vh HH Bodewes, Millingen, The Netherlands for *FMHE Res* of The Netherlands for a service across the River Maas between Cuijk and Middelaar. In 1987 a new bridge was opened and the service ceased. She was latterly used on contract work in the Elbe and then laid up. In 1996 acquired by *Valentia Island Ferries* and inaugurated a car ferry service to the island. **Note** This island never had a car ferry service before. A bridge was opened at the south end of the island in 1970; before that a passenger/cargo service operated between Reenard Point and Knightstown.

Jenack *(Nick Widdows)*

FBD Tintern *(Nick Widdows)*

Ikom K *(Nick Widdows)*

Canna *(Nick Widdows)*

WOOLWICH FREE FERRY

THE COMPANY The *Woolwich Free Ferry* is operated by *Briggs Marine*, a British private sector company on behalf of *Transport for London*.

MANAGEMENT Ferry Manager Jeremy Mccarthy.

ADDRESS New Ferry Approach, Woolwich, London SE18 6DX.

TELEPHONE Administration + 44 (0)20 8853 9400, **Reservations** Not applicable.

FAX Administration + 44 (0)20 8316 6096, **Reservations** Not applicable.

INTERNET Website www.tfl.gov.uk *(English)*

ROUTE OPERATED Woolwich - North Woolwich (free ferry) (5 mins; *ERNEST BEVIN, JAMES NEWMAN, JOHN BURNS*; every 10 mins (weekdays - two ferries in operation), every 15 mins (weekends - one ferry in operation)). **Note** One ferry is always in reserve/under maintenance.

1	ERNEST BEVIN	1194t	63	8.0k	56.7m	310P	32C	6L	BA	UK	5426998
2	JAMES NEWMAN	1194t	63	8.0k	56.7m	310P	32C	6L	BA	UK	5411905
3	JOHN BURNS	1194t	63	8.0k	56.7m	310P	32C	6L	BA	UK	5416010

ERNEST BEVIN, JAMES NEWMAN, JOHN BURNS Built by Robb Caledon Shipbuilders Ltd, Dundee, UK for the *London County Council* who operated the service when the vessels were new. In 1965 ownership was transferred to the *Greater London Council*. Following the abolition of the *GLC* in April 1986, ownership was transferred to the *Department of Transport* and in 2001 to *Transport for London*. The *London Borough of Greenwich* operated the service on their behalf. In 2008 the operation of the service was transferred to Serco. An alternative loading is 6 x 18m articulated lorries and 14 cars; lorries of this length are too high for the nearby northbound Blackwall Tunnel.

Rhum *(Arranmore Island Ferry Services)*

SECTION 2 – Minor Ferry Operators

CLdN/COBELFRET FERRIES

THE COMPANIES *Compagnie Luxembourgouise de Navigation SA (CLdN)* is a Luxemburg company. *Cobelfret Ferries NV* is a Belgian private sector company, a subsidiary of *Cobelfret NV* of Antwerp. The two companies operate as a single network with a single fleet.

MANAGEMENT C.RO Agencies NV (Zeebrugge) Tom De Wannemacker, CLdN Ro-Ro SA (Luxembourg) Caroline Dubois, Cobelfret Waterways SA (Vlissingen) Geert Bogaerts, CLdN ro-ro Agencies Ltd (UK) Martin Thompson.

ADDRESSES *Belgium* C.RO Ports Zeebrugge NV, Britannia Quay, 8380 Zeebrugge, Belgium *UK - Purfleet* C.RO Ports London Ltd, London Road, Purfleet, Essex RM19 1RP, *UK - Dartford (currently unused)* C.RO Ports Dartford Ltd, Clipper Boulevard, Crossways, Dartford, Kent DA2 6QB, *UK - Killingholme* C.RO Ports Killingholme Ltd, Clough Lane, North Killingholme, Immingham DN40 3JS, UK, *The Netherlands - Rotterdam* C.RO Ports Nederland BV, Merseyweg 70, Port no: 5230 Rotterdam, Botlek, *The Netherlands - Vlissingen* C.RO Ports Nederland BV, CdMR Terminal, 4389 PA Ritthem, Harbour No. 1125, Vlissingen Oost.

TELEPHONE Administration & Reservations *Belgium* +32 (0)3 829 9011, *UK (Purfleet, Ipswich & Killingholme)* +44 (0)1708 891199, *Luxembourg* +352 (0)26 44 66 288, *The Netherlands* +31 (0)118 480005.

FAX Administration & Reservations *Belgium* +32 (0)50 502219, *UK (Purfleet, Ipswich & Killingholme)* +44 (0)1708 890853, *Luxembourg* +352(0)26 44 66 299, *The Netherlands* +31 118480009.

INTERNET Website www.cldn.com www.cobelfret.com *(English)*

ROUTES OPERATED Cobelfret Ferries Services Zeebrugge - Purfleet (9 hrs; *ADELINE, CATHERINE, MAZARINE CLASS, VALENTINE, VICTORINE*; 2/3 per day), Zeebrugge - Killingholme (13 hrs; *PAULINE, YASMINE*; 6 per week), CLdN Services Rotterdam - Purfleet (14 hrs 30 mins; *MAZARINE CLASS*); 6 per week), Rotterdam - Killingholme (14 hrs; *OPALINE CLASS and MAZARINE CLASS*; 6 per week), Zeebrugge - Esbjerg (24hrs; *CATHERINE, CLEMENTINE, VALENTINE, VICTORINE*; 1 per week), Zeebrugge - Dublin (36 hrs; *MAZARINE CLASS and OPALINE CLASS*; 2 per week), Rotterdam - Dublin (38 hrs; *MAZARINE CLASS and OPALINE CLASS*; 2 per week), Zeebrugge - Gothenburg (32-33 hrs; *SCHIEBORG, SLINGEBORG, SPAARNEBORG*; 5 per week). MAZARINE CLASS = *MAZARINE, PALATINE, PEREGRINE, and VESPERTINE*; OPALINE CLASS = *AMANDINE and OPALINE*.

Note: The Zeebrugge - Gothenburg service is operated by CLdN and Wagenborg for the Stora-Enso paper and board group, for the conveyance of their products. CLdN act as handling agents at Zeebrugge and Gothenburg and market the surplus capacity on the vessels, which is available for general ro-ro traffic. Although this route is strictly outside the scope of this book it is included for the sake of completeness.

Contract Services for Ford Motor Company Vlissingen - Dagenham (11 hrs; *CYMBELINE, MELUSINE, UNDINE*; 2 per day).

1	ADELINE	21020t	12	15.8k	150.0m	12P	-	170T	A	LU	9539092
2	AMANDINE	33960t	11	18.5k	195.4m	12P	-	270T	A	LU	9424869
3	CATHERINE	21287t	02	18.0k	182.2m	12P	-	200T	A2	BE	9209453
4	CELANDINE	23987t	00	17.9k	162.5m	12P	630C	157T	A	BE	9183984
5	CELESTINE	23986t	96	17.8k	162.5m	24P	630C	157T	A	BE	9125372
6	CLEMENTINE	23986t	97	17.8k	162.5m	24P	630C	157T	A	BE	9125384
7	CYMBELINE	11866t	92	17.0k	147.4m	8P	350C	100T	A2	LU	9007764
8	HATCHE	29004t	09	21.5k	193.0m	12P	-	249T	A	LU	9457165
9	MAZARINE	25593t	09	18.5k	195.4m	12P	-	180T	A	LU	9376696
10	MELUSINE	23987t	99	17.8k	162.5m	12P	630C	157T	A	BE	9166637
11	OPALINE	33960t	10	18.5k	195.4m	12P	-	270T	A	MT	9424869
12	PALATINE	25593t	09	18.5k	195.4m	12P	-	180T	A	LU	9376701
13	PAQIZE	29429t	10	21.5k	193.0m	12P	-	249T	A	LU	9457206

14	PAULINE	49166t	06	21.7k	200.0m	12P	656C	258T	A	LU	9324473
15	PEREGRINE	25235t	10	18.5k	195.4m	12P	-	180T	A	MT	9376725
16	QEZBAN	29004t	10	21.5k	193.0m	12P	-	249T	A	LU	9457189
17	SCHIEBORG	21005t	00	18.0k	183.4m	12P	-	180T	A	NL	9188233
18	SLINGEBORG	21005t	00	18.0k	183.4m	12P	-	180T	A	NL	9188245
19	SPAARNEBORG	21005t	00	18.0k	183.4m	12P	-	180T	A	NL	9188221
20	UNDINE	11854t	91	15.0k	147.4m	8P	350C	100T	A2	LU	9006112
21	VALENTINE	23987t	99	18.0k	162.5m	12P	630C	157T	A	BE	9166625
22	VESPERTINE	25235t	10	18.5k	195.4m	12P	-	180T	A	LU	9376713
23	VICTORINE	23987t	00	17.8k	162.5m	12P	630C	157T	A	BE	9184029
24	YASMINE	49166t	07	21.7k	200.0m	12P	656C	258T	A	LU	9337353

ADELINE, Built by the Kyokuyo Shipyard, Shimonoseki, Japan. After competition, a additional deck and sponsons were retro-fitted at the Chengxi Shipyard, Jiangyin, China. In November 2012 chartered to *RMR Shipping* to operate between Western Europe and West Africa. In January 2013 sub-chartered to *Castor Shipping* of Bulgaria. In March undertook another trip to West Africa and then returned to the Zeebrugge - Purfleet route in April.

AMANDINE Built by Flensburger Schiffbau-Gesellschaft, Flensburg, Germany. Operates mainly between Rotterdam and Killingholme and Rotterdam/Zeebrugge and Dublin.

CATHERINE Built as the ROMIRA by Zhonghua Shipyard, Zhonghua, China for *Dag Engström Rederi* of Sweden. For six months engaged on a number of short-term charters, including *Cobelfret Ferries* who used her on both the Rotterdam - Immingham and Zeebrugge - Purfleet routes. In September 2002 purchased by *Cobelfret Ferries* and, in November 2002, renamed the CATHERINE and placed on the Rotterdam - Immingham service. In Spring 2003 chartered to the *US Defense Department* to convey materials to the Persian Gulf. Returned in late summer and operated thereafter on the Rotterdam - Immingham service. In January 2009 chartered to *CoTuNav* of Tunisia. In February 2010 returned to *Cobelfret* service and operated on the Rotterdam - Purfleet service. In March 2010 again chartered to *CoTuNav*. In March 2011 chartered to *RMR Shipping* to operate between Western Europe and Antwerp, Eemshaven, Harwich and Dublin to Lagos (Nigeria). In May 2011 returned to *Cobelfret Ferries* and used on the Zeebrugge - Gothenburg service UNTIL January 2013 when she began operating on the Purfleet route during the week and the Gothenburg route at weekend (one round trip). From April 2013 operated full-time on the Purfleet service.

CELANDINE, VALENTINE, VICTORINE Built by Kawasaki Heavy Industries, Sakaide, Japan for *Cobelfret*. The CELANDINE was originally to be called the CATHERINE and the VICTORINE the CELANDINE. The names were changed before delivery. Generally used on the Zeebrugge - Purfleet route. In May 2011 the CELANDINE was chartered to *RMR Shipping*.

CELESTINE Built by Kawasaki Heavy Industries, Sakaide, Japan as the CELESTINE. In 1996 chartered to the *British MoD* and renamed the SEA CRUSADER. She was originally expected to return to *Cobelfret Ferries* in early 2003 and resume the name CELESTINE; however, the charter was extended because of the Iraq war. Returned in September 2003 and placed on the Zeebrugge - Immingham service. In November 2006 moved to the Zeebrugge - Purfleet route. In November 2008 moved to the Ostend - Dartford service. In April 2009 the route became Ostend - Purfleet. In April 2010 chartered to *RMR Shipping*.

CLEMENTINE Built by Kawasaki Heavy Industries, Sakaide, Japan for *Cobelfret*. Mainly used on the Zeebrugge - Immingham service. In 2007 moved to the Zeebrugge - Purfleet route. In March 2013 chartered to *RMR Shipping*.

CYMBELINE, UNDINE Built by Dalian Shipyard, Dalian, China for *Cobelfret Ferries*. Currently mainly used on the Dagenham - Vlissingen route. They were occasionally used on a weekend Southampton - Vlissingen service but this ceased in 2012 following the closure of the Southampton Ford Transit factory.

HATCHE Built as the MAAS VIKING by Odense Staalskibsværft A/S, Odense, Denmark for *Epic Shipping* of the UK and chartered to *Norfolkline*. Charter taken over by *DFDS Seaways*. Operated between Vlaardingen and Killingholme. In September 2012 sold to *CLdN* of Luxembourg and renamed the KENT. At the end of the month the charter was ended. Operated from Rotterdam to Purfleet and Killingholme. In January 2013 renamed the HATCHE and chartered to *Ekol Lojistik* of Turkey to operate between Trieste in Italy and Haydarpasa (Istanbul) in Turkey.

MAZARINE, PALATINE, PEREGRINE, VESPERTINE Built by Flensburger Schiffbau-Gesellschaft, Flensburg, Germany.

MELUSINE Built by Kawasaki Heavy Industries, Sakaide, Japan for *Cobelfret*. Similar to the CLEMENTINE. Currently used on Zeebrugge - Purfleet or Rotterdam - Purfleet.

OPALINE Built by Flensburger Schiffbau-Gesellschaft, Flensburg, Germany. Operates mainly between Rotterdam and Killingholme and Rotterdam and Dublin.

PAQIZE Built as the MERCIA by Odense Staalskibsværft A/S, Odense, Denmark for *Epic Shipping* of the UK and chartered to *UN RoRo* of Turkey. Operated between Istanbul (Turkey) and Toulon (France). In February 2011 transferred to the Istanbul - Constanza (Romania) route. In May 2012 laid up in Greece. In September 2012 sold to *CLdN* of Luxembourg. In January 2013 renamed the PAQIZE and chartered to *Ekol Lojistik* of Turkey to operate between Trieste in Italy and Haydarpasa (Istanbul) in Turkey.

PAULINE, YASMINE Built by Flensburger Schiffbau-Gesellschaft, Flensburg, Germany to operate on the Zeebrugge - Killingholme route.

QEZBAN Built as the WESSEX by Odense Staalskibsværft A/S, Odense, Denmark for *Epic Shipping* of the UK and chartered to *UN RoRo* of Turkey. Operated between Istanbul (Turkey) and Toulon (France). In February 2011 chartered to *LD Lines* to operate between Marseilles and Tunis. In March 2011 returned to *UN RoRo*. In March 2012 laid up in Greece. In September 2012 sold to *CLdN* of Luxembourg. In January 2013 renamed the QEZBAN and chartered to *Ekol Lojistik* of Turkey to operate between Trieste in Italy and Haydarpasa (Istanbul) in Turkey.

SCHIEBORG, SLINGEBORG, Built by Flender Werft AG, Lübeck, Germany for *Wagenborg* of The Netherlands and time-chartered to *Stora-Enso* to operate between Zeebrugge and Gothenburg.

SPAARNEBORG Built by Flender Werft AG, Lübeck, Germany for *Wagenborg* of The Netherlands and time-chartered to *Stora-Enso* to operate between Zeebrugge and Gothenburg. She also operated between Tilbury and Gothenburg during 2010. In August 2011 chartered to the *Canadian MoD* to operate between Montreal and Cyprus in connection with the Libyan 'no fly zone'. On return in November she was laid up in Zeebrugge and in January 2012 moved to Gothenburg. In August 2012 chartered to *LD Lines* to operate between Marseilles and Tunis. In March 2013 returned to the Zeebrugge - Gothenburg route.

CLdN also own the CAPUCINE and SEVERINE, on charter to *Stena Line* and the WILHELMINE, on charter to *P&O Ferries*.

FINNLINES

THE COMPANY *Finnlines PLC* is a Finnish private sector company. Services to the UK are marketed by *Finnlines UK Ltd*, a British private sector company. From 1st January 2001, *Finncarriers* was merged into the parent company, trading as *Finnlines Cargo Service*.

MANAGEMENT *Finnlines* President & CEO Uwe Bakosch, **Vice-President** Simo Airas.

ADDRESS *Finland* PO Box 197, 00181 Helsinki, Finland, **UK** Finnlines UK Ltd, Finhumber House, Queen Elizabeth Dock, Hedon Road, HULL HU9 5PB.

TELEPHONE Administration & Reservations *Finland* + 358 (0)10 343 50, **UK** + 44 (0)1482 377 655

FAX Administration *Finland* + 358 (0)10 343 5200, **UK** + 44 (0)1482 787 229.

INTERNET Email *Finland* info.fi@finnlines.com **UK** customer.service.uk@finnlines.com

Website www.finnlines.com (*English, Finnish, German, Polish, Swedish*)

SECTION 3 – FREIGHT ONLY FERRIES

ROUTES OPERATED Irregular service from St Petersburg, Helsinki, Rauma and Kotka to Hull, Immingham, Amsterdam, Antwerp and Bilbao. For details see website. In view of the fact that ships are liable to be transferred between routes, the following is a list of all *Finnlines Cargo Service* ro-ro vessels, including those which currently do not serve the UK. Ro-pax vessels on Baltic services are listed in Section 6.

1	BALTICA	21224t	90	19.0k	157.7m	0P	-	163T	A	MT	8813154
2	CAROLINE RUSS	10488t	99	22.0k	153.5m	12P	-	134T	A2	AG	9197533
4	FINNBREEZE	28002t	11	20.0k	184.8m	12P	600C	200T	A	FI	9468889
5	FINNHAWK	11530t	01	20.0k	162.2m	12P	-	140T	A	FI	9207895
6	FINNKRAFT	11530t	00	20.0k	162.2m	12P	-	140T	A	FI	9207883
7	FINNMILL	25732t	02	20.0k	184.8m	12P	-	190T	A	SE	9212656
8	FINNPULP	25732t	02	20.0k	184.8m	12P	-	190T	A	SE	9212644
9	FINNSEA	28002t	11	21.0k	184.8m	12P	600C	200T	A	FI	9468891
10	FINNSKY	28002t	12	21.0k	184.8m	12P	600C	200T	A	LU	9468906
11	FINNSUN	28002t	12	21.0k	184.8m	12P	600C	200T	A	LU	9468918
12	FINNTIDE	28002t	12	21.0k	184.8m	12P	600C	200T	A	LU	9468920
13	FINNWAVE	28002t	12	21.0k	184.8m	12P	600C	200T	A	FI	9468932
14	MISANA	14100t	07	20.0k	163.9m	12P	-	150T	A	FI	9348936
15	MISIDA	14100t	07	20.0k	163.9m	12P	-	150T	A	FI	9348948

BALTICA Built by Hyundai Heavy Industries, Ulsan, South Korea as the AHLERS BALTIC for *Ahlers Line* and chartered to *Finncarriers*. In 1995 acquired by *Poseidon Schiffahrt AG* of Germany and renamed the TRANSBALTICA. She continued to be chartered to *Finncarriers* and was acquired by them when they purchased *Poseidon Schiffahrt AG* (now *Finnlines Deutschland AG*) in 1997. In 2003 sold to Norwegian interests and chartered back; She was renamed the BALTICA. In recent years she operated on the Helsinki - St Petersburg - Hamina - Helsinki - Zeebrugge - Tilbury – Amsterdam - Antwerp - service with the MERCHANT. During 2007 she operated Helsinki - Turku - Antwerp on a one-week cycle. In January 2008 moved to Baltic services. In April 2011 chartered to *Power Line* to operate between Helsinki and Travemünde. In January 2013 returned to *Finnlines*.

CAROLINE RUSS Built by J J Sietas KG, Hamburg, Germany for *Ernst Russ* of Germany and chartered to *Transfennica*. In January 2013 chartered to *Finnlines*.

FINNBREEZE, FINNSEA, FINNSKY, FINNSUN, FINNTIDE, FINNWAVE Built by Jinling Shipyard, Nanjing, China for *Finnlines*.

FINNHAWK Built by Jinling Shipyard, Nanjing, China for the *Macoma Shipping Group* and chartered to *Finnlines*. In April 2008 purchased by *Finnlines*. Currently operates used on service between Finland and The Netherlands, Belgium, the UK and Spain.

FINNKRAFT Built by Jinling Shipyard, Nanjing, China for the *Macoma Shipping Group* and chartered to *Finncarriers*. In April 2008 purchased by *Finnlines*. Currently operates on services between Finland and Germany.

FINNMILL, FINNPULP Built by Jinling Shipyard, Nanjing, China for the *Macoma Shipping Group* and chartered to *Finnlines*. In 2008 purchased by *Finnlines*. During Winter 2008/09 extra ramps were added at STX Europe Helsinki shipyard to enable ro-ro traffic to be conveyed on the weather deck.

MISANA, MISIDA Built by J J Sietas, Hamburg, Germany for *Godby Shipping AB* of Finland and time-chartered to *UPM-Kymmene* of Finland to operate between Finland, Spain and Portugal. In July 2013 charter taken over by *Finnlines*.

Adeline *(Cees de Bijl)*

Valentine *(Cees de Bijl)*

FORELAND SHIPPING

THE COMPANY *Foreland Shipping Limited* (formerly *AWSR Shipping Limited*) is a UK private sector company jointly owned by *Bibby Line*, *James Fisher*, *The Hadley Shipping Company* and *Andrew Weir*.

MANAGEMENT **Managing Director** Peter Morton.

ADDRESS Dexter House, 2 Royal Mint Court, London EC3N 4XX.

TELEPHONE +44 (0)20 7480 4140.

FAX +44 (0)20 7481 9940.

INTERNET Website www.foreland-shipping.co.uk *(English)*

ROUTES OPERATED No routes are operated. Four ships are for charter to the *UK Ministry of Defence* for their 'Strategic Sealift Capability'.

1	ANVIL POINT	23235t	03	17.1k	193.0m	12P	-	180T	A	UK	9248540
2	EDDYSTONE	23235t	02	17.1k	193.0m	12P	-	180T	A	UK	9234070
3	HARTLAND POINT	23235t	03	17.1k	193.0m	12P	-	180T	A	UK	9248538
4	HURST POINT	23235t	02	17.1k	193.0m	12P	-	180T	A	UK	9234068

ANVIL POINT, HARTLAND POINT Built by Harland & Wolff, Belfast, UK for *AWSR Shipping*.

EDDYSTONE, HURST POINT Built by Flensburger Schiffbau-Gesellschaft, Flensburg, Germany for *AWSR Shipping*.

Foreland Shipping Limited also owns the BEACHY HEAD and LONGSTONE, currently on charter to *DFDS Seaways*.

MANN LINES

THE COMPANY *Mann Lines* are owned by *Mann & Son (London) Ltd* of Great Britain. They replaced in 2001 *ArgoMann Ferry Service*, a joint venture between *Argo Reederei* of Germany and *Mann & Son*.

MANAGEMENT **Managing Director** Bill Binks.

ADDRESS *UK* Mann & Son (London) Ltd, The Naval House, Kings Quay Street, Harwich CO12 3JJ, *Germany* Mann Lines GmbH, Birkenstrasse 15, 28195 Bremen.

TELEPHONE **Administration & Reservations** *UK* +44 (0)1255 245200, *Germany* +49 (0)421 163850, *Finland* +358 (0)2 275 0000, *Estonia* +372 (0)679 1450.

FAX **Administration & Reservations** *UK* +44 (0)1255 245219, *Germany* +49 (0)421 1638520, *Finland* +358 (0)2 253 5905, *Estonia* +372 (0)679 1455.

INTERNET **Email** enquiry@manngroup.co.uk **Website** www.mannlines.com *(English, Finnish, Estonian, German, Russian)*

ROUTE OPERATED Harwich (Navyard) - Cuxhaven - Paldiski - Turku - Bremerhaven (Germany) – Harwich *(ESTRADEN*; weekly).

1	ESTRADEN	18205t	99	19.0k	162.7m	12P	130C	170T	A	FI	9181077

ESTRADEN Built as the ESTRADEN by Aker Finnyards, Rauma, Finland for *Rederi Ab Engship* (later *Bore Shipowners*) of Finland and chartered to *ArgoMann*. Later in 1999 renamed the AMAZON. In 2001 the charter was taken over by *Mann Lines* and later in the year she resumed the name ESTRADEN. In 2006 *Rederi AB Engship* was taken over by *Rettig Group Bore* and she remained on charter to *Mann Lines*.

SCA TRANSFOREST

THE COMPANY SCA Transforest is a Swedish company.

MANAGEMENT Managing Director (UK) Hugo Heij.

ADDRESS Sweden Box 805, 851 23, Sundsvall, Sweden, UK Interforest Terminal London Ltd, 44 Berth, Tilbury Dock, Essex RM18 7HR.

TELEPHONE Administration & Reservations Sweden +46 (0)60 19 35 00, UK +44 (0)1375 488501.

FAX Administration & Reservations Sweden +46 (0)60-19 35 65, UK +44 (0)1375 488503.

INTERNET Email Sweden info@transforest.sca.com UK interforest.london@sca.com

Website www.sca.com/transforest (English)

ROUTE OPERATED Umeå - Sundsvall - Helsingborg - Tilbury - Rotterdam (Eemhaven) - Helsingborg - Umeå (8/9 day round trip; OBBOLA, ORTVIKEN, ÖSTRAND; 2 per week).

1	OBBOLA	20168t	96	16.0k	170.6m	OP	-	-	A	SE	9087350
2	ORTVIKEN	20154t	97	16.0k	170.4m	OP	-	-	A	SE	9087374
3	ÖSTRAND	20171t	96	16.0k	170.6m	OP	-	-	A	SE	9087362

OBBOLA, ORTVIKEN, ÖSTRAND Built by Astilleros Españoles, Seville, Spain for Gorthon Lines and chartered to SCA Transforest. They are designed for the handling of forest products in non-wheeled 'cassettes' but can also accommodate ro-ro trailers; however, no trailer capacity is quoted. The ORTVIKEN was lengthened during Autumn 2000 and the OBBOLA and ÖSTRAND were lengthened during 2001. In June 2001 purchased by SCA Transforest.

SEA-CARGO

THE COMPANY Sea-Cargo AS of Norway is a joint venture between Nor-Cargo AS (a Norwegian company owned by Posten Norge, the Norwegian Postal Service.) and SeaTrans DS of Norway.

MANAGEMENT Managing Director Ole Saevild, Director Sales and Marketing Erik A Paulsen.

ADDRESS Norway Sea-Cargo AS, PO Box 353, Nesttun, 5853 Bergen, Norway, Immingham Sea-Cargo UK, West Riverside Road, Immingham Dock, Immingham DN40 2NT, Aberdeen Sea-Cargo Aberdeen Ltd, Matthews Quay, Aberdeen Harbour, Aberdeen, AB11 5PG.

TELEPHONE Administration & Bookings Bergen +47 85 02 82 16, Immingham +44 (0)1469 577119, Aberdeen +44 (0)1224 596481.

FAX Administration & Reservations Bergen +47 85 02 82 16, Immingham 44 (0)1469 577708, Aberdeen +44 (0)1224 582360.

INTERNET Email mail@sea-cargo.no Website www.sea-cargo.no (English)

ROUTES OPERATED Sea-Cargo operate a network of services from West Norway to Amsterdam, Aberdeen, Immingham and Esbjerg. The schedule varies from week to week and is shown on the company website. The BALTIC BRIGHT and NORRLAND are generally used on the twice-weekly Immingham - Tanager, Haugesund, Bergen and Odda service and the SEA-CARGO EXPRESS on the weekly Aberdeen - Tanager, Haugesund, Bergen, Florø, Aalesund, Kristiansund, Trondheim and Molde service.

1	BALTIC BRIGHT	9708t	96	15.0k	134.4m	12P	-	65T	A	SE	9129263
2	NORRLAND	5562t	90	14.5k	107.5m	OP	-	28T	A	AB	8818764
3•	SC ABERDEEN	4234t	79	16.0k	109.0m	OP	-	29T	AS	BS	7800540
4	SC AHTELA	8610t	91	14.8k	139.5m	12P	-	92T	A	MT	8911736
5	SC ASTREA	9528t	91	13.5k	129.1m	0p	-	58T	A	BS	8917895
6	SEA-CARGO EXPRESS	6693t	12	16.0k	117.4m	OP	-	35T	A	MT	9358060
7	TRANS CARRIER	9953t	94	14.5k	145.2m	OP	-	94T	A	BS	9007879

SECTION 3 – FREIGHT ONLY FERRIES

BALTIC BRIGHT Built for *Ab Kungsvik* of Sweden and chartered to *Holmen Papper AB* of Sweden (shipping division trading as *Holmen Carrier*) to operate on their private paper carrying service between Hallstavik and Södertälje in Sweden and Chatham in the UK. Later operated on a number of short-term charters. In November 2009 chartered to *Sea-Cargo* to operate between Western Norway and Immingham.

NORRLAND Built by J J Sietas KG, Hamburg, Germany for *Trailer Link* of Sweden. Chartered to *Sea-Cargo*.

SEA-CARGO EXPRESS One of two vessels ordered in 2005 from Bharati Ratnagiri Ltd, Mumbai, India for *Sea-Cargo*. The order for the second ship has been cancelled. Trailers are carried on the main deck only. Containers are carried on the weather deck and pallets on the lower decks. A crane is provided for the containers and a side door for pallets. She operates on the Aberdeen - Norway service.

SC ABERDEEN Con-ro vessel built by Fosen Mekaniske Verksteder, Rissa, Norway for *Nor-Cargo*. Launched as the ERIC JARL but renamed the ASTREA before entering service. In 1986 she sank and, after raising and refitting, she was, in 1992, renamed the TUNGENES. In 2001 she was renamed the SC ABERDEEN. In October 2012 laid up.

SC AHTELA Built as the AHTELA by Brodogradiliste "Sava", Macvanska Mitrovica, Yugoslavia, completed by Fosen Mekaniske Verksteder, Rissa, Norway for *Rederi AB Gustav Erikson* of Finland. Chartered to *Transfennica*. In 1995 chartered to DFDS Tor Line. In 1996 chartered to *Finncarriers Oy* of Finland and in 1997 renamed the FINNOAK. In 2007 sold to *Hollming Oy* of Finland and in 2008 the charter ended and she was renamed the AHTELA. Chartered to *Navirail* of Estonia to operate between Helsinki and Muuga (Estonia). Between February and May 2011 chartered to *Sea-Cargo* to operate between Esbjerg (Denmark) and Egersund (Norway). In October 2012 purchased by *Sea-Cargo* and renamed the SC AHTELA.

SC ASTREA Built as the ASTREA by Tangen Verft Kragerø A/S, Kragerø, Norway for *Finncarriers* of Finland. Operated between Finland and Spain - Portugal via Antwerp. In 2006 chartered to *Danish MoD*. In 2007 chartered to *Sea-Cargo*. In August 2011 purchased by *Sea-Cargo* and renamed the SC ASTREA. Currently chartered out.

TRANS CARRIER Built as the KORSNÄS LINK by Brodogradiliste Kraljevica, Kraljevica, Croatia for *SeaLink AB* of Sweden and due to be time-chartered to *Korsnäs AB*, a Swedish forest products company. However, due to the war in Croatia, delivery was seriously delayed and she was offered for sale. In 1994 sold to the *Swan Group* and renamed the SWAN HUNTER. She was placed on the charter market. In 1997 she was chartered to *Euroseabridge* and renamed the PARCHIM. In 1999 the charter ended and she resumed the name SWAN HUNTER. In 1999 she was sold to *SeaTrans* and renamed the TRANS CARRIER. She operated for *Sea-Cargo*. In 2005 chartered to *Finnlines* and used on the Finland to Spain/Portugal service. In 2006 returned to *Sea-Cargo*. In January and February 2009 lengthened by 18.9 metres in Poland.

Under Construction

8	SEA-CARGO INNOVATION	7695t	13	17.0k	132.8m	0P	-	80T	AS	NO	-
9	SEA-CARGO RENERGY	7695t	13	17.0k	132.8m	0P	-	80T	AS	MT	-

SEA-CARGO INNOVATION, SEA-CARGO RENERGY Con-ro vessels under construction at Bharati Ratnagiri Ltd, Mumbai, India for *Sea-Cargo*. They will be powered by a single Rolls-Royce LNG (liquefied natural gas) engine driving a single screw.

SEATRUCK FERRIES

THE COMPANY *Seatruck Ferries Ltd* is a British private sector company. It is part of the *Clipper Group*.

MANAGEMENT **Chairman** Ole Frie, **Managing Director** Alistair Eagles.

ADDRESSES *Heysham (HQ)* North Quay, Heysham Port, Heysham, Morecambe, Lancs LA3 2UH, *Warrenpoint* Seatruck House, The Ferry Terminal, Warrenpoint, County Down BT34 3JR, *Liverpool:* Seatruck Ferry Terminal, Brocklebank Dock, Port of Liverpool, L20 1DB, *Dublin:* Seatruck Dublin, Alexandra Road, Dublin 1 Irish Republic.

TELEPHONE Administration +44 (0)1524 855377, Reservations *Heysham* +44 (0)1524 853512. *Warrenpoint* +44 (0)28 754400, *Liverpool* + (0)151 9333660, *Dublin* + (0) 353 18230492.

FAX Administration +44 (0)28 4175 4545, Reservations *Warrenpoint* +44 (0)28 4177 3737, *Heysham* +44 (0)1524 853549.

INTERNET Email aje@seatruckgroup.co.uk Websites www.seatruckferries.com *(English)*

ROUTES OPERATED Heysham - Warrenpoint (9 hrs; *ANGLIA SEAWAYS, SEATRUCK PANORAMA*); 2 per day), Heysham - Dublin (1 per day; *CLIPPER RANGER*; 9 hrs), Liverpool - Dublin (9; *SEATRUCK POWER, SEATRUCK PROGRESS*; 1 or 2 per day).

1	ANGLIA SEAWAYS	13073t	00	18.5k	142.5m	12P	-	114T	A	DK	9186649
2	ARROW	7606t	98	17.0k	122.3m	12P	-	84T	A	IM	9119414
3	CLIPPER PENNANT	14759t	09	22.0k	142.0m	12P	-	120T	A	CY	9372688
4	CLIPPER RANGER	7606t	98	17.0k	122.3m	12P	-	84T	A	IM	9119402
5	SEATRUCK PACE	14759t	09	22.0k	142.0m	12P	-	120T	A	CY	9350678
6	SEATRUCK PANORAMA	14759t	09	22.0k	142.0m	12P	-	120T	A	CY	9372676
7	SEATRUCK POWER	19722t	11	21.0k	142.0m	12P	-	151T	A	IM	9506215
8	SEATRUCK PROGRESS	19722t	11	21.0k	142.0m	12P	-	151T	A	IM	9506203

ANGLIA SEAWAYS Built as the MAERSK ANGLIA by Guangzhou Shipyard International, Guangzhou, China for *Norfolkline*. Entered service as the GUANGZHOU 7130011 (unofficially the 'China II') but renamed shortly afterwards. Operated on the Scheveningen (from 2007 Vlaardingen) - Felixstowe service. In June 2009 moved to the Heysham - Dublin route. In August 2010 renamed the ANGLIA SEAWAYS. In January 2011 service withdrawn. In February 2011 chartered to *Seatruck Ferries* to inaugurate their new Heysham - Dublin service. In January 2012 returned to *DFDS Seaways* and placed on the Vlaardingen - Immingham route as an extra vessel. In April 2012 moved to the Zeebrugge - Rosyth service but proved too slow. In May chartered to *Seatruck Ferries* to operate between Heysham and Belfast. In August, this service ceased and she was switched to the Heysham - Dublin route and in September to the Heysham - Warrenpoint route. She is expected to remain with *Seatruck Ferries* until the end of 2013.

ARROW Built as the VARBOLA by Astilleros de Huelva SA, Huelva, Spain for the *Estonian Shipping Company*. On completion, chartered to *Dart Line* and placed on the Dartford - Vlissingen route. In 1999 she was renamed the DART 6. At the end of August 1999, the charter was terminated and she was renamed the VARBOLA. She undertook a number of short-term charters, including *Merchant Ferries*. In 2000 long-term chartered to *Merchant Ferries* to operate between Heysham and Dublin. In 2003 the charter ended and she was chartered to *Dart Line* to replace the DART 9; she was placed initially on the Dartford - Vlissingen route but later transferred to the Dartford - Dunkerque route. Later sub-chartered to *NorseMerchant Ferries* and placed on the Heysham – Dublin route. In 2004 the charter transferred to *NorseMerchant Ferries*. In 2005 sold to *Elmira Shipping* of Greece and renamed the RR ARROW. In October 2007 sold to *Seatruck Ferries* but the charter to *Norfolkline* continued. Renamed the ARROW. In June 2009 returned to *Seatruck Ferries*.

CLIPPER PENNANT Built by Astilleros Sevilla SA, Seville, Spain for *Seatruck Ferries*. In January 2013 chartered to *Stena RoRo*.

CLIPPER RANGER Built as the LEMBITU by Astilleros de Huelva SA, Huelva, Spain for the *Estonian Shipping Company*. On completion chartered to *P&O European Ferries (Irish Sea)* and placed on their Liverpool - Dublin route. In Autumn 1998 she was chartered to *Dart Line* and placed on the Dartford - Vlissingen route. In 1999 she was renamed the DART 7. In Autumn 1999 the charter was ended and she was chartered to *Cetam* of France, resumed the name LEMBITU and was used on services between Marseilles and Tunis. In 2000 she was chartered to *P&O European Ferries (Irish Sea)* and renamed the CELTIC SUN; she operated between Liverpool and Dublin. In 2001 the charter ended; she then reverted to the name LEMBITU and was chartered to *NorseMerchant Ferries* and placed on the Heysham - Dublin service. In late 2001 the charter ended and she returned to *ESCO* service in the Baltic. In 2003 chartered to *Scandlines AG* and placed on their Rostock - Helsinki - Muuga service. This service finished in December 2004 and she was chartered to *Channel Freight Ferries* in January 2005. In March 2005 chartered to *NorseMerchant Ferries* again and operated between Heysham and

SECTION 3 – FREIGHT ONLY FERRIES

Cragside (*Cees de Bijl*)

Obbola (*Cees de Bijl*)

Belfast. Later purchased by *Elmira Shipping* of Greece and renamed the RR CHALLENGE. In June 2005 chartered to *Seatruck Ferries*. In October 2007 sold to *Attica Group* of Greece and renamed the CHALLENGE. She continued to be chartered to *Seatruck Ferries*. In January 2008 she was transferred to the Liverpool - Dublin route and in April sold to *Seatruck Ferries*. In July renamed the CLIPPER RANGER. In June 2009 replaced the SHIELD (now the HILDASAY) until the new CLIPPER PENNANT took over in October. In May 2010 inaugurated a new Heysham - Larne service. Now generally used on the Heysham - Dublin service.

SEATRUCK PACE Built as the CLIPPER PACE by Astilleros Sevilla SA, Seville, Spain for *Seatruck Ferries*. In March 2012 renamed the SEATRUCK PACE. In January 2013 chartered to *Blue Water Shipping* of Denmark to carry wind turbine parts between Mostyn (Wales) and Esbjerg.

SEATRUCK PANORAMA Built by Astilleros de Huelva SA, Huelva Spain for *Seatruck Ferries*. Launched as the CLIPPER PENNANT and renamed the CLIPPER PANORAMA before delivery. In December 2011 renamed the SEATRUCK PANORAMA.

SEATRUCK POWER, SEATRUCK PROGRESS Built by Flensburger Schiffbau-Gesellschaft, Flensburg, Germany for *Seatruck Ferries*.

Seatruck Ferries also own the HELLIAR and HILDASAY, currently on charter to *NorthLink Ferries*, the STENA PERFORMER and STENA PRECISION, currently on charter to *Stena Line* and the CLIPPER POINT, currently on charter to *DFDS Seaways* in the Baltic.

FLOTA SUARDIAZ

THE COMPANY *Flota Suardiaz SL* is owned by *Grupo Suardiaz*, a Spanish private sector logistics company which operates divisions in ports, bunkering, warehousing, haulage, freight forwarding and shipping.

MANAGEMENT Presidente Juan Riva **Director General** Jesús Nieto.

ADDRESSES Spain Calle Ayala, 6 28001 Madrid, Spain, **UK** Suardiaz Shipping Ltd, Suardiaz House, 193 Shirley Road, Southampton, Hampshire, SO15 3FG.

TELEPHONE Spain +34 914 31 66 40, **UK** +44 (0) 2380 211 981.

FAX Spain +34 914 36 46 74, **UK** +44 (0) 2380 335309.

INTERNET Email infoweb@suardiaz.com, **Website** www.suardiaz.com *(Spanish)*.

ROUTES OPERATED Channel Line (3 times per week) Sheerness – Calais, Grimsby – Calais **Cantabrian Line** (weekly) Teesport – Zeebrugge - Southampton – Le Havre – Santander **Northern Sea Line** (twice weekly) Cuxhaven – Immingham **Línea del Atlántico / Barcelona - Inglaterra** (weekly) Vlissingen – Zeebrugge – Southampton – Vigo – Setubal – Las Palmas – Tenerife – Casablanca – Barcelona – Sete – Barcelona – Casablanca – Setubal – Sheerness – Newcastle **Biscay Line** (3 per week) St Nazaire – Vigo **Canaries Line** (weekly) Barcelona – Tarragona – Las Palmas – Tenerife **Italy Line** (3 per week) Barcelona – Livorno.

Services listed carry unaccompanied ro-ro cargo together with large volumes of trade cars for vehicle manufacturers and distributors. The Cantabrian and Channel Line services are operated by SCSC (Suardiaz CAT Shipping Co) a joint venture with European Car distributor CAT. The Biscay Line is operated under contract to GEFCO. Vessels are regularly transferred between routes and are often chartered out for short periods to other operators and vehicle manufacturers. In view of this the following is a list of all vessels in the *Flota Suardiaz* fleet at the present time including those that do not currently serve the UK.

#											
1	BOUZAS	15224t	02	18.5k	149.4m	12P	1265C	105T	A	ES	9249996
2	GALICIA	16361t	03	15.0k	149.4m	12P	1390C	110T	A	ES	9268409
3	GRAN CANARIA CAR	9600t	01	18.0k	132.5m	0P	1150C	42T	AS	ES	9218014
4	IVAN	8191t	96	14.6k	102.5m	0P	853C	73T	A	PT	9112040
5	L'AUDACE	15224t	99	18.5k	149.4m	12P	1233C	107T	A	ES	9187318
6	LA SURPRISE	15222t	00	18.5k	149.4m	12P	1233C	107T	A	ES	9198719

| 7 | SUAR VIGO | 16361t | 03 | 18.5k | 149.4m | 12P | 1356C | 118T | A | ES | 9250000 |
| 8 | TENERIFE CAR | 13122t | 02 | 20.0k | 149.4m | 12P | 1354C | 54T | AS | ES | 9249984 |

GRAN CANARIA CAR Built as HARALD FLICK by Hijos de J. Barreras SA, Vigo, Portugal for *Naviera del Odiel*, one of the shareholders in Barreras and placed on 10 year charter to *Flota Suardiaz* of Spain for use on services in the Mediterranean and to the Canaries, U.K. and Benelux. Renamed GRAN CANARIA CAR before entering service. In 2008 ownership passed to *Navicar SA* a subsidiary of *Flota Suardiaz*. In addition to operating for *Flota Suardiaz* has been chartered to UECC on a number of occasions.

BOUZAS, GALICIA, L'AUDACE, LA SURPRISE, SUAR VIGO Built by Hijos de J. Barreras SA, Vigo, Portugal for *Flota Suardiaz* of Spain for use on services in the Mediterranean and to the Canaries, U.K. and Benelux. In addition to operating for *Flota Suardiaz* a number of vessels have spent periods on charter to UECC.

IVAN Built by Astilleros De Murueta, Vizcaya, Spain for *Adamastor - Sociedade de Navegação, Lda* a subsidiary of *Flota Suardiaz* for use on short sea services. In recent years she has been used on services between Sheerness, Grimsby and Calais.

TENERIFE CAR Built by Hijos de J. Barreras SA, Vigo, Portugal for *Navicar SA* a subsidiary of *Flota Suardiaz* for use on services in the Mediterranean and to the Canaries, U.K. and Benelux.

TRANSFENNICA

THE COMPANY *Transfennica Ltd* is a Finnish private sector company wholly owned by *Spliethoff Bevrachtingskantoor* of The Netherlands.

MANAGEMENT **Managing Director** Dirk P. Witteveen, **Sales Director (UK)** Andrew Clarke.

ADDRESSES *Finland* Eteläranta 12, 00130 Helsinki, Finland, **UK** Finland House, 47 Berth, Tilbury Freeport, Tilbury, Essex RM18 7EH.

TELEPHONE **Administration & Reservations** *Finland* +358 (0)9 13262, **UK** +44 (0)1375 363 900.

FAX **Administration & Reservations** *Finland* +358 (0)9 652377, **UK** +44 (0)1375 840 888.

INTERNET **Email** *Finland* info@transfennica.fi **UK** info.uk@transfennica.com *(English)*

Website www.transfennica.com *(English)*

ROUTES OPERATED Tilbury (twice weekly) to various destinations in Finland and Russia. Please see the website. All *Transfennica* ships are listed below as ships are sometimes moved between routes. *Transfennica* also act as Tilbury agents for the *UPM-Kymmene Seaways* Kotka-Tilbury and v.v. service.

1	BIRKA CARRIER	12251t	98	20.0k	155.5m	12P	-	124T	A2	FI	9132002
2	BIRKA TRADER	12251t	98	20.0k	154.5m	12P	-	124T	A2	FI	9132014
3	FRIEDRICH RUSS	10471t	99	20.0k	153.5m	12P	-	120T	A2	AG	9186429
4	GENCA	28289t	07	22.0k	205.0m	12P	-	200T	A	NL	9307372
5	KRAFTCA	28289t	06	22.0k	205.0m	12P	-	200T	A	NL	9307360
6	PAULINE RUSS	10488t	99	22.0k	153.5m	12P	-	120T	A2	AG	9198989
7	PLYCA	28289t	09	22.0k	205.0m	12P	-	200T	A	NL	9345398
8	PULPCA	28289t	08	22.0k	205.0m	12P	-	200T	A	NL	9345386
9	SEAGARD	10488t	99	21.0k	153.5m	12P	-	134T	A2	FI	9198977
10	STENA CARRIER	21089t	04	20.5k	182.6m	12P	-	200T	A	UK	9138800
11	STENA FORECASTER	24688t	03	22.0k	195.3m	12P	-	210T	A2	SE	9214666
12	STENA FORERUNNER	24688t	02	22.0k	195.3m	12P	-	210T	A2	SE	9214666
13	STENA FORETELLER	24688t	02	22.0k	195.3m	12P	-	210T	A2	SE	9214666
14	STENA FREIGHTER	21104t	04	22.0k	182.6m	12P	-	200T	A	UK	9138795
15	TIMCA	28300t	06	22.0k	205.0m	12P	-	200T	A	NL	9307358
16	TRICA	28289t	07	22.0k	205.0m	12P	-	200T	A	NL	9307384

BIRKA CARRIER, BIRKA TRADER Built as the UNITED CARRIER and UNITED TRADER by Fosen Mekaniske Verksteder A/S, Rissa, Norway for *United Shipping* (a subsidiary of *Birka Shipping*) of Finland and chartered to *Transfennica*. During 2000 they were used on their Kemi - Oulu - Antwerp - Felixstowe service. In 2001 the route was transferred to *Finnlines* and the vessels used sub-chartered to them (charter later transferred to *Finnlines*). In 2002 *United Shipping* was renamed *Birka Cargo* and the ships were renamed the BIRKA CARRIER and BIRKA TRADER. In 2006 the service ceased. In 2008 the charter was extended a further four years. In January 2013 chartered to *Transfennica*.

FRIEDRICH RUSS, PAULINE RUSS, Built by J J Sietas KG, Hamburg, Germany for *Ernst Russ* of Germany and chartered to *Transfennica*.

GENCA, KRAFTCA, PLYCA, PULPCA, TIMCA, TRICA Built by New Szczecin Shipyard (SSN), Szczecin, Poland for *Spliethoff Bevrachtingskantoor*, owners of *Transfennica*.

SEAGARD Built by J J Sietas KG, Hamburg, Germany for *Bror Husell Chartering* of Finland (later acquired by *Bore Shipowning* of Finland) and chartered to *Transfennica*.

STENA CARRIER Laid down in 1998 by Societa Esercizio Cantieri SpA, Viareggio, Italy for *Stena RoRo*. In 1999 the builders went bankrupt and work ceased. The hull was purchased by *Enrico Bugazzi Shipmanagement*, named the ARONTE and in 2003 she was towed to Marina di Carrara, Italy for work to be completed. In 2003 she was sold to *Stena RoRo*; in 2004 she was transferred to *Stena Line* and was renamed the STENA CARRIER II. After further work at Gothenburg she entered service on the Gothenburg - Travemünde route. She was later renamed the STENA CARRIER. She replaced the STENA TRANSFER on Rotterdam - Harwich in September 2010. In September 2012 withdrawn. In January 2013, chartered to *Transfennica* and placed on the Zeebrugge - Bilbao service.

STENA FORECASTER, STENA FORERUNNER Built by Dalian Shipyard Co Ltd, Dalian, China for *Stena RoRo* and chartered to *Transfennica*.

STENA FORETELLER Built as the STENA FORETELLER by Dalian Shipyard Co Ltd, Dalian, China for *Stena RoRo*. Initially chartered to *Cetam* of France to operate between Marseilles and Tunis and renamed the CETAM MASSILIA. In November 2003 the charter ended and she resumed her original name. A number of short-term commercial and military charters followed until June 2006 when she was chartered to *StoraEnso* paper group to operate between Gothenburg and Finnish ports. In September 2009 she was chartered to *Rederi AB Transatlantic* who took over responsibility to operate all *StoraEnso's* Baltic services. In February 2012 she was chartered to *Transfennica*.

STENA FREIGHTER Laid down in 1998 by Societa Esercizio Cantieri SpA, Viareggio, Italy for *Stena RoRo*. Due to be called the SEA CHIEFTAIN for charter to the *British MoD*. In 1999 the builders went bankrupt and work ceased. In 2003 the incomplete vessel was purchased at auction by a *Stena* subsidiary, she was renamed the STENA SEAFREIGHTER and towed to Kraljevica, Croatia for work to be completed. In 2004 she was renamed the STENA FREIGHTER and entered service with *Stena Line* between Gothenburg and Travemünde. This route closed at the end of August 2010 and she was moved to the Gothenburg - Kiel route, running in tandem with the STENA SCANDINAVICA (1988). In April 2011 she moved to the Rotterdam - Harwich service. In September 2012 withdrawn. In January 2013, chartered to *Transfennica* and placed on the Zeebrugge - Bilbao service.

SECTION 3 – FREIGHT ONLY FERRIES

UECC

THE COMPANY *United European Car Carriers AS* is a Norwegian private sector company jointly owned in equal shares by *Nippon Yusen Kabushiki Kaisha* (NYK) of Japan and *Wallenius Lines* of Sweden. UECC consists of companies in Norway, Germany, Spain, France, Portugal and the UK. The fleet technical and ship management department is based in Grimsby (UK).

MANAGEMENT **Chief Executive Officer** Glenn Edvardsen **Senior Commercial Manager UK** Peter Pegg.

ADDRESSES **Norway** Karenlyst Allè 57, 0277 Oslo, **UK** 17 St. Helen's Place, London EC3A 6DG.

TELEPHONE **Norway** + 47 21 00 98 00, **UK** +44 (0)207 628 2855.

Seatruck Progress (*Cees de Bijl*)

Clipper Ranger (*Gordon Hislip*)

FAX Norway +47 21 00 98 01, UK +44 (0)207 628 2858.

INTERNET Email companymail@uecc.com, Website www.uecc.com (English).

ROUTES OPERATED Bristol Service Portbury - Pasajes (AUTOSUN; every 4 days) North Sea Line Sheerness – Emden, Southampton – Cuxhaven, Zeebrugge – Malmo (AUTOPRESTIGE; AUTOPRIDE; weekly or twice weekly, Biscay Services Pasajes – Zeebrugge – Southampton – Santander - Pasajes (AUTOSTAR; weekly) Pasajes – Rotterdam - Zeebrugge – Santander - Pasajes (AUTOSKY; weekly) Santander – Zeebrugge – Southampton – Le Havre – Santander (AUTOPREMIER; weekly) Atlantic Service Vigo – Le Havre – Zeebrugge – Sheerness – Vigo (VIKING CHANCE; weekly) Norway Service Bremerhaven – Oslo/Drammen (AUTORACER; twice weekly) Bremerhaven – Drammen – Cuxhaven – Southampton – Zeebrugge – Bremerhaven (AUTOPROGRESS; weekly) Baltic Long Loop Service Southampton – Zebrugge – Gydnia – Hanko – Kotka – St Petersburg – Cuxhaven – Southampton (ARABIAN BREEZE, ASIAN BREEZE; weekly) Baltic Short Loop Service Bremerhaven – Wallhamn – Kotka – St Petersburg – Ust Luga – Bremerhaven (AUTO BAY, AUTO BANK; every 5 days) Bremerhaven –Hanko – St Petersburg – Bremerhaven (AUTO BALTIC; weekly) North / South Service Bremerhaven - Zeebrugge - Portbury - Vigo - Malaga - Tarragona - Livorno - Piraeus - Derince - Yenikoy - Borusan - Vigo - Bremerhaven (OPAL LEADER, CORAL LEADER, EMERALD LEADER, MORNING MENAD, VIKING DRIVE; weekly) West-Med Service Vigo - Djen Djen (SPICA LEADER; 3 per month) Fos – Mostaganem (AUTORUNNER; every 4 days) Gioia Tauro – Misurata – Djen Djen - Gioia Tauro (BALTIC BREEZE; AEGEAN BREEZE; weekly).

Services listed carry unaccompanied ro-ro cargo together with large volumes of trade cars and may call at additional ports for an inducement and regular additional ports include Cork, Dublin, Immingham, Sheerness, Portbury, Tilbury, and Newcastle. A number of short-sea contract sailings for vehicle manufacturers and distributors are also operated and these serve many additional ports in Northern Europe. Vessels are regularly transferred between routes and contracts and in view of this the following is a list of all owned and long term chartered vessels in the UECC fleet at the current time including those that do not presently serve the UK. Additionally the fleet is regularly supplemented by short term chartered vessels from Flota Suardiaz and Fret Cetam (the Louis Dreyfus Armateurs and Höegh Auto-liners Airbus joint venture) and with deep sea ocean-going ro-ro vessels from parent companies NYK Line and Wallenius Lines and Eukor. Chartered vessels at the time of preparation and considered out of the scope of this book were the MORNING MENAD, CORAL LEADER, EMERALD LEADER, OPAL LEADER, SPICA LEADER, VIKING CHANCE and VIKING DRIVE.

1	AEGEAN BREEZE	27876t	83	18.0k	164.0m	OP	3070C	260T	QRS	SG	8202367
2	ARABIAN BREEZE	27876t	83	18.0k	164.0m	OP	3070C	260T	QRS	SG	8202355
3	ASIAN BREEZE	27876t	83	18.0k	164.0m	OP	3070C	260T	QRS	SG	8202381
4	AUTO BALTIC	18979t	96	20.0k	138.5m	12P	1452C	105T	A2	FI	9121998
5	AUTO BANK	19107t	96	20.0k	138.8m	12P	1610C	105T	A2	FI	9160774
6	AUTO BAY	19094t	96	20.0k	138.8m	12P	1610C	105T	A2	FI	9122007
7	AUTOPREMIER	11591t	97	20.0k	128.8m	OP	1220C	-	AS	PT	9131943
8	AUTOPRESTIGE	11591t	99	20.0k	128.8m	OP	1220C	-	AS	PT	9190157
9	AUTOPRIDE	11591t	97	20.0k	128.8m	OP	1220C	-	AS	PT	9131955
10	AUTOPROGRESS	11591t	98	20.0k	128.8m	OP	1220C	-	AS	PT	9131967
11	AUTORACER	9693t	94	20.0k	119.9m	OP	1060C	-	AS	PT	9079200
12	AUTORUNNER	9693t	94	20.0k	119.9m	OP	1060C	-	AS	PT	9079212
13	AUTOSKY	21010t	00	20.9k	140.0m	OP	1220C	-	AS	PT	9206774
14	AUTOSTAR	21010t	00	20.9k	140.0m	OP	1220C	-	AS	PT	9206786
15	AUTOSUN	21094t	00	20.9k	140.0m	OP	1220C	-	AS	PT	9227053
16	BALTIC BREEZE	29979t	83	18.0k	164.0m	OP	3070C	260T	QRS	SG	8312590

AEGEAN BREEZE, ARABIAN BREEZE, ASIAN BREEZE Built by Kurushima Dockyard, Onishi, Japan for Fuji Shipping of Tokyo. Sold in 1988 to Amon Shipping. In 1990 sold to Wallenius Lines, Singapore and later chartered to UECC. Of deep-sea ocean-going ro-ro design with quarter ramps, they are normally used on the Baltic Long Loop and Mediterranean services.

AUTO BALTIC Built as the TRANSGARD by Umoe Sterkoder, Kristiansund, Norway for *Bror Husell Chartering* of Finland for long-term charter to *Transfennica* and used between Rauma and Antwerp and Hamina and Lübeck. Later chartered to *Finncarriers*. In 2005 she underwent conversion in Poland to add a garage on top of the original weather deck and was placed on long-term charter to *UECC* with options to purchase. Generally used on the Baltic or Iberian services. In 2007 renamed AUTO BALTIC.

AUTO BANK Built as the SERENADEN by Umoe Sterkoder AS, Kristiansund, Norway for *Rederi AB Engship* of Finland and chartered to *Transfennica*. In 2006 *Rederi AB Engship* was taken over by *Rettig Group Bore*. In 2007 converted at COSCO Shipyard, Nantong, China to add a garage on top of the weather deck, renamed AUTO BANK and placed on long-term charter to *UECC*. Generally used on the Baltic or Iberian services.

AUTO BAY Built as the HERALDEN by Umoe Sterkoder AS, Kristiansund, Norway for *Rederi AB Engship* of Finland and chartered to *Transfennica*. In 2006 *Rederi AB Engship* was taken over by *Rettig Group Bore*. In 2007 converted at COSCO Shipyard, Nantong, China to add a garage on top of the weather deck, renamed AUTO BAY and placed on long-term charter to *UECC*. Generally used on the Baltic or Iberian services.

AUTOPREMIER, AUTOPRESTIGE, AUTOPROGRESS, AUTOPRIDE Built by Frisian Shipyard Welgelegen, Harlingen, the Netherlands for *UECC*. Designated P-class, they are an enlarged version of the R-class and built to a 'Grimsby-Max' specification with greater capacity for ro-ro cargo. Normally used on scheduled sailings between Iberia, Belgium, Ireland and UK.

AUTORUNNER, AUTORACER. Built by Brattvaag Skipsverft, Brattvaag, Norway for *UECC*. Designated as R-class, they are normally used on scheduled sailings between Iberia, Belgium, Ireland and UK.

AUTOSKY, AUTOSTAR, AUTOSUN Built by Tsuneishi Zosen, Tadotsu, Japan for *UECC*. Designated S-class, they are a further enlargement of the P-class and R-class designs and are normally used on the longer routes to Iberia and in the Baltic.

BALTIC BREEZE Built by Kurushima Dockyard, Onishi, Japan for *Fuji Shipping Co* of Tokyo. Sold in 1988 to *Amon Shipping*. Sold to *Wallenius Lines*, Singapore in 1990. Chartered to *Eukor* then to *UECC*. Of deep-sea ocean-going ro-ro design with a quarter ramp, she is normally used on the Mediterranean services.

SECTION 4 - GB & IRELAND - CHAIN, CABLE ETC FERRIES

CUMBRIA COUNTY COUNCIL

Address Environment Directorate, County Offices, Kendal, Cumbria LA9 4RQ **Tel** +44 (0)1539 713040, **Fax** +44 (0)1539 713035.

Internet Email tony.beaty@cumbria.gov.uk *(English)*

Website www.cumbria.gov.uk/roads-transport/highways-pavements/windermereferry.asp *(English)*

Route Bowness-on-Windermere - Far Sawrey.

1	MALLARD	-	90	-	25.9m	140P	18C	-	BA	

MALLARD Chain ferry built by F L Steelcraft, Borth, Dyfed for *Cumbria County Council*.

DARTMOUTH - KINGSWEAR FLOATING BRIDGE CO LTD

Address Dart Marina, Sandquay Road, Dartmouth, Devon TQ6 9PH. **Tel** +44 (0)1803 839622.

Website www.dartmouthhigherferry.com *(English)*

Route Dartmouth - Kingswear (Devon) across River Dart (higher route) (forms part of A379).

1	HIGHER FERRY	540t	09	-	52.7m	240P	32C	-	BA	

HIGHER FERRY Built by Ravestein BV, Deest, The Netherlands under contract to Pendennis Shipyard, Falmouth, who fitted the vessel out between January and June 2009.

ISLE OF WIGHT COUNCIL (COWES FLOATING BRIDGE)

Address Ferry Office, Medina Road, Cowes, Isle of Wight PO31 7BX. **Tel** +44 (0)1983 293041.

Route West Cowes - East Cowes.

1	NO 5	-	76	-	33.5m	-	15C	-	BA	

NO 5 Chain ferry built by Fairey Marine, East Cowes, UK for *Isle of Wight County Council*, now *Isle of Wight Council*.

KING HARRY FERRY AND CORNWALL FERRIES

Address Feock, Truro, Cornwall TR3 6QJ. **Tel** +44 (0)1872 862312, **Fax** +44 (0)1872 863355.

Internet Email info@falriver.co.uk **Website** www.falriver.co.uk *(English)*

Route Philliegh - Feock (Cornwall) (across River Fal)

1	KING HARRY FERRY	500t	06	-	55.2m	150P	34C	-	BA	UK	9364370

KING HARRY FERRY Chain ferry built by Pendennis Shipyard, Falmouth (hull constructed at Ravestein Shipyard, Deest, The Netherlands) to replace the previous ferry.

REEDHAM FERRY

Address Reedham Ferry, Ferry Inn, Reedham, Norwich NR13 3HA. **Tel** +44 (0)1493 700999.

Internet Email info@reedhamferry.co.uk **Website** www.reedhamferry.co.uk (English)

Route Acle - Reedham - Norton (across River Yare, Norfolk).

1	REEDHAM FERRY	-	84	-	11.3m	20P	3C	-	BA	

REEDHAM FERRY Chain ferry built by Newsons, Oulton Broad, Lowestoft, UK for Reedham Ferry. Maximum vehicle weight: 12 tons.

SANDBANKS FERRY

Address *Company* Bournemouth-Swanage Motor Road and Ferry Company, Shell Bay, Studland, Swanage, Dorset BH19 3BA. **Tel** +44 (0)1929 450203, **Fax** +44 (0)1929 450498), *Ferry* Floating Bridge, Ferry Way, Sandbanks, Poole, Dorset BH13 7QN. **Tel** +44 (0)1929 450203.

Internet Email email@sandbanksferry.co.uk **Website** www.sandbanksferry.co.uk (English)

Route Sandbanks - Shell Bay (Dorset).

1	BRAMBLE BUSH BAY	625t	93	-	74.4m	400P	48C	-	BA	UK	9072070

BRAMBLE BUSH BAY Chain ferry, built by Richard Dunston (Hessle) Ltd, Hessle, UK for the Bournemouth-Swanage Motor Road and Ferry Company.

SOUTH HAMS DISTRICT COUNCIL

Address Lower Ferry Office, The Square, Kingswear, Dartmouth, Devon TQ6 0AA. **Tel** +44 (0)1803 752342, **Fax** +44 (0)1803 752227.

Website www.southhams.gov.uk/sp-dartmouthlowerferry.htm (English)

Route Dartmouth - Kingswear (Devon) across River Dart (lower route).

1	THE TOM AVIS	-	94	-	33.5m	50P	8C	-	BA
2	THE TOM CASEY	-	89	-	33.5m	50P	8C	-	BA

THE TOM AVIS Float (propelled by tugs) built by Alan Toms, Fowey, UK for South Hams District Council.

THE TOM CASEY Float (propelled by tugs) built by Cozens, Portland, UK for South Hams District Council.

TORPOINT FERRY

Address 2 Ferry Street, Torpoint, Cornwall PL11 2AX. **Tel** +44 (0)1752 812233, **Fax** +44 (0)1752 816873.

Website www.tamarcrossings.org.uk (English)

Route Devonport (Plymouth) - Torpoint (Cornwall) across the Tamar. The three ferries operate in parallel, each on her own 'track'. Pre-booking is not possible and the above numbers cannot be used for that purpose.

1	LYNHER II	748t	06	-	73.0m	350P	73C	-	BA	UK	9310941
2	PLYM II	748t	04	-	73.0m	350P	73C	-	BA	UK	9310927
3	TAMAR II	748t	05	-	73.0m	350P	73C	-	BA	UK	9310939

LYNHER II, PLYM II, TAMAR II Chain ferries built by Ferguson Shipbuilders Ltd, Port Glasgow, UK to replace 1960s-built ships. Unlike previous ferries, they are registered as 'Passenger/Ro-Ro Cargo' ships and thus have gross tonnage, nation of registry and, being over 100t, an IMO number.

WATERFORD CASTLE HOTEL

Address The Island, Waterford, Irish Republic. **Tel** + 353 (0)51 878203.

Internet Email info@waterfordcastle.com **Website** www.waterfordcastle.com *(English (mainly about hotel; little about ferry)).*

Route Grantstown - Little Island (in River Suir, County Waterford).

1	LORELEY	110t	59	-	32.0m	57P	12C	-	BA

LORELEY Chain ferry built as the LORELEY V by Ruthof, Mainz, Germany to operate between St Goarshausen and St Goar on the River Rhine. In 2004 replaced by a new vessel (the LORELEY VI) and became a reserve vessel In 2007, sold to the *Waterford Castle Hotel* and renamed the LORELEY and, in 2008 replaced the previous ferry. She is self propelled and guided by cable.

SECTION 5 - GB & IRELAND - MAJOR PASSENGER-ONLY FERRIES

There are a surprisingly large number of passenger-only ferries operating in the British Isles, mainly operated by launches and small motor boats. There are, however, a few 'major' operators who operate only passenger vessels (of rather larger dimensions) and have not therefore been mentioned previously.

Aran Island Ferries CEOL NA FARRAIGE (234t, 2001, 37.4m, 294 passengers, IMO 9246750), DRAÍOCHT NA FARRAIGE (318t, 1999, 35.4m, 294 passengers, IMO 9200897), GLÓR NA FARRAIGE (170t, 1985, 33.5m, 244 passenger, IMO 8522391) (ex ARAN FLYER 2007), BANRÍON NA FARRAIGE (117t, 27.4m, 1984, 188 passengers, IMO 8407709) (ex ARAN EXPRESS 2007), SEA SPRINTER (16t, 11.6m, 35 passengers). **Routes operated** Rossaveal (Co Galway) – Inishmor, Rossaveal - Inis Meáin, Rossaveal - Inisheer. **Tel** + 353 (0)91 568903 (572273 after 19.00), **Fax** + 353 (0)91 568538, **Email** info@aranislandferries.com **Website** www.aranislandferries.com *(English).*

Bruce Watt Sea Cruises Ltd WESTERN ISLES (46t, 1969, 19.5m, 81 passengers). **Route Operated** Mallaig - Inverie (Knoydart) - Tarbet. **Tel** + 44 (0)1687 462320, **Email** brucewattcruises@aol.com, **Website** www.knoydart-ferry.co.uk *(English).*

Clydelink ISLAND PRINCESS (1996, 13.7m, 96 passengers), CAILIN OIR (1999, 15.2m, 72 passengers), **Route operated** Gourock - Kilcreggan (operated on behalf of *Strathclyde Partnership for Transport*) ISLAND TRADER (12 passengers), **Route operated** Renfrew - Yoker (operated on behalf of *Strathclyde Partnership for Transport*) **(Tel** 0871 705 088, **Website** www.clydelink.co.uk *(English).*

Clyde Cruises (Clyde Marine Services Ltd) CLYDE CLIPPER (125t, 2009, 27m, 250 passengers), CRUISER (ex POOLE SCENE, 2001, HYTHE HOTSPUR, 1995, SOUTHSEA QUEEN, 1978) (119t, 1974, 24.4m, 245 passengers), FENCER (18t, 1976, 11.0m, 33 passengers), ROVER (48t, 1964, 19.8m, 120 passengers), SEABUS (2007, 19.5m, 100 passengers), THE SECOND SNARK (45t, 1938, 22.9m, 120 passengers). **Routes operated** Glasgow – Braehead, Govan – Riverside Museum, Aberdeen Harbour Tours, Private charters around the Clyde area. **Tel** + 44 (0)1475 721281, **Email** julie@clydecruises.com & enquiries@clyde-marine.co.uk **Website** www.clydecruises.com www.clyde-marine.co.uk *(English).*

Dartmouth Steam Railway & Riverboat Company DARTMOUTH PRINCESS (22t, 1990, 18.3m, 156 passengers), EDGCUMBE BELLE (35t, 1957, 17.7m, 150 passengers), KINGSWEAR PRINCESS (27t, 1978, 19.1m, 150 passengers) **Route operated** Dartmouth - Kingswear., CARLINA (5t, 8.5m, 12 passengers), CHAMPION (4t, 1952, 9.7m, 12 passengers), WARRIOR (3.5t, 1947, 9.7m, 12 passengers). **Route operated** Dartmouth – Dittisham. **Note:** Pleasure craft owned by this operator are also used for the ferry service on some occasions. **Tel** + 44 (0)1803 834488, **Fax** + 44 (0)1803 835248, **Email** bookings@dsrrb.co.uk **Website** www.dartmouthrailriver.co.uk *(English).*

Doolin2Aran Ferries DOOLIN DISCOVERY (2009, 15.2m, 72 passengers), JACK B (2005, 15.2m, 67 passengers), HAPPY HOOKER (77t, 1989, 19.8m, 96 passengers), MACDARA (2010, 8.5m, 12 passengers), ROSE OF ARAN (113t, 1976, 20.1m, 96 passengers). IMO 7527916). **Routes operated**

Doolin - Inisheer, Doolin - Inishmore, Doolin - Inishmaan. **Tel** +353 (0)65 707 59 49, **Email** info@doolin2aranferries.ie **Website** www.doolin2aranferries.com *(English)*.

Exmouth to Sea Cruises MY QUEEN (1929, 37t, 18m, 127 passengers), ORCOMBE (1954, 14.3m, 100 passengers), PRINCESS MARINA (1936, 15.8m, 60 passengers). **Route operated** Exmouth - Starcross. **Tel** +44 (0)1626 774770, **Email** info@exe2sea.co.uk **Website** www.exe2sea.co.uk *(English)*.

Fleetwood - Knott End Ferry (operated by *Wyre Marine Services Ltd*) WYRE ROSE (2005, 32 passengers). **Route operated** Fleetwood - Knott End. **Route operated** Fleetwood - Knott End. **Tel** +44 (0) 7793 270934, **Fax** +44 (0)1253 87 79 74 **Email** info@wyremarine.co.uk **Website** www.wyremarine.co.uk *(English)*.

Gosport Ferry GOSPORT QUEEN (159t, 1966, 30.5m, 250 passengers, IMO 8633700), PORTSMOUTH QUEEN (159t, 1966, 30.5m, 250 passengers, IMO 8633695), SPIRIT OF GOSPORT (300t, 2001, 32.6m, 300 passengers, IMO 8972089), SPIRIT OF PORTSMOUTH (377t, 2005, 32.6m, 300 passengers, IMO 9319894). **Route operated** Gosport - Portsmouth. **Tel** +44 (0)23 9252 4551, **Email** admin@gosportferry.co.uk **Website** www.gosportferry.co.uk *(English)*.

Gravesend - Tilbury Ferry (operated by the *Lower Thames & Medway Passenger Boat Co Ltd*) DUCHESS M (ex VESTA 1979) (71t, 1956, 23.8m, 124 passengers), PRINCESS POCAHONTAS (ex FREYA II 1989, LABOE I 1985, LABOE 1984) (180t, 1962, 29.9m, 207 passengers, IMO 5201271). The PRINCESS POCAHONTAS is an excursion vessel operating regularly to Greenwich, Westminster, Chelsea and Southend, also occasionally to Rochester and Whitstable but sometimes covers the ferry roster. **Route operated** Gravesend (Kent) - Tilbury (Essex), **Tel** +44 (0)1732 353448, **Direct Line to Ferry** +44 (0)7973 390124, **Email** enquiry@princess-pocahontas.com **Websites** www.princess-pocahontas.com *(English)* www.gravesham.gov.uk/__data/assets/ pdf_file/ 0004/ 74965/ FerryTimetableSEPT2012.pdf *(English)*.

Hamble - Warsash Ferry CLAIRE (2.1t, 1985, 7,3m, 12 passengers), EMILY (3.7t, 1990, 8.5m, 12 passengers), **Route operated** Hamble - Warsash (across Hamble River) . **Tel** +44 (0)23 8045 4512, **Mobile** +44 (0) 7720 438402 **Email** mike@hamble-warsashferry.co.uk, **Website** www.hamble-warsashferry.co.uk *(English)*.

Hayling Ferry PRIDE OF HAYLING (1989, 11.9m, 63 passengers). **Route operated** Eastney – Hayling Island. **Tel** +44 (0)7702 928 154, **Email:** haylingferry@yahoo.co.uk **Website** www.haylingferry.co.uk *(English)*.

Hovertravel FREEDOM 90 (1990, 25.4m, 95 passengers, BHC AP1-88/100S hovercraft, converted from AP1-88/100 in 2000), ISLAND EXPRESS (ex FREJA VIKING, 2002) (1985, 25.4m, 95 passengers, BHC AP1-88/100S hovercraft, converted from BHC AP1-88/100 in 2001), SOLENT EXPRESS (2007, 29.5m, 130 passengers, BHT 130 hovercraft). **Route operated** Southsea - Ryde. **Tel** +44 (0)8434 878887, **Fax** +44 (0)1983 562216, **Email** barrie.jehan@hovertravel.com **Website** www.hovertravel.com *(English)*.

Hythe Ferry (White Horse Ferries) GREAT EXPECTATIONS (66t, 1992, 21.3m, 162 passengers - catamaran), HOTSPUR IV (50t, 1946, 19.5m, 125 passengers). **Route operated** Southampton - Hythe (Hants). *Head Office* **Tel.** +44 (0)1793 618566, **Fax** +44 (0)1793 488428, *Local Office* **Tel** +44 (0)23 8084 0722, **Fax** +44 (0)23 8084 6611, **Email** post@hytheferry.co.uk **Website** www.hytheferry.co.uk *(English)*.

Isle of Sark Shipping Company BON MARIN DE SERK (118t, 1983, 20.7m, 131 passengers, IMO 8303056), SARK VENTURE (133t, 1986, 21.3m, 122 passengers, IMO 8891986). **Route operated** St Peter Port (Guernsey) - Sark. **Tel** +44 (0) 1481 724059, **Fax** +44 (0) 1481 713999, **Email** info@sarkshippingcompany.com **Website** www.sarkshippingcompany.com *(English)*.

John O'Groats Ferries PENTLAND VENTURE (186t, 1987, 29.6m, 250 passengers, IMO 8834122). **Route operated** John O'Groats – Burwick (Orkney). **Tel** +44 (0)1955 611353, **Email** Office@jogferry.co.uk **Website** www.jogferry.co.uk *(English)*.

Kintyre Express KINTYRE EXPRESS (5.75t, 2006, 11.0m, 12 passengers), KINTYRE EXPRESS II (5.75t, 2011, 11.0m, 12 passengers), KINTYRE EXPRESS III (5.75t, 2012, 11.0m, 12 passengers),

Pentland Venture (*Matt Davies*)

Bramble Bush Bay (*Andrew Cooke*)

Higher Ferry (*John Hendy*)

Island Express (*Andrew Cooke*)

KINTYRE EXPRESS IV (5.75t, 2012, 11.0m, 12 passengers). **Routes operated** Campbeltown - Ballycastle, Campbeltown - Troon. **Tel** +44 (0) 1586 555895, **Fax** +44(0)1586 552344, **Email** info@kintyreexpress.com **Website** www.kintyreexpress.com *(English)*.

Lundy Company OLDENBURG (294t, 1958, 43.6m, 267 passengers, IMO 5262146). **Routes operated** Bideford - Lundy Island, Ilfracombe - Lundy Island. Also North Devon coastal cruises and River Torridge cruises. **Tel** +44 (0)1237 470074, **Fax** +44 (0)1237 477779, **Email** info@lundyisland.co.uk **Website** www.lundyisland.co.uk *(English)*.

Manche Iles Express (trading name of Société Morbihannaise de Navigation) VICTOR HUGO (ex SALTEN 2003) (387t, 1997, 35.0m, 195 passengers, IMO 9157806 - catamaran). **Routes operated** Portbail or Carteret – Jersey, Guernsey and Sark, Diélette - Alderney - Guernsey, MARIN MARIE (ex AREMETI 3 2003) (608t, 1994, 40.0m, 243 passengers, IMO 9112478), TOCQUEVILLE (269t, 2007, 37m, 260 passengers, IMO 9442823). **Route operated** Granville – Jersey - Sark - Guernsey. **Tel** *Jersey* +44 (0)1534 880756, *Guernsey* +44 (0)1481 701316, *Granville, Carteret, Diélette* +33 0825 131 050 **Email** mancheilesexpress@cwgsy.net **Website** www.manche-iles-express.com *(French, English)*.

Mersey Ferries ROYAL DAFFODIL (ex OVERCHURCH 1999) (751t, 1962, 46.6m, 860 passengers, IMO 4900868) (laid up), ROYAL IRIS OF THE MERSEY (ex MOUNTWOOD 2002) (464t, 1960, 46.3m, 750 passengers, IMO 8633712), SNOWDROP (ex WOODCHURCH 2004) (670t, 1960, 46.6m, 750 passengers, IMO 8633724). **Routes operated** Liverpool (Pier Head) - Birkenhead (Woodside), Liverpool - Wallasey (Seacombe) with regular cruises from Liverpool and Seacombe to Salford along the Manchester Ship Canal. **Tel** *Admin* +44 (0)151 639 0609, *Reservations* +44 (0)151 330 1444, **Fax** +44 (0)151 639 0578, **Email** info@merseyferries.co.uk **Website** www.merseyferries.co.uk *(English)*.

Mudeford Ferry (Derham Marine) FERRY DAME (4t, 1989, 9.1m, 48 passengers), JOSEPHINE (10t, 1997, 10.7m, 70 passengers - catamaran). **Route operated** Mudeford Quay - Mudeford Sandbank. **Tel** +44 (0)7968 334441 **Email** information@mudefordferry.co.uk **Website** www.mudefordferry.co.uk *(English)*.

Nexus (trading name of Tyne & Wear Integrated Transport Authority) PRIDE OF THE TYNE (222t, 1993, 24.0m, 240 passengers, IMO 9062166), SPIRIT OF THE TYNE (174t, 2006, 25.0m, 200 passengers). **Route operated** North Shields - South Shields. Also cruises South Shields - Newcastle. **Tel** +44 (0)191 2020747, **Fax** +44 (0)191 427 9510, **Website** www.nexus.org.uk *(English)*.

O'Brien Line QUEEN OF ARAN (113t, 1976, 20.1m, 96 passengers, IMO 7527928), TRANQUILITY (62t, 1988, 15.8m, 100 passengers). **Routes operated** Doolin - Inisheer, Doolin - Inishmaan, Doolin - Inishmore. **Tel** +353 (0)65 707 5555, **Fax** 00 353 (0)65 707 11 82, **Email** info@obrienline.com **Website** www.obrienline.com *(English)*.

Severn Link RAPPAREE (478t, 1996, 40.0m, 34.0k, 361 passengers, IMO 9144976) (ex WATER JET 1 1999, ex SUPERCAT 17 2000, ex FASTCAT RYDE 2010), FASTCAT SHANKLIN (482t, 1996, 40.0m, 34.0k, 361 passengers, IMO 8888513) (ex WATER JET 2 1999, ex SUPERCAT 18 2000). **Route operated:** None. Service unable to start in 2010 or 2011; vessels laid up.

SPT (trading name of Strathclyde Partnership for Transport) YOKER SWAN (65t, 1984, 21.9m, 50 passengers). **Route operated** None. Renfrew - Yoker service closed in March 2010. Vessels laid up.

Thames Clippers (trading name of Collins River Enterprises Ltd) AURORA CLIPPER (181t, 2007, 37.8m, 27.5k, 220 passengers, IMO 9451824), CYCLONE CLIPPER (181t, 2007, 37.8m, 27.5k, 220 passengers, IMO 9451880), HURRICANE CLIPPER (181t, 2002, 37.8m, 27.5k, 220 passengers, IMO 9249702), METEOR CLIPPER (181t, 2007, 37.8m, 27.5k, 220 passengers, IMO 9451812), MONSOON CLIPPER (181t, 2007, 37.8m, 27.5k, 220 passengers, IMO 9451795), MOON CLIPPER (ex DOWN RUNNER 2005) (98t, 2001, 32.0m, 25.0k, 138 passengers, IMO 9245586), SKY CLIPPER (ex VERITATUM 1995, SD10 2000) (60t, 1992, 25.0m, 62 passengers, IMO 9451??), STAR CLIPPER (ex CONRAD CHELSEA HARBOUR SD9 2000) (60t, 1992, 25.0m, 62 passengers), STORM CLIPPER (ex DHL WORLDWIDE EXPRESS 1995, SD11 2000) (60t, 1992, 25.0m, 62 passengers), SUN CLIPPER (ex ANTRIM RUNNER 2005) (98t, 2001, 32.0m, 25.0k, 138 passengers, IMO 9232292), TORNADO CLIPPER (181t, 2007, 37.8m, 27.5k, 220 passengers, IMO 9451783), TWIN STAR (45t, 1974, 19.2m, 120 passengers), TYPHOON CLIPPER (181t, 2007, 37.8m, 27.5k, 220 passengers, IMO 9451771). The

'Typhoon', 'Tornado', 'Cyclone' and 'Monsoon', 'Aurora' and 'Meteor' Clippers were designed by AIMTEK and built by Brisbane Ship Constructions in Australia in 2007. **Routes operated** Embankment - Waterloo - Blackfriars – Bankside - London Bridge - Tower - Canary Wharf – Greenland - Masthouse Terrace - Greenwich - North Greenwich – Woolwich, Bankside – Millbank - St George (Tate to Tate Service), Putney - Wandsworth - Chelsea Harbour - Cardogan - Embankment - Blackfriars, Canary Wharf - Rotherhithe Hilton Docklands Hotel (TWIN STAR). **Tel** +44 (0)870 781 5049, **Fax** +44 (0)20 7001 2222, **Email** sean.collins@thamesclippers.com **Website** www.thamesclippers.com *(English)*.

Travel Trident HERM TRIDENT V (79t, 1989, 25.9m, 250 passengers), TRIDENT VI (79t, 1992, 22.3m, 250 passengers). **Route operated** St Peter Port (Guernsey) - Herm. **Tel** +44 (0)1481 721379, **Fax** +44 (0)1481 700226, **Email** peterwilcox@cwgsy.net **Website** www.traveltrident.com *(English)*.

Waverley Excursions BALMORAL (735t, 1949, 62.2m, 683 passengers, IMO 5034927) (laid up during 2013), WAVERLEY (693t, 1947, 73.2m, 925 passengers, IMO 5386954). **Routes operated** Excursions all round British Isles. However, regular cruises in the Clyde, Bristol Channel, South Coast and Thames provide a service which can be used for transport purposes and therefore both vessels are, in a sense, ferries. The WAVERLEY is the only seagoing paddle steamer in the world. The BALMORAL will not operate during 2013, but may return in 2014. **Tel** +44 (0)845 130 4647, **Fax** +44 (0)141 248 2150, **Email** info@waverleyexcursions.co.uk **Website** www.waverleyexcursions.co.uk *(English)*.

Hotspur IV *(Andrew Cooke)*

Spirit of the Tyne *(Miles Cowsill)*

SCANDINAVIAN AND NORTHERN EUROPE REVIEW - 2012

The following geographical review again takes the form of a voyage along the coast of The Netherlands and Germany, round the southern tip of Norway, down the Kattegat, through the Great Belt and into the Baltic then up to the Gulf of Finland and Gulf of Bothnia.

FRISIAN ISLANDS

EVT, a private sector rival to Rederij Doeksen, introduced the 55 car *Spathoek* onto the Harlingen - Terschelling route, replacing the passenger only *Stortemelk*.

NORWEGIAN DOMESTIC

Hurtigruten's *Finnmarken*, having returned from her two year charter as an accommodation vessel in Australia in November 2012, re-entered service in February 2013, allowing the elderly *Nordstjernen* to finally be retired from the daily Bergen - Kirkenes service.

In September Bastø Fosen, operators of the Moss-Horten service, acquired a fifth vessel in the form of the *Bastø V*, formerly the *Tranøy* of Torghatten Nord A/S.

SKAGERRAK & KATTEGAT

Fjord Lines' first newbuilding, the *Stavangerfjord* did not enter service in October as originally planned following a decision to build her with liquefied natural gas (LNG) engines rather than bring her into service with diesel engines and then convert her later. She entered service in July 2013 and will be followed by the second newbuild, the *Bergensfjord*, in December. Consequently the new service from Hirtshals to Langesund was also delayed. A contract for the conversion of the existing *Bergensfjord* to a day ferry to operate on the popular Sandefjord - Strömstad route in competition with Color Line was signed in June 2013.

In March, Color Line announced plans for a new LNG vessel to replace the 1971 built *Bohus* on the Sandefjord - Strömstad service in 2014. However, to date no contract has been signed.

DANISH DOMESTIC

Danish domestic routes saw the introduction of two new fast ferries during 2012. The first to enter service was the *KatExpress 1* of Mols-Linien. The 112 metre Incat, previously the *Norman Arrow* of LD Lines, entered service between Odden and Århus and Ebeltoft in May, replacing the 1996 built SeaJets *Mai Mols* and *Mie Mols*. A second model of this type, the *KatExpress 2*, was acquired for service in 2013.

Less successful was rival operator FRS's attempts to launch a similar service using the Austal built *Tanger Jet II*, renamed the *Dolphin Jet*, on their Kattegat-Ruten Kalundborg - Århus service. Although she arrived in Denmark in May, she did not get permission to enter service until July. Then severe speed restrictions were imposed on the operation which meant that crossing took two hours, almost twice as long as Mols-Linen's service to Odden. After less than a month's operation, the service was suspended and the ship laid-up. Attempts by the operator to operate to Odden instead of Kalundborg in 2013 were also frustrated, on the ground of safety - having two operators service the same port was deemed unsafe by the port authorities, despite this happening in many other ports. In May 2013 she returned to the Mediterranean.

Færgen introduced their two delayed German built ferries *Langeland* and *Lolland* on the Spodsbjerg - Tårs service in March and May respectively. They replaced the *Frigg Sydfyen* and *Odin Sydfyen*, which were moved to the Fynshav - Bøjden route. The older *Thor Sydfyen* was sold.

SOUTH BALTIC

In the spring Stena Line reached agreement with Scandlines to take over their services from Germany to Sweden and Latvia and the vessels involved, some owned and some chartered. During the rest of

Bohus (*Matthew Punter*)

Baltic Princess (*Miles Cowsill*)

Isabelle (*Kim Viktor*)

Stena Carisma and **Margrethe Laeso** (*Matthew Punter*)

the year, the new services and vessels were absorbed into Stena Lines' network. At the same time, their own Swedish Scandlines operation was absorbed and ceased to be operated as a separate brand. Several of the ships were repainted into Stena Line colours, with some just having Scandlines branding removed and funnels repainted, but none received Stena names, all retaining their previous names. Exceptionally the Helsingør - Helsingborg service continued to be branded as Scandlines, despite three of the four vessels employed being owned and operated by Stena.

The saga of the *Berlin* and *Copenhagen*, two ferries being built by Volkswerft Stralsund, Stralsund, Germany for Scandlines to operate on the Gedser - Rostock route continued throughout the year. Not only were the two vessels seriously delayed but found to be overweight and therefore did not meet the specification. In August the yard went bankrupt and whilst work continued to try to lighten the ships, in November Scandlines formally cancelled the contract and the yard began looking for alternative buyers, so far without success.

Meanwhile, the former train ferries *Kronprins Frederik* and *Prins Joachim* soldiered on. During the peak summer period, the HH-Ferries spare 'Superflex', the *Mercandian VIII* was chartered to provide additional capacity, mainly for freight.

CROSS BALTIC

Scandlines also disposed of their Rostock - Hanko freight service, not to Stena Line but to SOL Continent Line which, in September 2010, replaced the Stena Line Travemünde - Gothenburg service with a Travemünde - Helsingborg service. This subsequently ceased in April 2013. The *Aurora* was renamed the *Vikingland* whilst the *Merchant* was not renamed.

In June a new train ferry, freight and passenger service was inaugurated between Sassnitz and Ust Luga (near St Petersburg). It was operated by Black Sea Ferry in partnership with Russian Railways and AnRuss Trans and utilises the former Mukran - Klaipėda vessel *Petersburg*.

In October, Finnlines sold the 2007 built the *Europalink* to Atlantica Navigazione of Italy, another company within the Grimaldi Group. At the same time, their thrice weekly Helsinki - Gydnia - Rostock service operated by a 'Star' class vessel was split, with separate services to Poland and Germany, each operating with a single ship, twice weekly. The Polish service became freight only.

NORTH BALTIC

Viking Line took delivery of their newbuild *Viking Grace* for the Turku - Stockholm route during December, although she did not enter service until January 2013. Powered by LNG, she replaced the *Isabella* which was laid up. It was planned that the *Isabella* would operate between Helsinki and Tallinn during summer 2013. However, in April 2013 she was sold to Tallink Grupp to operate on the Silja Line branded route between Stockholm and Riga, replacing the *Silja Festival*. She was renamed the *Isabelle*.

In March Eckerö Line purchased a new vessel to replace the aging *Nordlandia* on the Helsinki - Tallinn route. She was the 2001 built *Moby Freedom* of Italian Moby Lines. Renamed first the *Freedom* and then the *Finlandia* she underwent a major refit in Landskrona to convert her from a Mediterranean cruise ferry to a vessel suitable for the very different and highly competitive Baltic route. She eventually entered service in December.

The services of RG-Line, which filed for bankruptcy in November 2011, were, during 2012, taken over by NLC Ferry Oy Ab, a Finnish company, jointly owned by the cities of Vaasa and Umeå. They continued to operate the *RG1* and trade as RG-Line. However, in October 2012 they purchased the *Betancuria* from Rederi AB Gotland and renamed her the *Wasa Express*. She entered service in January 2013, her entry coinciding with the relaunching of the company as Vasabåtarna (Vaasanlaivat in Finnish), the name of the traditional operator of this service before it was taken over by Silja Line in 1993. This was later changed to Wasaline.

Nick Widdows

BASTØ FOSEN

THE COMPANY Bastø Fosen is a Norwegian private sector company, a subsidiary of Fosen Trafikklag of Trondheim.

MANAGEMENT Managing Director Olav Brein.

ADDRESS PO Box 94, 3191 Horten, Norway.

TELEPHONE Administration +47 33 03 17 40, Reservations +47 33 03 17 40 (buses only).

FAX Administration +47 33 03 17 49, Reservations +47 33 03 17 49 (buses only).

INTERNET Email bastohorten@fosen.no Website www.basto-fosen.no (Norwegian)

ROUTE OPERATED Moss - Horten (across Oslofjord, Norway) (30 mins; BASTØ I, BASTØ II, BASTØ III, BASTØ IV, BASTØ IV up to every 15 mins).

1	BASTØ I	5505t	97	14.0k	109.0m	550P	200C	18L	BA	NO	9144081
2	BASTØ II	5505t	97	14.0k	109.0m	550P	200C	18L	BA	NO	9144093
3	BASTØ III	7310t	05	18.0k	116.2m	540P	212C	18L	BA	NO	9299408
4	BASTØ IV	2835t	86	13.5k	80.1m	456P	140C	12L	BA	NO	8512114
5	BASTØ V	3397t	90	16.0k	92.0m	650P	155C	-	BA	NO	8917340

BASTØ I, BASTØ II Built by Fosen Mekaniske Verksteder, Frengen, Norway for Bastø Fosen.

BASTØ III Built by Stocznia Remontowa, Gdansk, Poland for Bastø Fosen.

BASTØ IV Built as the AUSTRHEIM by Trønderverftet A/S, Hommelvik, Norway for A/S Bergen-Nordhordland Rutelag (BNR), operating between Steinestø and Knarvik. In 1993 chartered to Rogaland Trafikkselskap A/S and operated between Stavanger and Tau. In 1995 sold to Hardanger Sunnhordlandske Dampskibsselskap (HSD) of Norway and renamed the BJØRNEFJORD. Operated between Valevåg and Skjersholmane. In 2001 sold to Boknafjorden Ferjeselskap A/S and renamed the BOKNAFJORD. Later transferred to Båtbygg A/S and operated between Mortaviken and Arsvågen. In 2002 transferred to Rogaland Trafikkselskap Ferjer A/S and in 2003 transferred to Stavangerska Ferjer A/S. In 2008 and 2009 she was briefly chartered to a number of operators and in 2008 sold to Tide Sjø AS. In December 2010 she was sold to Bastø Fosen and renamed the BASTØ IV.

BASTØ V Built as the NORDKAPPHORN by Trønderverftet A/S, Hommelvik, Norway for Finnmark Fylkesrederi og Ruteselskap AS of Norway. In 1992 chartered to Rogaland Trafikkselskap A/S and renamed the RENNESØY. In January 2012 sold to Torghatten Nord A/S and renamed the TRANØY. In September 2012 sold to Bastø Fosen and renamed the BASTØ V.

COLOR LINE

THE COMPANY Color Line ASA is a Norwegian private sector stock-listed limited company. The company merged with Larvik Scandi Line of Norway (which owned Larvik Line and Scandi Line) in 1996. In 1997 the operations of Larvik Line were incorporated into Color Line; Scandi Line continued as a separate subsidiary until 1999, when it was also incorporated into Color Line. The marketing name Color Scandi Line was dropped at the end of 2000.

MANAGEMENT Managing Director Trond Kleivdal.

ADDRESS Commercial Postboks 1422 Vika, 0115 Oslo, Norway, Technical Management Color Line Marine AS, PO Box 2090, 3210 Sandefjord, Norway.

TELEPHONE Administration & Reservations +47 22 94 42 00.

INTERNET Email servicecenter@colorline.de

Website www.colorline.com (English, Danish, German, Norwegian, Swedish).

ROUTES OPERATED Conventional Ferries Oslo (Norway) - Kiel (Germany) (19 hrs 30 mins; COLOR FANTASY, COLOR MAGIC; 1 per day), Kristiansand (Norway) - Hirtshals (3 hrs 15 mins; SUPERSPEED 1; 4 per day), Larvik (Norway) - Hirtshals (Denmark) (3 hrs 45 mins; SUPERSPEED 2;

up to 2 per day), Sandefjord (Norway) - Strömstad (Sweden) (2 hrs 30 mins; *BOHUS, COLOR VIKING*; up to 4 per day).

1	BOHUS	9149t	71	20.5k	123.4m	1165P	240C	34T	BA	NO	7037806
2	COLOR FANTASY	75027t	04	22.3k	224.0m	2750P	750C	90T	BA	NO	9278234
3	COLOR MAGIC	75100t	07	22.3k	223.7m	2750P	550C	90T	BA	NO	9349863
4	COLOR VIKING	19763t	85	16.4k	134.0m	2000P	320C	40T	BA2	NO	8317942
5	SUPERSPEED 1	36822t	08	27.0k	211.3m	2250P	525C	121T	BA2	NO	9374519
6	SUPERSPEED 2	34231t	08	27.0k	211.3m	1800P	525C	121T	BA2	NO	9378682

BOHUS Built as the PRINSESSAN DESIREE by Aalborg Værft A/S, Aalborg, Denmark for *Rederi AB Göteborg-Frederikshavn Linjen* of Sweden (trading as *Sessan Linjen*) for their service between Gothenburg and Frederikshavn. In 1981 the company was taken over by *Stena Line* and she became surplus to requirements. During 1981 she had a number of charters including *B&I Line* of Ireland and *Sealink UK*. In 1982 she was chartered to *Sally Line* to operate as second vessel on the Ramsgate - Dunkerque service between June and September. She bore the name 'VIKING 2' in large letters on her hull although she was never officially renamed. In September 1982 she returned to *Stena Line* and in 1983 she was transferred to subsidiary company *Varberg-Grenaa Line* for their service between Varberg (Sweden) and Grenaa (Denmark), renamed the EUROPAFÄRJAN. In 1985 she was renamed the EUROPAFÄRJAN II. In 1986, following a reorganisation within *Stena Line*, ownership was transferred to subsidiary company *Lion Ferry AB* and she was named the LION PRINCESS. In 1993 she was sold to *Scandi Line* and renamed the BOHUS. In 1999 *Scandi Line* operations were integrated into *Color Line*.

COLOR FANTASY Built by Kværner Masa-Yards, Turku, Finland for *Color Line* to replace the PRINSESSE RAGNHILD on the Oslo – Kiel service.

COLOR MAGIC Built by Aker Yards, Turku, Finland (hull construction) and Rauma, Finland (fitting out), for the Oslo - Kiel route.

COLOR VIKING Built as the PEDER PAARS by Nakskov Skibsværft A/S, Nakskov, Denmark for *DSB (Danish State Railways)* for their service between Kalundborg (Sealand) and Århus (Jutland). In 1990 purchased by *Stena Line* of Sweden for delivery in 1991. In that year renamed the STENA INVICTA and entered service on the *Sealink Stena Line* Dover - Calais service. She was withdrawn from the route in February 1998, before the formation of *P&O Stena Line*, but ownership was transferred to that company. In Summer 1998, she was chartered to *Silja Line* to operate between Vaasa and Umeå under the marketing name 'WASA JUBILEE'. In Autumn 1998 she was laid up at Zeebrugge. She remained there until Autumn 1999 when she was chartered to *Stena Line* to operate between Holyhead and Dublin. In 2000 she was chartered to *Color Line*, renamed the COLOR VIKING and in April entered service on the Sandefjord - Strömstad service. In 2002 purchased by *Color Line*.

SUPERSPEED 1, SUPERSPEED 2 Built by Aker Yards, Rauma, Finland for the Kristiansand - Hirtshals and Larvik - Hirtshals routes. In January 2011, the SUPERSPEED 1 was modified to provide additional facilities and increase passenger capacity.

DESTINATION GOTLAND

THE COMPANY *Destination Gotland AB* is a Swedish private sector company owned by *Rederi AB Gotland*.

MANAGEMENT **Managing Director** Christer Bruzelius, **Marketing Manager** Per-Erling Evensen.

ADDRESS PO Box 1234, 621 23 Visby, Gotland, Sweden.

TELEPHONE **Administration** + 46 (0)498-20 18 00, **Reservations** + 46 (0)771-22 33 00.

FAX **Administration & Reservations** + 46 (0)498-20 18 90.

INTERNET **Email** info@destinationgotland.se **Website** www.destinationgotland.se (*Swedish, English, Finnish, German*).

Superspeed 1 *(John Bryant)*

Color Magic *(Miles Cowsill)*

ROUTES OPERATED Fast Conventional Ferries Visby (Gotland) - Nynäshamn (Swedish mainland) (3 hrs 15 mins; GOTLAND, VISBY; 1/2 per day), Visby - Oskarshamn (Swedish mainland) (2 hrs 55 mins; GOTLAND, VISBY; 1/4 per day). Fast Ferries (Summer only) Visby - Nynäshamn (3 hrs 15 mins; GOTLANDIA II; up to 3 per day), Visby - Oskarshamn (Swedish mainland) (2 hrs 55 mins; GOTLANDIA; 1 per day (selected).

1	GOTLAND	29746t	03	28.5k	195.8m	1500P	500C	118T	BAS2	SE	9223796
2»	GOTLANDIA	5632t	99	35.0k	112.5m	700P	140C	-	A	SE	9171163
3»	GOTLANDIA II	6554t	06	36.0k	122.0m	780P	160C	-	A	SE	9328015
4	VISBY	29746t	03	28.5k	195.8m	1500P	500C	118T	BAS2	SE	9223784

GOTLAND, VISBY Built by Guangzhou Shipyard International, Guangzhou, China for *Rederi AB Gotland* for use on *Destination Gotland* services.

GOTLANDIA Alstom Leroux Corsair 11500 monohull vessel built as the GOTLAND at Lorient, France for *Rederi AB Gotland* and chartered to *Destination Gotland*. In 2003 renamed the GOTLANDIA. In 2006 laid up. In 2007 inaugurated a new route between Visby and Grankullavik (Öland). In 2013 will operate between Visby and Oskarshamn.

GOTLANDIA II Fincantieri SF700 monohull fast ferry built at Riva Trigoso, Italy for *Rederi AB Gotland* for use by *Destination Gotland*.

DFDS SEAWAYS

THE COMPANY *DFDS Seaways* is a division of *DFDS A/S*, a Danish private sector company.

MANAGEMENT CEO DFDS A/S Niels Smedegaard, Head of Shipping Division Peder Gellert Pedersen, Head of Baltic Sea Business Area Anders Refsgaard, Head of Passenger Business Area Kim Heiberg.

ADDRESS *Copenhagen* Sundkrogsgade 11, 2100 Copenhagen Ø, Denmark.

TELEPHONE Administration +45 33 42 33 42, Reservations *Denmark* +45 33 42 30 10, *Germany* +49 (0)431 20976 420, *Lithuania* +370 46 393616, *Sweden* +46 454 33680.

FAX Administration +45 33 42 33 41.

INTERNET   Administration   incoming@dfdsseaways.dk,   Reservations   *Denmark* incoming@dfdsseaways.dk *Germany* passage.kiel@dfds.com, *Lithuania* booking.lt@dfds.com, *Sweden* pax@dfds.com.

Website www.dfdsseaways.com (*English, Danish, Dutch, German, Italian, Japanese, Norwegian, Polish, Swedish*)

ROUTES OPERATED *Passengers services* Copenhagen - Oslo (Norway) (16 hrs 30 mins; *CROWN SEAWAYS, PEARL SEAWAYS*; 1 per day), Klaipėda (Lithuania) - Kiel (Germany) (21 hrs; *REGINA SEAWAYS, VICTORIA SEAWAYS*; 6 per week), Klaipėda - Karlshamn (Sweden) (14 hrs; *LIVERPOOL SEAWAYS, OPTIMA SEAWAYS*; 7 per week), Klaipėda - Sassnitz (Germany) (18 hrs; *KAUNAS SEAWAYS*; 2 per week), Paldiski (Estonia) - Kapellskär (Sweden) (10 hrs; *PATRIA SEAWAYS*; 1 or 2 per day) (joint with *Baltic Scandinavia Line*), **Freight only Services** Fredericia - Copenhagen - Klaipėda (call at Aarhus once per week) (*CORONA SEAWAYS*; 2 per week), Kiel - Klaipėda - Ust Luga - St Petersburg, (*BOTNIA SEAWAYS, CLIPPER POINT*; 2 per week).

See Section 1 for services operating to Britain.

1F	BOTNIA SEAWAYS	11530t	00	20.0k	162.2m	12P	-	140T	A	LT	9192129
2F	CLIPPER POINT	14759t	08	22.0k	142.0m	12P	-	120T	A	CY	9350666
3F	CORONA SEAWAYS	25609t	08	20.0k	184.8m	12P	-	250T	AS	UK	9357597
4	CROWN SEAWAYS	35498t	94	22.0k	169.4m	1940P	450C	50T	BA	DK	8917613
5	KAUNAS SEAWAYS	25606t	89	16.3k	190.9m	262P	460C	93Tr	A2	LT	8311924
6	LIVERPOOL SEAWAYS	21856t	97	20.0k	186.0m	320P	100C	135T	A	LT	9136034
7	OPTIMA SEAWAYS	25206t	99	21.5k	186.3m	327P	164C	150T	A	LT	9188427

8	PATRIA SEAWAYS	18332t	92	17.0k	154.0m	242P	-	114T	BA2	LT	8917390
9	PEARL SEAWAYS	40039t	89	21.0k	178.4m	2090P	350C	70T	BA	DK	8701674
10	REGINA SEAWAYS	25518t	10	24.0k	199.1m	600P	-	190T	A	IT	9458535
11	VICTORIA SEAWAYS	24950t	09	23.0k	199.1m	600P	-	190T	A	LT	9350721
12	VILNIUS SEAWAYS	22341t	87	16.3k	190.9m	132P	460C	112Tr	A2	LT	8311900

BOTNIA SEAWAYS Built as the FINNMASTER by Jinling Shipyard, Nanjing, China for the *Macoma Shipping Group* and chartered to *Finncarriers*. In 2008 sold to *DFDS Lisco* and in January 2009 delivered, chartered to *DFDS Tor Line* and renamed the TOR BOTNIA. Operated on the Immingham - Rotterdam route until December 2010. In January 2011 moved to the Kiel - St Petersburg route. In January 2013 renamed the BOTNIA SEAWAYS.

CLIPPER POINT Built by Astilleros de Huelva SA, Huelva, Spain for *Seatruck Ferries*. In May 2012 chartered to *DFDS Seaways* and placed on the Immingham-Cuxhaven route. In April 2013 chartered to the organisers of the 'SATA Rally Azores 2013' car rally to take cars from Portugal to the Azores. In May began operating for *DFDS Seaways* in the Baltic. She is likely to be replaced with an ice-class vessel in autumn 2013 but could be re-deployed on a North Sea route.

CORONA SEAWAYS Built as the TOR CORONA by Jinling Shipyard, Nanjing, China for *Macoma Shipping Ltd* of the UK and time-chartered to *DFDS Tor Line* for ten years. Used on the Fredericia – Copenhagen - Klaipėda service. In April 2012 renamed the CORONA SEAWAYS.

CROWN SEAWAYS Launched as the THOMAS MANN by Brodogradevna Industrija, Split, Croatia for *Euroway AB* for their Lübeck - Travemünde - Malmö service. However, political problems led to serious delays and, before delivery, the service had ceased. She was purchased by *DFDS*, renamed the CROWN OF SCANDINAVIA and introduced onto the Copenhagen - Oslo service. In January 2013 renamed the CROWN SEAWAYS.

KAUNAS SEAWAYS Train ferry built as the KAUNAS by VEB Mathias-Thesen-Werft, Wismar, Germany (DDR) for *Lisco* of the former Soviet Union and operated between Klaipėda and Mukran in Germany (DDR). She was part of a series of vessels built to link the USSR and Germany (DDR), avoiding Poland. In 1994/95 she was modified to offer passenger facilities and placed on the Klaipėda – Kiel service. In 2003 transferred to the Klaipėda – Karlshamn route. Early in 2004 chartered to *DFDS Tor Line* to operate between Lübeck and Riga. In 2005 returned to the Klaipėda – Karlshamn route. In May 2009 replaced by the LISCO OPTIMA and laid up. In October 2009 placed on the Travemünde - Riga route; this route ceased in January 2010 and she was laid up again. In May 2010 chartered to *Scandlines* and placed on a new Travemünde - Liepaja (Latvia) service. In December 2010 returned to *DFDS Seaways*. In March 2011 chartered to *Baltic Scandinavian Line* to operate between Paldiski (Estonia) and Kapellskär In May returned to *DFDS Seaways* and inaugurated a new service between Kiel and Ust Luga (Russia). In May 2012 she was renamed the KAUNAS SEAWAYS and in June transferred to the Klaipėda - Sassnitz route.

LIVERPOOL SEAWAYS Built as the LAGAN VIKING by CN Visentini, Donada, Italy for *Levantina Trasporti* of Italy and chartered to *Norse Irish Ferries*, operating between Liverpool and Belfast. In 1999 the charter was taken over by *Merchant Ferries*. Purchased by *NorseMerchant Ferries* in 2001. In 2002 the service transferred to Twelve Quays River Terminal, Birkenhead. In January 2005 renamed the LIVERPOOL VIKING and in December moved to the Birkenhead – Dublin route. In August 2010 renamed the LIVERPOOL SEAWAYS. In February 2011 moved to the Klaipėda - Karlshamn service.

OPTIMA SEAWAYS Ro-pax vessel built as the ALYSSA by C N Visentini di Visentini Francesco & C Donada, Italy for *Levantina Trasporti* of Italy for charter. Initially chartered to *CoTuNav* of Tunisia for service between Marseilles, Genoa and Tunis and in 2000 to *Trasmediterranea* of Spain for service between Barcelona and Palma de Mallorca. In 2001 chartered to *Stena Line Scandinavia AB*, renamed the SVEALAND and placed as second vessel on the *Scandlines AB* freight-only Trelleborg - Travemünde service. In 2003 sub-chartered to *Scandlines AG* and placed on the Kiel - Klaipėda route, replacing the ASK and PETERSBURG. In 2004 sold to *Rederia AB Hornet*, a *Stena* company. In late 2005 the *Scandlines* Kiel - Klaipėda service ended. In early 2006 she was chartered to *TT-Line* to cover for the rebuilding of the engines of their four newest vessels. Later sold to *DFDS*, renamed the LISCO OPTIMA and returned to the Kiel - Klaipėda route in Spring 2006. In May 2009 moved to the Klaipėda

Regina Seaways (*Cees de Bijl*)

Pearl Seaways (*Miles Cowsill*)

– Karlshamn route and in February 2011 moved to the Klaipėda - Kiel route but in September moved back. In April 2012 renamed the OPTIMA SEAWAYS.

PATRIA SEAWAYS Ro-pax vessel built as the STENA TRAVELLER by Fosen Mekaniske Verksteder, Trondheim, Norway for *Stena RoRo*. After a short period with *Stena Line* on the Hook of Holland - Harwich service, she was chartered to *Sealink Stena Line* for their Southampton - Cherbourg route, initially for 28 weeks. At the end of the 1992 summer season she was chartered to *TT-Line* to operate between Travemünde and Trelleborg and was renamed the TT-TRAVELLER. In late 1995, she returned to *Stena Line*, resumed the name STENA TRAVELLER and inaugurated a new service between Holyhead and Dublin. In Autumn 1996 she was replaced by the STENA CHALLENGER (18523t, 1991). In early 1997 she was again chartered to *TT-Line* and renamed the TT-TRAVELLER. She operated on the Rostock - Trelleborg route. During Winter 1999/2000 her passenger capacity was increased to 250 and passenger facilities renovated. In early 2002 the charter ended and she was renamed the STENA TRAVELLER, chartered to *Stena Line* and placed on their Karlskrona - Gdynia service. This charter ended in May 2003 and she was sold to *Lisco Baltic Service* and renamed the LISCO PATRIA. Placed on the Klaipėda - Karlshamn service. In January 2006 transferred to the Klaipėda - Kiel service to replace the *Scandlines* vessel SVEALAND following that company's withdrawal from the joint route. In Spring 2006 returned to the Klaipėda – Karlshamn route. In May 2011 chartered to *Baltic Scandinavia Lines* and placed on their Paldiski - Kapellskär service. In September 2011 a controlling interest in this service was acquired by *DFDS Seaways*. In January 2012 renamed the PATRIA SEAWAYS.

PEARL SEAWAYS Built as the ATHENA by Wärtsilä Marine, Turku, Finland for *Rederi AB Slite* of Sweden (part of *Viking Line*) and used on 24-hour cruises from Stockholm to Mariehamn (Åland). In 1993 the company went into liquidation and she was sold to *Star Cruises* of Malaysia for cruises in the Far East. She was renamed the STAR AQUARIUS. Later that year she was renamed the LANGKAPURI STAR AQUARIUS. In February 2001 sold to *DFDS* and renamed the AQUARIUS. After rebuilding, she was renamed the PEARL OF SCANDINAVIA and introduced onto the Copenhagen - Oslo service. In January 2011 renamed the PEARL SEAWAYS.

REGINA SEAWAYS Built as the ENERGIA by Nuovi Cantieri Apuani, Marina di Carrara, Italy for *Grimaldi Holdings* of Italy. In August 2011 chartered to DFDS Seaways and moved to Klaipėda for modifications. In September 2011 renamed the REGINA SEAWAYS and placed on the Klaipėda - Kiel service.

VICTORIA SEAWAYS Built by Nuovi Cantieri Apuani, Marina di Carrara, Italy. Launched as the FORZA. Fifth of an order of eight vessels for *Grimaldi Holdings* of Italy. Whilst under construction, sold to *DFDS Tor Line*. On delivery renamed the LISCO MAXIMA. In March/April 2012 renamed the VICTORIA SEAWAYS. Operates between Kiel and Klaipėda.

VILNIUS SEAWAYS Train ferry as KAUNAS SEAWAYS. Built as the VILNIUS. In 1993 rebuilt in Liverpool to convert from a 12 passenger freight vessel to a 120 passenger ro-pax vessel. Operated on the Klaipėda – Kiel service until June 2003. Later chartered to *DFDS Tor Line* to operate between Lübeck and Riga. In Summer 2006 transferred to the *DFDS Lisco* Klaipėda - Sassnitz route. In January 2011 renamed the VILNIUS SEAWAYS. In June 2012 she was transferred to the Kiel - Ust Luga service. In June 2013 she was chartered to *Ukrferry* of the Ukraine for service in the Black Sea.

REDERIJ DOEKSEN

THE COMPANY *Koninklijke Doeksen BV* is a Dutch private sector company. Ferries are operated by subsidiary *Terschellinger Stoomboot Maatschappij*, trading as *Rederij Doeksen*.

MANAGEMENT **Managing Director** P Melles, **Marketing Manager** Irene Smit.

ADDRESS Waddenpromenade 5, 8861 NT Harlingen, The Netherlands.

TELEPHONE *In The Netherlands* 0900-DOEKSEN (3635736), *From abroad* +31 562 442 002.

FAX +31 (0)517 413303.

INTERNET Email info@rederij-doeksen.nl Website www.rederij-doeksen.nl *(Dutch, English, German).*

ROUTES OPERATED Conventional Ferries Harlingen (The Netherlands) - Terschelling (Frisian Islands) (2 hrs; *FRIESLAND, MIDSLAND*) (up to 6 per day), Harlingen - Vlieland (Frisian Islands) (1 hr 45 mins; *VLIELAND*; 3 per day). Fast Passenger Ferries Harlingen - Terschelling (45 mins; *KOEGELWIECK, TIGER*; 3 to 6 per day), Harlingen - Vlieland (45 mins; *KOEGELWIECK, NAJADE, TIGER*; 2 per day), Vlieland - Terschelling (30 mins; *KOEGELWIECK, NAJADE, TIGER*; 2 per day). Freight Ferry Harlingen - Terschelling (2 hrs; *NOORD-NEDERLAND*), Harlingen - Vlieland (1hr 45 mins; *NOORD-NEDERLAND*).

1	FRIESLAND	3583t	89	14.0k	69.0m	1350P	122C	12L	BA	NL	8801058
2»p	KOEGELWIECK	439t	92	33.0k	35.5m	315P	0C	0L	-	NL	9035527
3	MIDSLAND	1812t	74	15.5k	77.9m	1200P	55C	6L	BA	NL	7393066
4F	NOORD-NEDERLAND	361t	02	14.0k	48.0m	12P	-	9L	BA	NL	9269611
5»p	TIGER	660t	02	37.0k	52.0m	414P	0C	0L	BA	NL	9179191
6	VLIELAND	2726t	05	15.0k	64.1m	1300P	58C	4L	BA	NL	9303716

FRIESLAND Built by Van der Giessen-de Noord, Krimpen aan den IJssel, Rotterdam, The Netherlands for *Rederij Doeksen*. Used on the Harlingen - Terschelling route.

KOEGELWIECK Harding 35m catamaran built at Rosendal, Norway for *Rederij Doeksen* to operate between Harlingen and Terschelling, Harlingen and Vlieland and Terschelling and Vlieland.

MIDSLAND Built as the RHEINLAND by Werftunion GmbH & Co, Cassens-Werft, Emden, Germany for *AG Ems* of Germany. In 1993 purchased by *Rederij Doeksen* and renamed the MIDSLAND. Used mainly on the Harlingen - Terschelling route but also used on the Harlingen - Vlieland service. She is now a reserve vessel.

NOORD-NEDERLAND Catamaran built by ASB, Harwood, New South Wales, Australia for *Rederij Doeksen*. Used on freight services from Harlingen to Terschelling and Vlieland.

TIGER Catamaran built as the SUPERCAT 2002 by FBMA Babcock Marine, Cebu, Philippines for *SuperCat* of the Philippines. In 2007 purchased by *Rederij Doeksen* and renamed the TIGER. Operates from Harlingen to Terschelling and Vlieland.

VLIELAND Catamaran built by FBMA Babcock Marine, Cebu, Philippines for *Rederij Doeksen* to operate between Harlingen and Vlieland.

REDERI AB ECKERÖ

THE COMPANY *Rederi AB Eckerö* is an Åland Islands company. It operates two ferry companies, a cruise operation from Stockholm (*Birka Cruises*), a ro-ro time chartering company (*Birka Cargo*) and a bus company on Åland (*Williams*).

ADDRESS PB 158, AX-22101 Mariehamn, Åland, Finland.

TELEPHONE Administration + 358 (0)18 28 030.

FAX Administration + 358 (0)18 12 011.

INTERNET Email info@rederiabeckero.ax Website www.rederiabeckero.ax *(Swedish)*

ECKERÖ LINE

THE COMPANY *Eckerö Line Ab Oy* is a Finnish company, 100% owned by *Rederi Ab Eckerö* of Åland, Finland. Until January 1998, the company was called *Eestin-Linjat*.

MANAGEMENT Managing Director Irja Hanelius, Marketing Director Ida Toikka-Everi.

ADDRESS PO Box 307, 00181 Helsinki, Finland.

TELEPHONE Administration & Reservations + 358 9 2288 544 (in Finland: + 358 6000 4300).

FAX Administration & Reservations + 358 (0)9 22885541.

INTERNET Email info@eckeroline.fi Website www.eckeroline.fi *(Swedish, Finnish, English)*

Gotlandia II (*Miles Cowsill*)

Finlandia (*William Barham*)

Eckero *(Miles Cowsill)*

ROUTE OPERATED **Passenger Service** Helsinki (Länsisatama) - Tallinn (Estonia) (2 hrs 30 mins; *FINLANDIA*; up to 2 per day).

1	FINLANDIA	36093t	01	27.0k	175.0m	1880P	665C	116T	BA	FI	9214379
2•	NORDLANDIA	21473t	81	21.0k	153.4m	2000P	400C	40T	BA	FI	7928811

FINLANDIA Built as the MOBY FREEDOM by Daewoo Shipbuilding & Heavy Machinery Ltd., Okpo, South Korea for *Moby SpA (Moby Line)* of Italy. Operated on their Genoa/Civitavecchia/Livorno - Olbia routes. In March 2012 sold to *Eckerö Line*, and renamed the FREEDOM. Refitted at Landskrona and, in June, renamed the FINLANDIA. She entered service on 31st December 2012.

NORDLANDIA Built as the OLAU HOLLANDIA by AG Weser Seebeckwerft, Bremerhaven, Germany for *Olau Line* of Germany for the service between Vlissingen (The Netherlands) and Sheerness (England). In 1989 she was replaced by a new vessel of the same name and she was sold to *Nordström & Thulin*. She was renamed the NORD GOTLANDIA and introduced onto *Gotlandslinjen* services between Gotland and the Swedish mainland. In 1997 she was purchased by *Rederi Ab Eckerö* of Åland for delivery in early 1998, following the ending of *Nordström & Thulin's* concession to operate the Gotland services. She was renamed the NORDLANDIA and placed on the *Eckerö Line* Helsinki - Tallinn service, operating day trips. Replaced by the FINLANDIA and laid up for sale. In June sold (see Late News).

ECKERÖ LINJEN

THE COMPANY *Eckerö Linjen* is an Åland Islands company 100% owned by *Rederi AB Eckerö*.

MANAGEMENT **Managing Director** Tomas Karlsson, **Marketing Manager** Maria Hellman.

ADDRESS Torggatan 2, Box 158, AX-22100 Mariehamn, Åland.

TELEPHONE **Administration** and **Reservations** + 358 (0)18 28000.

FAX **Administration & Reservations** + 358 (0)18 28380.

INTERNET **Website** www.eckerolinjen.se *(Swedish, Finnish, English)*.

ROUTE OPERATED Eckerö (Åland) - Grisslehamn (Sweden) (2 hrs; *ECKERÖ*; 3 per day).

1	ECKERÖ	12358t	79	19.5k	121.1m	1500P	265C	34T	BA	SE	7633155

ECKERÖ Built as the JENS KOFOED by Aalborg Værft A/S, Aalborg, Denmark for *Bornholmstrafikken*. Used on the Rønne - Copenhagen, Rønne - Ystad and (until December 2002) Rønne - Sassnitz services. Rønne - Copenhagen service became Rønne – Køge in September 2004. In October 2004 sold to *Eckerö Linjen* for delivery in May 2005. Renamed the ECKERÖ and substantially rebuilt before entering service in early 2006. In January 2009 transferred from the Finnish to the Swedish flag.

AG EMS

THE COMPANY *AG Ems* is a German public sector company.

MANAGEMENT **Managing Director & Chief Executive** B W Brons, **Marine Superintendent** Knut Gerdes, **Operations Manager** Hans-Jörd Oltmanns.

ADDRESS Am Aussenhafen, Postfach 1154, 26691 Emden, Germany.

TELEPHONE **Administration & Reservations** + 49 (0)1805-180182.

INTERNET **Email** info@ag-ems.de **Website** www.ag-ems.de *(German)* www.borkumlijn.nl *(Dutch)* www.helgolandlinie.de *(German)*

ROUTES OPERATED **Conventional Ferries** Emden (Germany) - Borkum (German Frisian Islands) (2 hrs; *MÜNSTERLAND, OSTFRIESLAND*; up to 4 per day), Eemshaven (The Netherlands) - Borkum (55 mins; *GRONINGERLAND*; up to 4 per day), Wilhelmshaven - Heligoland (3 hrs; *HELGOLAND*; 1 per day) (Operated by subsidiary *Helgoland Linie* - tourist cars not conveyed). **Fast Ferries** Emden - Borkum (1 hr; *NORDLICHT* up to 4 per day), Eemshaven - Borkum (30 mins; *NORDLICHT*; 1 per week in summer).

Leonora Christina *(John Bryant)*

Hammerodde *(Peter Therkildsen)*

1	GRONINGERLAND	1070t	91	12.0k	44.4m	621P	30C	-	BA	DE	9002465
2	HELGOLAND	1812t	72	15.5k	77.9m	1200P	65C	10L	BA	DE	7217004
3	MÜNSTERLAND	1859t	86	15.5k	78.7m	1200P	70C	10L	BA	DE	8601989
4p»	NORDLICHT	435t	89	33.0k	38.8m	272P	0C	0L	-	DE	8816015
5	OSTFRIESLAND	1859t	85	15.5k	78.7m	1200P	70C	10L	BA	DE	8324622
6p	WAPPEN VON BORKUM	287t	76	11.5k	42.8m	358P	0C	0L	-	DE	7525918

GRONINGERLAND Built by Husumer Schiffswerft, Husum, Germany as the HILLIGENLEI for *Wyker Dampfschiffs-Reederei Föhr-Amrum GmbH* of Germany. Operated Schlüttsiel - Halligen – Wittdün (North Frisian Islands). In 2004 laid up. In late 2005 sold to *AG Ems*. In 2006 renamed the GRONINGERLAND and placed on the Eemshaven – Borkum route.

HELGOLAND Built by as the WESTFALEN C Cassens Schiffswerft, Emden, Germany for *AG Ems*. Rebuilt in 1994. In 2006 renamed the HELGOLAND and inaugurated a new Wilhelmshaven - Heligoland service for subsidiary *Helgoland Linie*.

MÜNSTERLAND, OSTFRIESLAND Built by Martin Jansen GmbH & Co KG Schiffswerft, Leer, Germany for *AG Ems*.

NORDLICHT Fjellstrand 38m passenger-only catamaran built at Mandal, Norway for *AG Ems*.

WAPPEN VON BORKUM Built as the HANNOVER by Schiffswerft Schlömer GmbH & Co KG, Oldersum, Germany for *Friesland Fahrlinie* of Germany. In 1979 sold to *AG Ems* and renamed the STADT BORKUM. In 1988 sold to *ST-Line* of Finland, operating day trips from Rauma and renamed the PRINCESS ISABELLA. In 1994 returned to *AG Ems* and renamed the WAPPEN VON BORKUM.

EVT

THE COMPANY *rederij Eigen Veerdienst Terschelling (EVT)* is a Dutch private sector company. There are 21 share-holders, all residents of the Island of Terschelling.

MANAGEMENT Managing Director E A Rob.

ADDRESS Postbus 81, 8880 AB Terschelling West, Netherlands.

INTERNET Email info@evt.nl Website www.evt.nl *(Dutch)*

ROUTE OPERATED Harlingen (The Netherlands) - Terschelling (Frisian Islands) (2 hrs; *SPATHOEK*; up to 3 per day).

1	SPATHOEK	1743t	88	12.0k	67.4m	975P	55C	-	BA	NL	8800975

SPATHOEK Built by Husumer Schiffswerft, Husum, Germany as the SCHLESWIG-HOLSTEIN for *Wyker Dampfschiffs-Reederei Föhr-Amrum GmbH* of Germany. She operated between Föhr and Amrum. In March 2011 sold to *EVT* and renamed the SPATHOEK. In March 2012 began operating between Harlingen and Terschelling.

FÆRGEN

THE COMPANY *Danske Færger A/S* trading as *Færgen (previously Nordic Ferry Services A/S)* is a Danish mixed public and private sector company.

MANAGEMENT CEO John Steen-Mikkelsen.

ADDRESSES Dampskibskajen 3, 3700 Rønne, Denmark.

TELEPHONE Administration + 45 56 56202404. Reservations *(BornholmerFaergen* only) + 45 70 10 18 66.

INTERNET Website www.faergen.com *(Danish, German, English)*

ROUTES OPERATED *AlsFærgen* Fynshav (Als) - Bøjden (Fyn) (50 mins; *FRIGG SYDFYEN, ODIN SYDFYEN*; hourly (summer) two-hourly (winter)), *BornholmerFærgen* Conventional Ferries Rønne (Bornholm, Denmark) - Køge (6 hrs 30 mins; *HAMMERODDE*; 1 per day, *April-October only:* Rønne – Sassnitz (Germany) (3 hrs 30 mins; *POVL ANKER*; 1 per day). Fast Ferry Rønne - Ystad (Sweden) (1 hr 20 mins; *LEONORA CHRISTINA, VILLUM CLAUSEN*; Peak season: departure every 2 hours. Low season: 3 trips a day), *FanøFærgen* Esbjerg (Jutland) - Nordby (Fanø) (12 mins; *FENJA, MENJA, SØNDERHO*; every 20-40 mins), *LangelandsFærgen* Spodsbjerg (Langeland) - Tårs (Lolland) (40 mins; *LANGELAND, LOLLAND*; hourly), *SamsøFærgen* Hou - Sælvig (Samsø) (50 min; *KANHAVE*; up to 8 per day), Kalundborg - Koby Kås (Samsø) (1 hr 50 min; *KYHOLM*; up to 4 per day).

1	FENJA	751t	98	11.5k	49.9m	396P	34C	4L	BA	DK	9189378
2	FRIGG SYDFYEN	1676t	84	13.5k	70.1m	338P	50C	8L	BA	DK	8222824
3	HAMMERODDE	13906t	05	18.5k	124.9m	400P	342C	106T	A	DK	9323699
4	KANHAVE	4250t	08	16.0k	91.4m	600P	122C	30L	BA	DK	9548562
5	KYHOLM	3380t	98	14.5k	69.2m	450P	96C	8L	BA	DK	9183025
6	LANGELAND	4500t	12	16.0k	99.9m	600P	122C	36L	BA	DK	9596428
7»	LEONORA CHRISTINA	8235t	11	40.0k	112.6m	1400P	359C	-	BA	DK	9557848
8	LOLLAND	4500t	12	16.0k	99.9m	600P	122C	36L	BA	DK	9594690
9	MENJA	751t	98	11.5k	49.9m	396P	34C	4L	BA	DK	9189380
10	ODIN SYDFYEN	1698t	82	12.5k	70.4m	338P	50C	8L	BA	DK	8027896
11	POVL ANKER	12131t	78	19.5k	121.0m	1500P	262C	26T	BA	DK	7633143
12p	SØNDERHO	93t	62	10.0k	26.3m	163P	0C	0L	-	DK	
13»	VILLUM CLAUSEN	6402t	00	40.0k	86.6m	1055P	200C	-	BA	DK	9216250

FENJA Built by Morsø Værft A/S, Nykøbing Mors, Denmark for *Scandlines Sydfyenske A/S* for the Esbjerg - Nordby service.

FRIGG SYDFYEN Built by Svendborg Skibsværft A/S, Svendborg, Denmark for *Sydfyenske Dampskibsselskab (SFDS)* of Denmark for the service between Spodsbjerg and Tårs. In June 2012 moved to the Fynshav - Bøjden route.

HAMMERODDE Built by Merwede Shipyard, Hardinxveld-Giessendam, The Netherlands for *Bornholmstrafikken*. In Winter 2010 an additional vehicle deck was added for freight and some additional cabins.

KANHAVE Built by Frantzis Shipyard, Perama, Greece. Used on the Hou - Sælvig route.

KYHOLM Built by Ørskov Staalskibsværft, Frederikshavn, Denmark for *Samsø Linien* of Denmark. In October 2008 chartered to *Samsøtrafikken* (now *SamsøFærgen*).

LANGELAND Built by Sietas Werft, Hamburg, Germany for the Spodsbjerg - Tårs route.

LEONORA CHRISTINA Austal Auto-Express 113 catamaran built at Fremantle, Australia for *Færgen*. Used on the Rønne - Ystad route.

LOLLAND Built by Sietas Werft, Hamburg, Germany. She was launched as the SAMSØ and it was intended that she would be operated on the Hou - Sælvig service, being owned by *Samsø Linien* and operated by *Færgen*. However, these plans were dropped and in February 2012 she was renamed the LOLLAND. After delivery in March 2012 she was, in April, placed on the Spodsbjerg - Tårs route.

MENJA Built by Morsø Værft A/S, Nykøbing Mors, Denmark for *Scandlines Sydfyenske A/S* for the Esbjerg - Nordby service.

ODIN SYDFYEN Built by Svendborg Skibsværft A/S, Svendborg, Denmark for *Sydfyenske Dampskibsselskab (SFDS)* of Denmark for the service between Spodsbjerg and Tårs. In June 2012 moved to the Fynshav - Bøjden route.

POVL ANKER Built by Aalborg Værft A/S, Denmark for *Bornholmstrafikken*. Used on the Rønne - Copenhagen (until September 2004), Rønne - Køge (October 2004-date), Rønne - Ystad and Rønne - Sassnitz services. In recent years she has operated between Rønne and Sassnitz and Rønne and Ystad in the peak summer period.

SØNDERHO Passenger-only ferry built by Esbjerg Jernstøberi & Maskinfabrik A/S, Esbjerg, Denmark for *Post & Telegrafvæsenet* (Danish Post Office). In 1977 taken over by *DSB*. Used on extra peak sailings and late night and early morning sailings between Esbjerg and Nordby.

VILLUM CLAUSEN Austal Auto-Express 86 catamaran built at Fremantle, Australia for *Bornholmstrafikken*. Used on the Rønne - Ystad service. Car capacity increased in 2005.

FINNLINES

THE COMPANY *Finnlines plc* is a Finnish private sector company. The Italian company *Grimaldi Compagnia de Navigazione SpA* has a controlling interest. It operates four passenger brands: *Finnlines HansaLink*, *Finnlines NordöLink* and *FinnLink* and *TransRussiaExpress*.

MANAGEMENT President and CEO Uwe Bakosch, Vice-President Mrs Seija Turunen.

ADDRESS PO Box 197, 00180 Helsinki, Finland.

TELEPHONE Administration + 358 (0)10 343 50, Reservations + 358 (0)10 343 4500.

FAX Administration + 358 (0)10 343 520.

INTERNET *Finnlines* Email info.fi@finnlines.com Website *Finnlines* www.finnlines.com *(English, Finnish, German, Polish, Swedish)*.

ROUTES OPERATED *Finnlines Hansalink branded routes* Helsinki - Travemünde (27 hrs; FINNLADY, FINNMAID, FINNSTAR; 7 per week), Helsinki - Rostock (32 hrs; *TRANSEUROPA*; 2 per week).

Finnlines NordöLink branded route Malmö - Travemünde (9 hrs; FINNCLIPPER, FINNPARTNER, FINNTRADER, NORDLINK; up to 4 per day).

FinnLink branded route Naantali (Finland) - Kapellskär (Sweden) (6 hrs; FINNEAGLE FINNFELLOW, FINNSAILOR; up to 3 per day).

TranRussia Express branded route Lübeck - Sassnitz - Ventspils - St Petersburg - (60 hours; FINNCLIPPER or FINNPARTNER or FINNTRADER, TRANSRUSSIA; 2 per week).

1	EUROFERRY BRINDISI	25996t	96	21.0k	168.0m	200P	800C	154T	BA2	SE	9010814
2	FINNCLIPPER	29841t	99	22.0k	188.3m	440P	-	210T	BA2	SE	9137997
3	FINNEAGLE	29841t	99	22.0k	188.3m	440P	-	185T	BA2	SE	9138006
4	FINNFELLOW	33769t	00	22.0k	188.3m	452P	-	220T	BA	SE	9145164
5	FINNLADY	45923t	07	25.0k	216.0m	500P	-	300T	BA2	FI	9336268
6	FINNMAID	45923t	06	25.0k	216.0m	500P	-	300T	BA2	FI	9319466
7	FINNPARTNER	32534t	94	21.3k	183.0m	90P	-	236T	A2	SE	9010163
8	FINNSAILOR	20783t	87	20.3k	157.6m	119P	-	146T	A	SE	8401444
9	FINNSTAR	45923t	06	25.0k	216.0m	500P	-	300T	BA2	FI	9319442
10	FINNTRADER	32534t	95	21.3k	183.0m	114P	-	220T	BA2	SE	9017769
11	NORDLINK	45923t	07	25.0k	216.0m	500P	-	300T	BA2	SE	9336256
12	TRANSEUROPA	32534t	95	21.3k	183.0m	90P	-	236T	A2	DE	9010175
13	TRANSLUBECA	24727t	90	20.5k	157.0m	84P	-	152T	A	DE	8706040
14	TRANSRUSSIA	32531t	94	21.3k	183.0m	90P	-	236T	A2	DE	9010151

EUROFERRY BRINDISI Built as the GOTLAND by Pt Dok Kodja Bahri, Kodja, Indonesia for *Rederi AB Gotland* for charter. In 1997 briefly chartered to *Tor Line* and then to *Nordic Trucker Line*, to operate between Oxelösund and St Petersburg (a ro-ro service). In June 1997 she was chartered to *SeaWind Line*, enabling a twice-daily passenger service to be operated. In late 1997 she was sold to *Finnlines* and renamed the FINNARROW. She started operating twice weekly between Helsinki and Travemünde. During Summer 1998 she was transferred to *FinnLink*; a bow door was fitted and she was modified to allow for two-level loading. In 2003 transferred to *Nordö Link*. In 2005 returned to *FinnLink*. In 2006 transferred to *Finnlines Nordö Link* again. In 2007 chartered to *Stena Line* to operate between Karlskrona and Gdynia. In December 2011 transferred to the Hook of Holland - Killingholme route. In March 2011 replaced by the STENA TRANSPORTER and returned to *Finnlines*. Placed on the

Travemünde - Malmö service. In October 2011 transferred to *FinnLink*. Between January and March 2013 chartered to *Stena Line* to cover Irish Sea routes during the refit period but withdrawn from service prematurely following an accident. In April 2013 chartered to *Grimaldi Line* of Italy for five years. In July, renamed the EUROFERRY BRINDISI.

FINNCLIPPER 'Ro-pax' ferry built by Astilleros Españoles, Cadiz, Spain. Ordered by *Stena RoRo* of Sweden and launched as the STENA SEAPACER 1. In 1998 sold, before delivery, to *Finnlines* and renamed the FINNCLIPPER. Entered service on the Helsinki - Travemünde route in 1999. During Winter 1999/2000 she was converted to double-deck loading. In 2003 transferred to *FinnLink*. In 2007 an additional freight deck was added. Currently operating on the Travemünde - Malmö and Lübeck - St Petersburg services.

FINNEAGLE 'Ro-pax' vessel built by Astilleros Españoles, Cadiz, Spain. Ordered by *Stena RoRo* of Sweden and launched as the STENA SEAPACER 2. In 1998 sold, before delivery, to *Finnlines* and renamed the FINNEAGLE. Although expected to join her sister the FINNCLIPPER on the Helsinki - Travemünde route, on delivery in November 1999 she entered service with *FinnLink*. During Winter 1999/2000 she was modified for two-deck loading. She has operated on both the *FinnLink* and *Finnlines NordöLink* services.

FINNFELLOW 'Ro-pax' ferry built as the STENA BRITANNICA by Astilleros Españoles, Cadiz, Spain for *Stena RoRo* and chartered to *Stena Line BV* to operate between Hook of Holland and Harwich. In 2003 replaced by a new STENA BRITANNICA, sold to *Finnlines*, renamed the FINNFELLOW and placed on the Helsinki - Travemünde route. In 2004 transferred to *FinnLink*.

FINNLADY, FINNMAID Built by Fincantieri-Cantieri Navali Italiani SpA, Ancona, Italy to operate between Helsinki and Travemünde.

FINNPARTNER 'Ro-pax' vessel built by Stocznia Gdanska SA, Gdansk, Poland for *Finnlines Oy* of Finland to provide a daily service conveying both freight and a limited number of cars and passengers on the previously freight-only route between Helsinki and Travemünde. In February 2007 replaced by the FINNLADY and placed on the Turku - Travemünde freight service; in May sent to the Remontowa Shipyard in Gdansk for rebuilding to increase passenger capacity and allow for two-deck through loading. Currently operating on the Travemünde - Malmö and Lübeck - St Petersburg services.

FINNSAILOR Built by Gdansk Shipyard, Gdansk, Poland for *Finnlines* of Finland for freight service between Finland and Germany. In 1996 converted to ro-pax format to inaugurate a new passenger/freight service between Helsinki and Norrköping (Sweden) for subsidiary *FinnLink*. In 1997 this service was transferred to the Kapellskär - Naantali route and passengers (other than lorry drivers) ceased to be conveyed. In 2000 she was chartered to *Nordö-Link* to operate between Travemünde and Malmö. In 2002 she returned to *FinnLink*. In 2004 transferred to *Nordö-Link*. In 2007 returned to *FinnLink* as fourth ship. In early 2009 transferred to *Finnlines'* freight service operating between Helsinki, Turku and Travemünde but in April transferred back. In March 2011 moved back to *Finnlines NordöLink*.

FINNSTAR Built by Fincantieri-Cantieri Navali Italiani SpA, Castellamare, Italy to operate between Helsinki and Travemünde.

FINNTRADER 'Ro-pax' vessel built by Stocznia Gdanska SA, Gdansk, Poland for *Finnlines Oy* of Finland to provide a daily service conveying both freight and a limited number of cars and passengers on the previously freight-only route between Helsinki and Travemünde. In 2006/07 rebuilt to increase passenger capacity and allow for two-deck through loading. In 2007 transferred to the Malmö - Travemünde route. Currently operating on the Travemünde - Malmö and Lübeck - St Petersburg services.

NORDLINK Built by Fincantieri-Cantieri Navali Italiani SpA, Castellamare, Italy for *Finnlines* to operate for *Finnlines NordöLink* between Travemünde and Malmö. Currently operating on the Travemünde - Malmö service.

TRANSEUROPA 'Ro-pax' vessel built by Stocznia Gdanska SA, Gdansk, Poland for *Poseidon Schiffahrt* of Germany to operate on a joint service between Lübeck and Helsinki. In 1997 *Poseidon Schiffahrt* was acquired by *Finnlines* and in 2001 renamed *Finnlines Deutschland AG*. She remained on the Helsinki -

Finnsailor (*Miles Cowsill*)

Stavangerfjord (*Fjord Line*)

Travemünde route until February 2009, and was then transferred to *TransRussia Express*. In October 2012 transferred to the Helsinki - Gydnia service and in January 2013 to Helsinki - Rostock.

TRANSLUBECA Built by Gdansk Shipyard, Gdansk, Poland for *Poseidon Schiffahrt OHG* of Germany and used on *Poseidon-Finncarriers* service in the Baltic. In 1999 chartered to *DFDS Tor Line* and operated between Harwich and Gothenburg. In 2001 transferred to *TransRussia Express*. In June 2010 returned to *Finnlines* and operated on the Travemünde - Turku service. In November 2010 returned to *TransRussia Express* as third vessel. In November 2011 chartered to *Grimaldi Lines* and to operate on the Civitavecchia – Catania – Malta service. In June 2012 chartered to *Navirail* of Estonia to operate between Paldiski and Hanko.

TRANSRUSSIA 'Ro-pax' vessel built as the FINNHANSA by Stocznia Gdanska SA, Gdansk, Poland for *Finnlines Oy* of Finland to operate between Helsinki - Travemünde. In April 2009 sold to Finnlines' parent company, *Grimaldi PLC* of Italy and renamed the EUROFERRY SICILIA. Operated between Genoa and Catania. In May 2010 sold back to *Finnlines* and in July 2010 renamed the TRANSRUSSIA and placed on the *TransRussia Express* service.

FJORD LINE

THE COMPANY *Fjord Line* is a Norwegian company. During 2007 most of the shares of the company were purchased by *Frode and Ole Teigen*. The company bought and merged with *Master Ferries* during December 2007 and all operations are branded as *Fjord Line*.

MANAGEMENT **Managing Director** Ingvald Fardal, **Sales and Marketing Director** Eva Sørås Mellgren, **CFO** Svein Ege, **Director Fjord Line Denmark** Gert Balling, **Technical & Nautical Director** Morten Larsen.

ADDRESS PO Box 513, 4379 Egersund, Norway.

TELEPHONE **Administration** + 47 55 54 87 00, **Reservations** + 47 51 46 40 99.

FAX **Administration & Reservations** + 47 51 49 24 30.

INTERNET **Email** info@fjordline.com **Website** www.fjordline.com *(English, Danish, German, Dutch, Polish, Norwegian).*

ROUTE OPERATED **Conventional Ferry** *Until January 2014* Bergen (Norway) – Stavanger - Hirtshals (Denmark) (19 hrs 30 mins; *BERGENSFJORD (1993)*; 3 per week (plus 3 Stavanger - Hirtshals only (12 hrs), Bergen (Norway) – Stavanger - Hirtshals (Denmark) (17 hrs; *STAVANGERFJORD*; 3 per week, Langesund (Norway) - Hirtshals (4 hrs 30 mins; *STAVANGERFJORD*, 3 per week), (plus 1 Stavanger - Hirtshals only (9 hrs). *From January 2014* Bergen (Norway) – Stavanger - Hirtshals (Denmark) (17 hrs; *BERGENSFJORD (2013)*, *STAVANGERFJORD*; daily), Langesund (Norway) - Hirtshals (4 hrs 30 mins; *BERGENSFJORD (2013)*, *STAVANGERFJORD*, daily). **Fast Ferry** *May-August* Kristiansand (Norway) - Hirtshals (Denmark) (2 hrs 15 min; *FJORD CAT*; up to 3 per day).

1	BERGENSFJORD	16794t	93	19.0k	134.4m	882P	350C	44T	BA	DK	9058995
2»	FJORD CAT	5619t	98	43.0k	91.3m	663P	220C	-	A	DK	9176060
3	STAVANGERFJORD	20000t	13	21.5k	170.0m	1500P	600C	90T	BA	NO	9586605

STAVANGERFJORD Built by Bergen Group Fosen AS, Rissa, Norway for *Fjord Line*. Operates on LNG.

BERGENSFJORD Built by Fosen Mekaniske Verksteder, Rissa, Norway for *Rutelaget Askøy-Bergen* as the BERGEN and used on the *Fjord Line* Bergen - Egersund - Hanstholm service. In April 2003 chartered to *DFDS Seaways*, renamed the DUCHESS OF SCANDINAVIA and, after modifications, introduced onto the Harwich - Cuxhaven service. In 2004 sold to *Bergensfjord KS* of Norway and chartered to *DFDS Seaways*. In 2005 sub-chartered to *Fjord Line* for 5 months (with *DFDS* officers and deck-crew) and renamed the ATLANTIC TRAVELLER. In 2006 chartered directly to *Fjord Line*. In March 2008 purchased by *Fjord Line* and renamed the BERGENSFJORD. To be renamed the OLSOFJORD when the new BERGENSFJORD is delivered in 2013, she will be rebuilt as a day ferry and will operate between Sandefjord (Norway) and Strömstad (Sweden).

FJORD CAT Incat 91-metre catamaran, built speculatively at Hobart, Tasmania, Australia. In Spring 1998.

following *Incat's* acquisition of a 50% share in *Scandlines Cat-Link A/S*, she was chartered by *Nordic Catamaran Ferries K/S* to that company, operating between Århus and Kalundborg and named the CAT-LINK V. She is the current holder of the Hales Trophy for fastest crossing of the Atlantic during her delivery voyage between the USA and Falmouth, UK (although this claim is disputed because it was not a genuine commercial service). In 1999 the charter was transferred to *Mols-Linien*, she was renamed the MADS MOLS and operated between Århus and Odden. Charter ended in July 2005. Laid up and renamed the INCAT 049. In 2006 sold to *Gabriel Scott Rederi (Master Ferries)* and renamed the MASTER CAT. In December 2008 purchased by *Fjord Line* renamed the FJORD CAT. Did not operate in 2009 but service resumed in 2010.

Under construction

4	BERGENSFJORD	20000t	13	21.5k	170.0m	1500P	600C	90T	BA	NO	-

BERGENSFJORD Under construction by Bergen Group Fosen AS, Rissa, Norway for *Fjord Line*. Operates on LNG.

FRS GROUP

KATTEGAT-RUTEN

THE COMPANY *Kattegatruten A/S* is a Danish private sector company owned by *FRS (Förde Reederei Seetouristik)* of Germany.

MANAGEMENT Managing Director Ulrik Rasmussen.

ADDRESS Sverigesgade 4, 8000 Aarhus C, Denmark.

TELEPHONE Administration & Reservations + 45 38 111 222.

FAX Administration & Reservations + 45 86 205 981.

INTERNET Email info@kattegat-ruten.dk **Website** www.kattegat-ruten.dk *(Danish, English, German)*

ROUTE OPERATED *Ro-Pax Ferry* Århus (Jutland) - Kalundborg (Sealand) (2 hr 40 mins; *KATTEGAT*; 3 per day).

1	KATTEGAT	14379t	96	19.0k	136.4m	600P	344C	82L	BA2	DK	9112765

KATTEGAT Ro-pax vessel built as the MAREN MOLS by Ørskovs Christensens Staalskibsværft A/S, Frederikshavn, Denmark for *Mols-Linien*. Initially operated on the Ebeltoft - Odden route. In January 2000 switched to the Århus - Kalundborg route. In August 2011 sold to *FRS* and renamed the KATTEGAT In September 2011 continued to operate on the same route for *Kattegat-Ruten*.

Sister vessel TANGER EXPRESS (previously the METTE MOLS) operates for *FRS* between Tarifa (Spain) and Tangiers (Morocco).

RØMØ-SYLT LINIE

THE COMPANY *Römö-Sylt Linie GmbH* is a German company, a subsidiary of *FRS (Förde Reederei Seetouristik)* of Flensburg. (Note: Although, being a German company, the company's official name uses the German version of 'o-umlaut' (ö), the company trades in both Denmark and Germany using the Danish version (ø).

MANAGEMENT Managing Director P Rathke.

ADDRESS *Germany* Am Fähranleger, 25992 List, Germany, *Denmark* Kilebryggen, 6792 Rømø, Denmark.

TELEPHONE Administration *Germany* + 49 (0)4651 870475, **Reservations** *Denmark* + 45 73 75 53 03, *Germany* + 49 (0)180 310 30 30.

FAX Administration *Germany* + 49 (0)4651 871446, **Reservations** *Denmark* + 45 73 75 53 05.

INTERNET Email romo-sylt@post12.tele.dk **Website** www.romo-sylt.dk *(Danish, English, German)*

ROUTE OPERATED List (Sylt, Germany) - Havneby (Rømø, Denmark) (35 mins; *SYLT EXPRESS*; variable - approx two-hourly). **Note**: The island of Rømø is linked to the Danish mainland by a road causeway; the island of Sylt is linked to the German mainland by a rail-only causeway on which cars are conveyed on shuttle wagons.

1	SYLT EXPRESS	3650t	05	16.0k	88.2m	600P	80C	10L	BA	CY	9321823

SYLT EXPRESS Built by Fiskerstrand Verft A/S, Aalesund, Norway for *Rømø-Sylt Linie*.

HURTIGRUTEN

THE COMPANY *Hurtigruten ASA* is a Norwegian private sector company. The service was originally provided by a consortium of companies. By 2006, through mergers and withdrawal from the operation, there were just two companies - *Troms Fylkes D/S* and *Ofotens og Vesteraalens D/S* and in that year *Hurtigruten ASA* was formed.

MANAGEMENT Chairman Trygve Hegnar, **Managing Director** Daniel Skjeldam.

ADDRESS Kirkegata 1 Postboks 6144 Tromsø, Norway.

TELEPHONE Administration +47 97 05 70 30, **Reservations** *Norway* +47 81 00 30 30, *UK* +44 (0)20 8846 2666.

FAX Administration & Reservations +47 97 05 70 31 Reservations (UK) +44 (0)20 8846 2677.

INTERNET Email firmapost@hurtigruten.com **Websites** www.hurtigruten.co.uk *(English)* www.hurtigruten.no *(Norwegian)* www.hurtigruten.de *(German)*.

ROUTE OPERATED The 'Hurtigruten' - Bergen - Kirkenes with many intermediate calls. Daily departures throughout the year. The round trip takes just under 11 days.

1	FINNMARKEN	15539t	02	18.0k	138.5m	1000P	50C	0L	S	NO	9231951
2P	FRAM	11647t	07	18.0k	110.0m	500P	47C	0L	S	NO	9370018
3	KONG HARALD	11204t	93	18.0k	121.8m	691P	50C	0L	S	NO	9039119
4	LOFOTEN	2621t	64	16.0k	87.4m	410P	4C	0L	C	NO	5424562
5	MIDNATSOL	16151t	03	18.0k	135.7m	1000P	50C	0L	S	NO	9247728
6	NORDKAPP	11386t	96	18.0k	123.3m	691P	50C	0L	S	NO	9107772
7	NORDLYS	11204t	94	18.0k	121.8m	691P	50C	0L	S	NO	9048914
8	NORDNORGE	11384t	97	18.0k	123.3m	691P	50C	0L	S	NO	9107784
9	POLARLYS	11341t	96	18.0k	123.0m	737P	50C	0L	S	NO	9107796
10	RICHARD WITH	11205t	93	18.0k	121.8m	691P	50C	0L	S	NO	9040429
11	TROLLFJORD	16140t	02	18.0k	135.7m	822P	50C	0L	S	NO	9233258
12	VESTERÅLEN	6262t	83	18.0k	108.6m	560P	40C	0L	S	NO	8019368

FINNMARKEN Built by Kværner Kleven Skeppsvarv, Ulsteinvik, Norway for *Ofotens og Vesteraalens D/S*. In October 2009 chartered as a support vessel for the Gorgon Project (natural gas) in Western Australia. In November 2011 returned to *Hurtigruten* and, in February 2012, returned to service.

FRAM Built by Fincantieri-Cantieri Navali Italiani SpA at Trieste for *Hurtigruten Group ASA* (ordered by *OVDS*). Since 2007 she has operated cruises around Greenland during the summer period and in South America during the winter and this has been the pattern since. It was originally proposed that she would operate on the Hurtigruten during the winter and this may happen in future years.

KONG HARALD Built by Volkswerft, Stralsund, Germany for *Troms Fylkes D/S*.

LOFOTEN Built by A/S Aker Mekaniske Verksted, Oslo, Norway for *Vesteraalens D/S*. In 1988 she was sold to *Finnmark Fylkesrederi og Ruteselskap*. In 1996 she was sold to *Ofotens og Vesteraalens D/S*. In 2002 she was replaced by the FINNMARKEN but she then operated summer cruises and in the winter months substituted for the NORDNORGE when that vessel was sailing in the Chilean Fjords and Antarctica. Since 2008 she has operated on the main Hurtigruten roster.

MIDNATSOL Built by Fosen Mekaniske Verksteder, Rissa, Norway for *Troms Fylkes D/S*.

Fram (*John Bryant*)

Vesteralen (*John Bryant*)

NORDKAPP Built by Kværner Kleven Skeppsvarv, Ulsteinvik, Norway for *Ofotens og Vesteraalens D/S*. During the winters of 2005/06 and 2006/07 she operated cruises in South America but following the delivery of the FRAM she now remains on the Hurtigruten throughout the year.

NORDLYS Built by Volkswerft, Stralsund, Germany for *Troms Fylkes D/S*. In 2002 sold to *Kilberg Shipping KS* of Norway and leased back on 15 year bareboat charter with options to repurchase. She was laid up during winter 2008/09 until required to replace the damaged RICHARD WITH from the end of January. She now operates full-time on the Hurtigruten roster.

NORDNORGE Built by Kværner Kleven, Ulsteinvik, Norway for *Ofotens og Vesteraalens D/S*. During winters 2002/03 - 2007/08 she operated cruises in South America. During most of Winter 2008/09 she was used as an accommodation vessel for a liquefied natural gas field. Laid up at Bremerhaven during winter 2009/10.

POLARLYS Built by Ulstein Verft A/S, Ulsteinvik, Norway for *Troms Fylkes D/S*.

RICHARD WITH Built by Volkswerft, Stralsund, Norway for *Ofotens og Vesteraalens D/S*. In 2002 sold to *Kystruten KS*, of Norway and leased back on 15 year bareboat charter with options to re-purchase.

TROLLFJORD Built by Fosen Mekaniske Verksteder, Rissa, Norway for *Troms Fylkes D/S*.

VESTERÅLEN Built by Kaarbös Mekaniske Verksted A/S, Harstad, Norway for *Vesteraalens D/S*. From 1987 owned by *Ofotens og Vesteraalens D/S* and from 2006 by *Hurtigruten Group ASA*.

LD LINES

THE COMPANY *LD Lines* is a French company, a subsidiary of *Louis Dreyfus Armateurs*.

MANAGEMENT **LD Lines Managing Director** Christophe Santoni.

ADDRESS 28 Quai Galliéni 92100 Suresnes.

TELEPHONE **Administration & Reservations** + 33 (0) 2 32 14 52 09, *Freight Reservations* + 33 (0)2 32 14 52 05.

INTERNET **Email** ferry@ldlines.com **Websites** www.ldlines.com *(English, French, Spanish)*

ROUTE OPERATED St-Nazaire (France) - Gijón (Spain) (14 hrs; *NORMAN ASTURIAS*; 3 per week).

1	NORMAN ASTURIAS	26500t	07	24.0k	186.5m	1000P	170C	140L	BA	IT	9349760

NORMAN ASTURIAS Built by CN Visentini, Porto Viro, Italy. Whilst under construction, sold to *Stena RoRo* of Sweden and provisionally named the STENA AUSONIA. However, before delivery a charter was arranged with *Balearia* of Spain and she was delivered as the BORJA. Operated between Barcelona and Palma (Majorca). In February 2010 the charter ended and she was laid up at Rotterdam. In April 2010 chartered to *Ave Line* and renamed the BALTIC AMBER. In October 2010 chartered to *DFDS Seaways* to replace the fire-damaged LISCO GLORIA. In February 2011 chartered to *LD Lines* to operate between Marseilles and Rades (Tunisia). In June 2011 renamed the NORMAN ASTURIAS. In October 2011 the charter was ended but resumed the following month.

Services operated jointly with *DFDS Seaways* are shown in section 1 under *DFDS Seaways France*.

MOLS-LINIEN

THE COMPANY Mols-Linien A/S is a Danish private sector company; previously a subsidiary of J Lauritzen A/S, it was sold in 1988 to DIFKO No LXII (Dansk Investeringsfond). Since 1994 shares in the company have been traded on the Stock Exchange. In January 1999 a 40% share in the company was acquired by Scandlines Danmark A/S. Their Scandlines Cat-Link Århus - Kalundborg service became part of Mols-Linien in February 1999 and the service was switched from Kalundborg to Odden in April 1999. The Scandlines share in the company was acquired by the Clipper Group in 2007.

MANAGEMENT **Managing Director** Preben Wolff, **Marketing Manager** Mikkel Hybel.

ADDRESS Færgehavnen, 8400 Ebeltoft, Denmark.

TELEPHONE **Administration** + 45 89 52 52 00, **Reservations** + 45 70 10 14 18 (press 8).

FAX **Administration** + 45 89 52 53 93.

INTERNET **Email** mols-linien@mols-linien.dk **Website** www.mols-linien.dk (Danish, English, German).

ROUTES OPERATED Århus - Odden (Sealand) (1 hr 5 mins; KATEXPRESS 1, KATEXPRESS 2, MAX MOLS; up to 7 per day), Ebeltoft (Jutland) - Odden (45 mins; KATEXPRESS 1, KATEXPRESS 2, MAX MOLS; up to 4 per day).

1»	KATEXPRESS 1	10841	09	40.0k	112.6m	1200P	417C	34L	A	DK	9501590
2»	KATEXPRESS 2	10841	13	40.0k	112.6m	1000P	417C	34L	A	DK	9561356
3»•	MAI MOLS	3971t	96	43.4k	76.1m	450P	120C	-	BA	DK	9112997
4»	MAX MOLS	5617t	98	43.0k	91.3m	800P	220C	-	A	DK	9176058
5»•	MIE MOLS	3971t	96	43.4k	76.1m	450P	120C	-	BA	DK	9113006

KATEXPRESS 1 Incat 112m catamaran built by Incat Tasmania Pty Ltd for MGC Chartering of the Irish Republic. Launched as the INCAT 066. On completion, sold to for MGC Chartering of the Irish Republic and renamed the MGC 66. In April 2009 chartered to LD Lines, renamed the NORMAN ARROW and, in June, placed on the Dover - Boulogne route. In November 2009 withdrawn and laid up for the winter. In April 2010 began operating on the Portsmouth Le Havre - route. In March 2012 chartered to Mols-Linien and renamed the KATEXPRESS 1 (Note: in upper and lower case spelt 'KatExpress 1'). Entered service in May 2012.

KATEXPRESS 2 Incat 112m catamaran built by Incat Tasmania Pty Ltd. Launched as INCAT 067. In March 2013 chartered to Mols-Linien and renamed the KATEXPRESS 2 for ten years with a purchase option. (Note: in upper and lower case spelt 'KatExpress 2'). Entered service in May 2013.

MAI MOLS, MIE MOLS Danyard SeaJet 250 catamaran built by Danyard-Aalborg A/S, Aalborg, Denmark for Mols-Linien. In May 2012 withdrawn and laid up.

MAX MOLS Incat 91-metre catamaran, built speculatively at Hobart, Tasmania, Australia. In Spring 1998, following Incat's acquisition of a 50% share in Scandlines Cat-Link A/S, she was sold to that company and named the CAT-LINK IV. In 1999 purchased by Mols-Linien and renamed the MAX MOLS. In 2000 chartered to Marine Atlantic of Canada to operate between Port aux Basques (Newfoundland) and North Sydney (Nova Scotia). Returned to Mols-Linien in Autumn 2000. In Summer 2002 chartered to Riga Sea Lines to operate between Riga and Nynäshamn. Returned to Mols-Linien in Autumn 2002. In 2004 chartered to P&O Ferries to operate between Portsmouth and Caen. Operated under the marketing name 'Caen Express'. In November 2004 returned to Mols-Linien and placed on the Århus – Odden route to enhance the service as second vessel.

REEDEREI NORDEN-FRISIA

THE COMPANY *Aktiengesellschaft Reederei Norden-Frisia* is a German public sector company.

MANAGEMENT President/CEO C LI Stegmann, Managing Director/CFO Prok. Graw, Technical Manager Prok. H Stolle.

ADDRESS Postfach 1262, 26534 Norderney, Germany.

TELEPHONE Administration +49 (0)4931 987 0

FAX Administration +49 (0)4931 987 1131.

INTERNET Email info@reederei-frisia.de Website www.reederei-frisia.de *(German)*

ROUTES OPERATED Car Ferries & Passenger Ferries Norddeich (Germany) - Norderney (German Frisian Islands) (1 hr; *FRISIA I, FRISIA IV, FRISIA VI*; up to 15 per day), Norddeich - Juist (German Frisian Islands) (1 hr 20 mins; *FRISIA II, FRISIA V, FRISIA VII*; up to 15 per day). Excursion Vessels *(FRISIA IX, FRISIA X, WAPPEN VON NORDENEY*; varies).

1	FRISIA I	1020t	70	12.3k	63.7m	1500P	53C	-	BA	DE	7018604
2	FRISIA II	1125t	78	12.0k	63.3m	1340P	53C	-	BA	DE	7723974
3	FRISIA IV	1574t	02	12.0k	71.7m	1342P	60C	-	BA	DE	9246839
4	FRISIA V	1007t	65	11.0k	63.8m	1442P	53C	-	BA	DE	8827181
5	FRISIA VI	768t	68	12.0k	54.9m	1096P	35C	-	BA	DE	8827179
6F	FRISIA VII	363t	84	12.0k	53.0m	12P	30C	-	BA	DE	8891807
7p	FRISIA IX	571t	80	11.0k	57.0m	785P	0C	-	-	DE	7924310
8p	FRISIA X	187t	72	12.0k	36.3m	290P	0C	-	-	DE	7222308
9p	WAPPEN VON NORDENEY	154t	67	14.0k	31.1m	200P	0C	-	-	DE	7935395

FRISIA I, FRISIA II, FRISIA V, FRISIA VI Built by Jos L Meyer Werft, Papenburg, Germany for *Reederei Norden-Frisia*. Passenger capacities relate to the summer season. Capacity is reduced during the winter.

FRISIA IV Built by Schiffswerft und Maschinenfabrik Cassens GmbH, Emden, Germany for *Reederei Norden-Frisia* to replace the FRISIA VIII.

FRISIA VII Built by Schlömer Werft, Oldersum, Germany for *Reederei Norden-Frisia*. Conveys ro-ro freight to Norderney and Juist.

FRISIA IX, FRISIA X Built by Schiffswerft Julius Diedrich GmbH & Co. KG, Oldersum, Germany for *Reederei Norden-Frisia*. The FRISIA IX was built to convey 9 cars at the bow end but is now used in passenger-only mode. These ships are generally used for excursions.

WAPPEN VON NORDENEY Built by Cassens-Werft, Emden, Germany for *Reederei Norden-Frisia*. Used for excursions.

POLFERRIES

THE COMPANY *Polferries* is the trading name of *Polska Zegluga Baltycka SA (Polish Baltic Shipping Company)*, a Polish state-owned company.

MANAGEMENT Financial Director and Board Member Piotr Redmerski.

ADDRESS ul Portowa 41, PL 78-100 Kolobrzeg, Poland.

TELEPHONE Administration +48 94 35 52 103, +48 94 35 52 102, Passenger Reservations *Swinoujscie* +48 91 32 26 140, *Gdansk* +48 58 34 31 887, *Ystad* +46 40 97 61 80, *Nynäshamn* +46 8 520 686 60 Freight Reservations *Swinoujscie* +48 91 32 26 104, *Gdansk* +48 58 34 30 212, *Ystad* +46 411 55 88 50, *Nynäshamn* +46 8 520 202 60.

FAX Administration +48 94 35 52 208, Passenger Reservations *Swinoujscie* +48 91 32 26 168, *Gdansk* +48 58 34 36 574, *Ystad* +46 411 55 88 51, *Nynäshamn* +46 8 520 172 54 Freight

Wawel *(John Bryant)*

Scandinavia *(William Barham)*

Reservations *Swinoujscie* +48 91 32 26 169, *Gdansk* +48 58 34 30 975, *Ystad* +46 411 55 88 51, *Nynäshamn* +46 8 520 178 01

INTERNET Email info@polferries.pl **Passenger Reservations** *Swinoujscie* boas.pax@polferries.pl *Gdansk*   pax.gdansk@polferries.pl,   *Ystad*   info@polferries.se,   *Nynäshamn* *pax.nynashamn@polferries.se* **Freight Reservations** *Swinoujscie* boas.cargo@polferries.pl, *Gdansk* cargo.gdansk@polferries.pl, *Ystad*spedition@polferries.se, *Nynäshamn* frakt@polferries.se **Website** www.polferries.pl *(Polish, Danish, English, German, Swedish)*

ROUTES OPERATED Swinoujscie - Ystad (7 hrs; *BALTIVIA*, *WAWEL*; 2 per day), Gdansk - Nynäshamn (Sweden) (18 hrs; *SCANDINAVIA*; 3 per week.

1	BALTIVIA	17790t	81	19.0k	146.9m	250P	30C	80L	BA	BS	7931997
2	SCANDINAVIA	23842t	80	20.0k	146.1m	1800P	510C	38L	BA2	BS	7826788
3	WAWEL	25318t	80	19.0k	163.9m	900P	550C	75L	A2	BS	7814462

BALTIVIA Built as the SAGA STAR by Fartygsentreprenader AB, Kalmar, Sweden for *TT-Saga-Line* and, from 1982, used on freight services between Travemünde and Trelleborg/Malmö. (Originally ordered by *Rederi AB Svea* as the SAGALAND). In 1989 sold to *Cie Meridionale* of France, renamed the GIROLATA and used on *SNCM* (later *CMR*) services in the Mediterranean. In 1993 she was chartered back to *TT-Line*, resumed her original name and was used on the Travemünde - Trelleborg service. Following delivery of the ROBIN HOOD and the NILS DACKE in 1995, she was transferred to the Rostock - Trelleborg route. In July 1997 she was purchased by *TT-Line* and in 1998 passenger facilities were completely renovated to full ro-pax format; following the delivery of the TOM SAWYER she was transferred back to the Travemünde - Trelleborg route, operating additional freight sailings. Briefly transferred back to Rostock - Trelleborg when the charter of the TT-TRAVELLER ended. Withdrawn in 2002, sold to Transmanche Ferries and renamed the DIEPPE. In 2006 replaced by the SEVEN SISTERS, sold to *Polferries*, renamed the BALTIVIA and, in 2007, placed on the Gdansk - Nynäshamn route. In February 2013 transferred to the Swinoujscie – Ystad service.

SCANDINAVIA Built as the VISBY by Öresundsvarvet AB, Landskrona, Sweden for *Rederi AB Gotland* of Sweden for their services between the island of Gotland and the Swedish mainland. In 1987 the franchise to operate these services was lost by the company and awarded to *Nordström & Thulin* of Sweden. A subsidiary called *N&T Gotlandslinjen AB* was formed to operate the service. The VISBY was chartered to this company and managed by *Johnson Line*, remaining owned by *Rederi AB Gotland*. In early 1990 she was chartered to *Sealink* and renamed the FELICITY. After modifications, she was, in March 1990, introduced onto the Fishguard - Rosslare route. Later in 1990 she was renamed the STENA FELICITY. In Summer 1997 she was returned to *Rederi AB Gotland* for rebuilding, prior to her entering service with *Destination Gotland* in January 1998. She was renamed the VISBY. In late 2002 she was renamed the VISBORG. In March 2003 replaced by the new VISBY and laid up for sale or charter. In July sold to *Polferries*, renamed the SCANDINAVIA and placed on the Gdansk - Nynäshamn route.

WAWEL Built as the SCANDINAVIA by Kockums Varvet AB, Malmö, Sweden for *Rederi AB Nordö* of Sweden. After service in the Mediterranean for *UMEF*, she was, in 1981, sold to *SOMAT* of Bulgaria, renamed the TZAREVETZ and used on *Medlink* services between Bulgaria and the Middle East, later on other routes. In 1986 she was chartered to *Callitzis* of Greece for a service between Italy and Greece. In 1988 she was sold to *Sealink*, re-registered in The Bahamas and renamed the FIESTA. She was then chartered to *OT Africa Line*. During Autumn 1989 she was rebuilt at Bremerhaven to convert her for passenger use and in March 1990 she was renamed the FANTASIA and placed on the Dover - Calais service. Later in 1990 she was renamed the STENA FANTASIA. In 1998 transferred to *P&O Stena Line*. In 1999 she was renamed the P&OSL CANTERBURY. In 2002 renamed the PO CANTERBURY. In Spring 2003 replaced by the PRIDE OF CANTERBURY and laid up at Dunkerque. Later in the year sold to *GA Ferries* and renamed the ALKMINI A. In 2004 moved to Greece and, after a partial rebuild (including the welding up of the bow door) placed on the Igoumenitsa – Brindisi route. Later in 2004 sold to *Polferries* and renamed the WAWEL; rebuilt to increase the number of cabins. In 2005 placed on the Swinoujscie – Ystad service.

SAAREMAA LAEVAKOMPANII

THE COMPANY Saaremaa Laevakompanii AS is an Estonian company, founded in 1992.

MANAGEMENT General Director Tõnis Rihvk.

ADDRESS Kohtu 1, 93819 Kuressaare, Estonia.

TELEPHONE Administration +372 452 4350, **Reservations** +372 452 4444.

FAX Administration +372 452 4355.

INTERNET Email slk@laevakompanii.ee **Website** www.tuulelaevad.ee (Estonian, English).

ROUTES OPERATED Vehicle Ferries Kuivastu - Virtsu (30 mins, MUHUMAA, SAAREMAA, up to 27 per day), Heltermaa (Hiiumaa) – Rohuküla (1 hr 30 mins; HIIUMA, REGULA; up to 10 per day), Triigi - Sõru (1 hr 5 mins; KÕRGELAID; up to 8 per day).

1P•	AEGNA	101t	79	18.0k	25.9 m	93P	0C	0L	-	EE	8874366
2	HARILAID	1028t	85	9.9k	49.9m	120P	35C	0L	BA	EE	8727367
3	HIIUMAA	5900t	11	15.0k	97.9m	600P	150C	12L	BA	EE	9481805
4	KÕRGELAID	1028t	87	9.9k	49.9m	200P	35C	0L	BA	EE	8725577
5	MUHUMAA	5900t	10	15.0k	97.9m	600P	150C	12L	BA	EE	9474060
6	OFELIA	3638t	68	14.4k	74.4m	600P	110C	12L	BA	EE	6809771
7	REGULA	3774t	71	14.5k	71.2m	580P	105C	12L	BA	EE	7051058
8	SAAREMAA	5900t	10	15.0k	97.9m	600P	150C	12L	BA	EE	9474072
9•	ST OLA	4833t	71	16.0k	85.9m	500P	140C	12L	BA	EE	7109609

AEGNA Built as the RÅSA by Fjellstrand, Omastrand, Norway for Helgeland Trafikkselskap of Norway. In 2003 sold to Jan og Torleif Charter DA. In 2005 sold to Saaremaa Laevakompanii and renamed the AEGNA. Inaugurated a passenger-only service between Saaremaa and Ruhnu and Pärnu. This no longer operates and she is now laid up.

HARILAID, KÕRGELAID Built by Riga Shiprepair Yard, Riga, Latvia (USSR) for ESCO of Estonia. In 1994 transferred to Saaremaa Laevakompanii. The HARILAID is now a spare vessel.

HIIUMAA, MUHUMAA, SAAREMAA Built by Fiskerstrand Verft A/S, Aalesund, Norway for Saaremaa Laevakompanii.

OFELIA Built by Krögerwerft GmbH, Rendsburg, Germany for Svenska Rederi-AB Öresund of Sweden and used on the Limhamn - Dragør service. In 1980 sold to Scandinavian Ferry Lines. In 1990 transferred to SweFerry and later to Scandlines AB. In 1997 sold to Saaremaa Laevakompanii. Now a spare vessel.

REGULA Built by Jos L Meyer, Papenburg, Germany for Stockholms Rederi AB Svea of Sweden for the service between Helsingborg and Helsingør operated by Linjebuss International AB (a subsidiary company). In 1980 she was sold to Scandinavian Ferry Lines. During Winter 1984/85 she was rebuilt to increase vehicle and passenger capacity. In 1991 ownership was transferred to SweFerry and operations to ScandLines on the Helsingborg - Helsingør service. Ownership later transferred to Scandlines AB. In 1997 sold to Saaremaa Laevakompanii. Now a spare vessel.

ST OLA Built as the SVEA SCARLETT for by Jos L Meyer, Papenburg, Germany Stockholms Rederi AB Svea of Sweden and used on the SL (Skandinavisk Linjetrafik) service between Copenhagen (Tuborg Havn) and Landskrona (Sweden). In 1980 she was sold to Scandinavian Ferry Lines of Sweden and Dampskibsselskabet Øresund A/S of Denmark (jointly owned). Initially she continued to serve Landskrona but later that year the Swedish terminal became Malmö. In 1981 she operated on the Helsingborg - Helsingør service for a short while, after which she was withdrawn and laid up. In 1982 she was sold to Eckerö Linjen of Finland, renamed the ECKERÖ and used on services between Grisslehamn (Sweden) and Eckerö (Åland Islands). In 1991 she was sold to P&O Scottish Ferries and renamed the ST OLA. In March 1992 she replaced the previous ST OLA (1345t, 1974) on the Scrabster - Stromness service. In September 2002 withdrawn and sold to Saaremaa Laevakompanii. In 2011 laid up.

SASSNITZ - UST LUGA FERRY

THE COMPANY The *Sassnitz - Ust Luga Ferry* is operated by *Black Sea Ferry* in partnership with *Russian Railways* and *AnRuss Trans*. *Trans-Exim* act as agents.

ADDRESS Trans-Exim, 45 Suvorova street, Kaliningrad, Russia.

TELEPHONE Administration and Reservations + 7 4012 66 04 68.

FAX Administration and Reservations + 7 4012 66 04 69.

INTERNET Email ferrytransexim.ru **Website** www.transexim.ru/eng *(English, Russian)*

ROUTE OPERATED Ust Luga (Russia) - Baltiysk (Kaliningrad, Russia) - Sassnitz (Germany) (*PETERSBURG*; 1 per week).

1	PETERSBURG	25353t	86	16.0k	190.8m	144P	329C	110T	A2	RU	8311883

PETERSBURG Built Mathias Thesen Werft, Wismar, East Germany as the MUKRAN for *DSR* of Germany (DDR) to operate between Mukran (Sassnitz) and Klaipėda, a joint service with *Lisco* of Lithuania. In 1994 the service was taken over by *Euroseabridge*. In 1995 she was rebuilt to introduce road vehicle and additional passenger capacity and was renamed the PETERSBURG. In 2001 she was transferred to the Kiel - Klaipėda service, replacing the sister vessel GREIFSWALD whose charter was ended. In April 2003, the service became part of *Scandlines* and she was transferred to transferred to the Karlshamn - Liepaja (Latvia) route. In 2009, the charter ended and she returned to her owners. In October 2010 she was sold to *Baltic Fleet LLC* of Russia and the following month placed on a service between Baltiysk (Kaliningrad) and Ust Luga. In June 2012 she inaugurated a new service between Sassnitz and Ust Luga via Baltiysk.

SCANDLINES

THE COMPANY In 2007, the owners of *Scandlines AG*, the Danish Ministry of Transport and Energy and Deutsche Bahn AG, decided to sell their shares. The new owner was a consortium of the 3i Group, Allianz Capital Partners GmbH (40% of the shares each) and Deutsche Seereederei GmbH (20% of the shares). The company was subsequently transformed into a private limited company and now trades under the name Scandlines GmbH, uniting the companies *Scandlines Deutschland GmbH* and *Scandlines Danmark A/S*. With *Deutsche Seereederei GmbH* selling its shares in *Scandlines GmbH* in 2010, 3i and Allianz Capital Partners now hold 50% of the shares each. During 2012 *Stena Line* took over the Travemünde - Ventspils, Travemünde - Liepaja and Nynäshamn - Ventspils routes, took full control of the joint routes - Rostock - Trelleborg and Sassnitz - Trelleborg and took over the vessels used. The freight-only route between Rostock and Hanko passed to *SOL*. The Helsingborg - Helsingør service remains jointly operated with *Stena Line* and continues to be branded *Scandlines*.

MANAGEMENT CEO Søren Poulsgaard Jensen, **CCO** – Morten Haure-Petersen, **Business Development** Volker Schiemann.

TELEPHONE Administration *Denmark* + 45 33 15 15 15, *Germany* + 49 (0)381 5435899,

Reservations *Denmark* + 45 33 15 15 15, *Germany* + 49 (0)1802 116699.

FAX Administration *Denmark*, + 45 72 68 64 80, *Germany* + 49 (0)381 5435 678.

INTERNET Email info@scandlines.com **Website** www.scandlines.com *(Danish, German, English)*,

ROUTES OPERATED Helsingør (Sealand, Denmark) - Helsingborg (Sweden) (25 mins; *HAMLET, TYCHO BRAHE*; every 20 mins) (joint with *Scandlines AB* of Sweden), Rødby (Lolland, Denmark) - Puttgarden (Germany) (45 mins; *DEUTSCHLAND, HOLGER DANSKE, PRINS RICHARD, PRINSESSE BENEDIKTE, SCHLESWIG-HOLSTEIN (HOLGER DANSKE* specially for dangerous goods); half-hourly train/vehicle ferry + additional road freight-only sailings), Gedser (Falster, Denmark) - Rostock (Germany) (2 hours; *KRONPRINS FREDERIK, PRINS JOACHIM*; every 2 hours.

1	DEUTSCHLAND	15187t	97	18.5k	142.0m	1200P	364C	30Lr	BA2	DE	9151541
2	HAMLET	10067t	97	13.5k	111.2m	1000P	244C	34L	BA	DK	9150030

Princess Maria (*Miles Cowsill*)

Norrona (*Smyril Line*)

3F	HOLGER DANSKE	2779t	76	14.9k	86.8m	12P	-	12L	BA	DK	7432202
4	KRONPRINS FREDERIK	16071t	81	20.5k	152.0m	1082P	210C	46T	BA	DK	7803205
5	PRINS JOACHIM	16071t	80	21.0k	152.0m	922P	210c	46Lr	BA	DK	7803190
6	PRINS RICHARD	14822t	97	18.5k	142.0m	1100P	364C	36Lr	BA2	DK	9144419
7	PRINSESSE BENEDIKTE	14822t	97	18.5k	142.0m	1100P	364C	36Lr	BA2	DK	9144421
8	SCHLESWIG-HOLSTEIN	15187t	97	18.5k	142.0m	1200P	364C	30Lr	BA2	DE	9151539
9	TYCHO BRAHE	11148t	91	14.5k	111.2m	1250P	240C	35Lr	BA	DK	9007116

DEUTSCHLAND Train/vehicle ferry built by Van der Giessen-de Noord, Krimpen aan den IJssel, Rotterdam, The Netherlands for DFO for the Puttgarden - Rødby service. During Winter 2003/04 a new hoistable deck was added for cars by Neptun Yard Rostock, (Germany).

HAMLET Road vehicle ferry built by Finnyards, Rauma, Finland for Scandlines (50% owned by Scandlines AG and 50% owned by Scandlines AB of Sweden) for the Helsingør - Helsingborg service. Sister vessel of the TYCHO BRAHE but without rail tracks.

HOLGER DANSKE Built by Aalborg Værft A/S, Aalborg, Denmark as a train/vehicle ferry for DSB for the Helsingør - Helsingborg service. In 1991 transferred to the Kalundborg - Samsø route (no rail facilities). In 1997 transferred to subsidiary SFDS A/S. Withdrawn at the end of November 1998 when the service passed to Samsø Linien. In 1999 began operating between Rødby and Puttgarden as a road-freight-only vessel, carrying, among others, loads which cannot be conveyed on passenger vessels.

KRONPRINS FREDERIK Train/vehicle ferry built by Nakskov Skibsværft A/S, Nakskov, Denmark for DSB for the Nyborg - Korsør service. Withdrawn in 1997. After conversion to a car/lorry ferry, she was transferred to the Gedser - Rostock route (no rail facilities).

PRINS JOACHIM Train/vehicle ferry, built by Nakskov Skibsværft A/S, Nakskov, Denmark for DSB for the Nyborg - Korsør service. Withdrawn in 1997 and laid up. During Winter 2000/2001 modified in the same way as KRONPRINS FREDERIK and transferred to the Gedser - Rostock route.

PRINS RICHARD, PRINSESSE BENEDIKTE Train/vehicle ferries, built by Ørskov Christensen Staalskibsværft A/S, Frederikshavn, Denmark for Scandlines A/S for the Rødby - Puttgarden service. During Winter 2003/04 a new hoistable deck was added for cars by Neptun Yard Rostock, (Germany).

SCHLESWIG-HOLSTEIN Train/vehicle ferry built by Van der Giessen-de Noord, Krimpen aan den IJssel, Rotterdam, The Netherlands for DFO for the Puttgarden - Rødby service. During Winter 2003/04 a new hoistable deck was added for cars by Neptun Yard Rostock, (Germany).

TYCHO BRAHE Train/vehicle ferry, built by Tangen Verft A/S, Tomrefjord, Norway for DSB for the Helsingør - Helsingborg service.

SMYRIL LINE

THE COMPANY Smyril Line is a Faroe Islands company.

MANAGEMENT Adm. Director Mr. Rúni Vang Poulsen, Accounting and Department Manager, Ms. Nina Djurhuus.

ADDRESS Yviri við Strond 1, PO Box 370, 110 Tórshavn, Faroe Islands.

TELEPHONE Administration & Reservations + 298-345900.

FAX + 298-345901.

INTERNET Email office@smyrilline.com Website www.smyrilline.com (English, Danish, Faroese, German, Icelandic)

ROUTES OPERATED Winter/Early Spring Tórshavn (Faroes) - Hirtshals (Denmark) (36 hrs; NORRÖNA; 1 per week), Spring/Early Summer/Autumn Tórshavn - Hirtshals (36 hrs; NORRÖNA; 1 per week), Tórshavn - Seyðisfjördur (Iceland) (19 hrs; NORRÖNA; 1 per week), Summer Tórshavn -

Hirtshals (Denmark) (30 hrs; *NORRÖNA*; 2 per week), Tórshavn - Seyðisfjördur (Iceland) (19 hrs; *NORRÖNA*; 2 per week).

1	NORRÖNA	35966t	03	21.0k	164.0m	1482P	800C	134T	BA	FO	9227390

NORRÖNA Built by Flender Werft, Lübeck, Germany for *Smyril Line*, to replace the existing NORRÖNA. Originally due to enter service in Summer 2002, start of building was delayed by financing difficulties. She was to have been built at Flensburger Schiffbau-Gesellschaft, Flensburg, Germany, but delays in arranging finance led to change of shipyard.

ST. PETER LINE

THE COMPANY *St. Peter Line* is a Russian owned, EU registered private sector company.

MANAGEMENT CEO Andrey Mushkarev.

ADDRESS 1, ul. Karavannaya, St Petersburg, Russia.

TELEPHONE *Russia* +7 812 702-07-77, *Finland* +358 (0)9 6187 2000.

FAX *Russia* +7 812 322-66-99, *Finland* +358 10 3467 801.

INTERNET Email sales@stpeterline.ru Website www.stpeterline.ru *(Russian, English, Finnish, Swedish)*

ROUTES OPERATED Helsinki (Finland) - St Petersburg (Russia) (12 hours 30 mins; *PRINCESS MARIA*; 3/4 per week), St Petersburg - Helsinki - Stockholm - Tallinn - St Petersburg; *SPL PRINCESS ANASTASIA*; 1/2 per week).

1	PRINCESS MARIA	34093t	81	20.0k	168.1m	1638P	360C	54T	A	MT	7911533
2	SPL PRINCESS ANASTASIA	37583t	86	22.0k	177.0m	2500P	380C	42L	BA	MT	8414582

PRINCESS MARIA Built as the FINLANDIA by Oy Wärtsilä Ab, Turku, Finland for *EFFOA* of Finland for *Silja Line* services between Helsinki and Stockholm. In 1990 she was sold to *DFDS*, renamed the QUEEN OF SCANDINAVIA and introduced onto the Copenhagen - Helsingborg - Oslo service. In 2000 rebuilt at Gdynia. In 2001 transferred to the Newcastle - IJmuiden route. In May 2007 moved to the Newcastle - Norway route. This service ended at the end of August 2008 and she was laid up. In 2009 used for ten weeks as an accommodation vessel at Oskarshamn and in December in Copenhagen. In April 2010 time chartered to *Inflot Cruise and Ferry Ltd* of Russia for three years for use by *St. Peter Line* and in renamed the PRINCESS MARIA.

SPL PRINCESS ANASTASIA Built as the OLYMPIA by Oy Wärtsilä Ab, Turku, Finland for *Rederi AB Slite* of Sweden for *Viking Line* service between Stockholm and Helsinki. In 1993 she was chartered to *P&O European Ferries* to inaugurate a new service between Portsmouth and Bilbao. Renamed the PRIDE OF BILBAO. During the summer period she also operated, at weekends, a round trip between Portsmouth and Cherbourg. In 1994 she was purchased by the *Irish Continental Group* and re-registered in the Bahamas. *P&O* have since entered her into the British bareboat register. In 2002 her charter was extended for a further five years and again for a further three years from October 2007. The Cherbourg service ended at the end of 2004. In September 2010 redelivered to *Irish Continental Group*. In October 2010 renamed the BILBAO. In November 2010 chartered to *St. Peter Line*, in February 2011 renamed the SPL PRINCESS ANASTASIA and in April 2011 inaugurated a new Stockholm - St Petersburg service. In February 2011 purchased by an associated company of *St. Peter Line*.

STENA LINE

THE COMPANY *Stena Line Scandinavia AB* is a Swedish private sector company. During 2012, the operations of subsidiary *Scandlines AB* of Sweden were absorbed and some of the Baltic operations and vessels of *Scandlines GmbH* of Germany were taken over.

MANAGEMENT CEO Carl-Johan Hagman, Ship Management Director Bjarne Koitrand, Area Director Scandinavia Fredrik Lantz, Director Group Business Development Peter Arvidsson, Financial Director Ola Helgesson, Communication Director Joakim Kenndal.

ADDRESS 405 19 Gothenburg, Sweden (*Visitors' address* Danmarksterminalen, Masthuggskajen, Gothenburg, Sweden).

TELEPHONE Administration + 46 (0)31-85 80 00, Reservations + 46 (0)31-704 00 00.

FAX Administration & Reservations + 46 (0)31-24 10 38.

INTERNET Email info@stenaline.com Website www.stenaline.com (*Danish, Dutch, English, French, German, Norwegian, Polish, Swedish*).

ROUTES OPERATED *Stena Line branded routes* Conventional Ferries Gothenburg (Sweden) - Frederikshavn (Denmark) (3 hrs 15 mins; *STENA DANICA, STENA JUTLANDICA*; up to 6 per day), Gothenburg - Kiel (Germany) (14 hrs; *STENA GERMANICA, STENA SCANDINAVICA*; 1 per day), Frederikshavn - Oslo (Norway) (8 hrs 45 mins; *STENA SAGA*; 1 per day), Varberg (Sweden) - Grenaa (Denmark) (4 hrs; *STENA NAUTICA*; 2 per day), Karlskrona (Sweden) - Gdynia (Poland) (10 hrs 30 mins; *STENA ALEGRA, STENA SPIRIT, STENA VISION*; 2 per day), Rostock (Germany) - Trelleborg (Sweden) (5 hrs 45 mins (7 hrs night); *MECKLENBURG-VORPOMMERN, SKÅNE*; 3 per day)), Sassnitz (Germany) - Trelleborg (3 hrs 45 mins; *SASSNITZ, TRELLEBORG*; 4-5 per day), Travemünde (Germany) - Ventspils (Latvia) (28 hrs 30 mins; *STENA FLAVIA*; 2 per week), Travemünde (Germany) - Liepaja (Latvia) (28 hrs 30 mins; *ASK, URD*; 4 per week), Nynäshamn (Sweden) – Ventspils (Latvia) (12 hrs; *SCOTTISH VIKING*; 5 per week). Fast Ferry Gothenburg - Frederikshavn (2 hrs; *STENA CARISMA*; 4 per day). Freight Ferry Gothenburg - Frederikshavn (Train Ferry) (3 hrs 45 mins; *STENA SCANRAIL*; 2 per day).

Scandlines branded route (joint with Scandlines) Helsingør (Sealand, Denmark) - Helsingborg (Sweden) (25 mins; *AURORA AF HELSINGBORG, HAMLET, MERCANDIA IV*; up to every 15 mins).

1	ASK	13144t	82	18.0k	171.0m	186P	-	104T	AS	DK	7826867
2	AURORA AF HELSINGBORG	10918t	92	14.0k	111.2m	1250P	225C	25Lr	BA	SE	9007128
3	MECKLENBURG-VORPOMMERN	36185t	96	22.0k	199.9m	600P	445C	230Tr	A2	DE	9131797
4	MERCANDIA IV	4296t	89	13.0k	95.0m	420P	170C	18L	BA	DK	8611685
5	MERCANDIA VIII	4296t	87	13.0k	95.0m	420P	170C	18L	BA	DK	8611623
6	SASSNITZ	21154t	89	18.5k	171.5m	875P	314C	50Tr	BA2	DE	8705383
7	SCOTTISH VIKING	26500t	09	24.0k	186.5m	800P	185C	120L	A	IT	9435454
8	SKÅNE	42705t	98	21.0k	200.2m	600P	520C	240Tr	AS2	SE	9133915
9	STENA ALEGRA	22152t	98	22.5k	180.0m	250P	-	144T	BA	UK	9147291
10	STENA CARISMA	8631t	97	40.0k	88.0m	900P	210C	-	A	SE	9127760
11	STENA DANICA	28727t	83	19.5k	154.9m	2274P	555C	120T	BAS2	SE	7907245
12	STENA FLAVIA	26904t	08	24.0k	186.5m	852P	185C	120L	A	UK	9417919
13	STENA GERMANICA	44372t	01	22.0k	240.1m	900P	-	250L	BA	SE	9145176
14	STENA JUTLANDICA	29691t	96	21.5k	183.7m	1500P	550C	156T	BAS2	SE	9125944
15	STENA NAUTICA	19504t	86	19.4k	134.0m	700P	330C	70T	BA2	SE	8317954
16	STENA SAGA	33750t	81	22.0k	166.1m	2000P	510C	76T	BA	SE	7911545
17	STENA SCANDINAVICA	55050t	03	22.0k	240.1m	900P	-	260L	BA	SE	9235517
18	STENA SCANRAIL	7504t	73	16.5k	142.4m	65P	-	64Tr	A	SE	7305772
19	STENA SPIRIT	39169t	88	20.0k	175.4m	2400P	550C	120T	BAS2	BS	7907661

Stena Jutlandica (*Miles Cowsill*)

Stena Danica (*Miles Cowsill*)

20	STENA VISION	39178t	87	20.0k	175.4m	2400P	550C	120T	BAS2 SE	7907659
21	TRELLEBORG	20028t	82	21.0k	170.2m	900P	200C	90Tr	A2 SE	7925297
22	URD	13144t	81	17.5k	171.0m	186P	-	104T	AS DK	7826855

ASK Built as the LUCKY RIDER by Nuovi Cantieri Apuania S.P.A., Marina De Carrara, Italy, a ro-ro freight ferry, for *Delpa Maritime* of Greece. In 1985 she was acquired by *Stena Line* and renamed the STENA DRIVER. Later that year she was acquired by *Sealink British Ferries* and renamed the SEAFREIGHT FREEWAY to operate freight-only services between Dover and Dunkerque. In 1988 she was sold to *SOMAT* of Bulgaria for use on *Medlink* services in the Mediterranean and renamed the SERDICA. In 1990 she was sold and renamed the NORTHERN HUNTER. In 1991 she was sold to *Blæsbjerg* of Denmark, renamed the ARKA MARINE and chartered to *DSB*. She was then converted into a ro-pax vessel, renamed the ASK and introduced onto the Århus - Kalundborg service. Purchased by *Scandlines A/S* of Denmark in 1997. In 1999 she was, after some modification, transferred to *Scandlines Euroseabridge* and placed on the Travemünde - Klaipéda route. In 2000 she was transferred to the Rostock - Liepaja route. Lengthened by 20m in 2001 and, in late 2001, chartered to *Nordö Link* to operate between Travemünde and Malmö. In late 2002 replaced by the FINNARROW and returned to *Scandlines*. She was transferred to the Rostock - Trelleborg route whilst the MECKLENBURG-VORPOMMERN was being rebuilt. She was then transferred to the Kiel - Klaipéda route. In 2003 chartered to *Scandlines AB* to operate on the Trelleborg - Travemünde route. In April 2005 the charter ended and she returned to *Scandlines AG*. Initially she was due to replace the FELLOW on the Nynäshamn – Ventspils route during her annual refit. In Autumn 2005 moved to the Rostock - Ventspils route. In January 2009 moved to the Nynäshamn – Ventspils route. In January 2011 moved to the Travemünde - Liepaja route. In May 2011 laid up. In November introduced as second vessel. In September 2013 sold to *Stena Line*.

AURORA AF HELSINGBORG Train/vehicle ferry built by Langsten Verft A/S, Tomrefjord, Norway for *SweFerry* for *ScandLines* joint *DSB/SweFerry* service between Helsingør and Helsingborg. Now owned by *Scandlines AB* (subsidiary of *Stena Line*) (previously leased from finance company).

MECKLENBURG-VORPOMMERN Train/vehicle ferry built by Schichau Seebeckwerft, Bremerhaven, Germany for *DFO* for the Rostock - Trelleborg service. During Winter 2002/03 modified to increase freight capacity and reduce passenger capacity. In September 2013 sold to *Stena Line*.

MERCANDIA IV Built as the SUPERFLEX NOVEMBER by North East Shipbuilders Ltd, Sunderland, UK for *Vognmandsruten* of Denmark. In 1989 sold to *Mercandia* and renamed the MERCANDIA IV. In 1990 she began operating on their *Kattegatbroen* Juelsminde - Kalundborg service. In 1996 she was transferred to their *Sundbroen* Helsingør - Helsingborg service. In 1997 the service and vessel were leased to *HH-Ferries*. In 1999 she was purchased by *HH-Ferries*. She has been equipped to carry dangerous cargo.

MERCANDIA VIII Built as the SUPERFLEX BRAVO by North East Shipbuilders Ltd, Sunderland, UK for *Vognmandsruten* of Denmark and used on their services between Nyborg and Korsør and Copenhagen (Tuborg Havn) and Landskrona (Sweden). In 1991 she was chartered to *Scarlett Line* to operate on the Copenhagen and Landskrona route. In 1993 she was renamed the SVEA SCARLETT but later in the year the service ceased and she was laid up. In 1996 she was purchased by *Mercandia*, renamed the MERCANDIA VIII and placed on their *Sundbroen* Helsingør - Helsingborg service. In 1997 the service and vessel were leased to *HH-Ferries*. In 1999 she was purchased by *HH-Ferries*. Now reserve vessel.

SASSNITZ Train/vehicle ferry built by Danyard A/S, Frederikshavn, Denmark for *Deutsche Reichsbahn*. In 1993 ownership transferred to *DFO*. Used on the Sassnitz - Trelleborg service. In September 2013 sold to *Stena Line*.

SCOTTISH VIKING Built by CN Visentini, Porto Viro, Italy for *Epic Shipping* of the UK and chartered to *Norfolkline*. Operated between Zeebrugge and Rosyth until December 2010. In January 2010 chartered to *Scandlines* and placed on the Nynäshamn-Ventspils service. In September 2013 charter transferred to *Stena Line*.

SKÅNE Train/vehicle ferry built by Astilleros Españoles, Cadiz, Spain for an American trust and chartered to *Scandlines*. She is used on the Trelleborg - Rostock service.

STENA ALEGRA Built as the DAWN MERCHANT by Astilleros Españoles SA, Seville, Spain for parent company Cenargo and chartered to Merchant Ferries. On delivery in autumn 1998, chartered to UND RoRo Isletmeri of Turkey to operate between Istanbul and Trieste. Returned to Merchant Ferries in late 1998 and in February 1999, inaugurated a new service between Liverpool and Dublin. In April 2002 chartered to Norfolkline and operated on the Liverpool - Dublin route. In October transferred the Dunkerque - Dover service. In October 2005 briefly returned to the Liverpool - Dublin route before being sold to Daybreak Shipping of the UK and renamed the EUROPAX APPIA. In 2006 chartered to Balearia of Spain and renamed the PAU CASALS. Operated between Valencia - Palma de Majorca. In 2008 chartered to Caronte & Tourist of Italy and operated between Messina - Salerno. After a period of lay-up she was chartered to Ave Trans Group, renamed the AVE LUEBECK and in January 2009 left for Travemünde. However, during the course of her voyage orders were changed and she spent several weeks laid up off Sheerness UK and Cuxhaven, Germany before returning to the Mediterranean where, in April, she was chartered to T-Link Line of Italy. She was renamed the T REX and operated between Genoa Voltri (Italy) and Termini Imerese (Sicily). In December 2099 she was chartered to CoTuNav of Tunisia. In April 2010 she was chartered to Norfolkline to cover for refits of their Liverpool based ships. In May 2010 she was chartered to LD Lines to operate between Dover and Boulogne and renamed the NORMAN TRADER. This service ended in September 2010. Since then she has been chartered back to LD Lines to cover for refits and also to P&O Ferries to operate provide refit cover on the Irish Sea. In April 2013 sold to Stena RoRo. In May renamed the STENA ALEGRA. In July 2013 chartered to Stena Line and placed on the Karlskrona - Gdynia route.

STENA CARISMA Westamarin HSS 900 craft built at Kristiansand, Norway for Stena Line for the Gothenburg - Frederikshavn service. Work on a sister vessel, approximately 30% completed, was ceased.

STENA DANICA Built by Chantiers du Nord et de la Méditerranée, Dunkerque, France for Stena Line for the Gothenburg - Frederikshavn service.

STENA FLAVIA Built by CN Visentini, Porto Viro, Italy for Epic Shipping of the UK. Launched as the WATLING STREET. On delivery, chartered to ISCOMAR of Spain and renamed the PILAR DEL MAR. In 2009 laid up until February 2010 when she was chartered to Acciona Trasmediterranea of Spain and operated between Barcelona and Tangiers. Later that month, chartered to T-Link and renamed the name WATLING STREET. In May 2011 chartered to Scandlines and placed on the Travemünde - Ventspils service. In April 2012, sold to Stena RoRo; she continued to be chartered to Scandlines. In September 2013 charter transferred to Stena Line. In April 2013 renamed the STENA FLAVIA.

STENA GERMANICA Ro-pax ferry built as the STENA HOLLANDICA by Astilleros Españoles, Cadiz, Spain for Stena RoRo and chartered to Stena Line BV to operate between Hook of Holland and Harwich. In 2007 lengthened by 50m at Lloyd Werft, Bremerhaven and passenger capacity increased to 900. Between May and August 2010 refurbished at Gdansk and had an 100 additional cabins added. At the end of August entered service on the Gothenburg - Kiel route, renamed the STENA GERMANICA III. In September, after the previous STENA GERMANICA had been renamed the STENA VISION, she was renamed the STENA GERMANICA.

STENA JUTLANDICA Train/vehicle 'ro-pax' vessel built by Van der Giessen-de Noord, Krimpen aan den IJssel, Rotterdam, The Netherlands for Stena Line to operate between Gothenburg and Frederikshavn. She was launched as the STENA JUTLANDICA III and renamed on entry into service.

STENA NAUTICA Built as the NIELS KLIM by Nakskov Skibsværft A/S, Nakskov, Denmark for DSB (Danish State Railways) for their service between Århus (Jutland) and Kalundborg (Sealand). In 1990 she was purchased by Stena Rederi of Sweden and renamed the STENA NAUTICA. In 1992 she was chartered to B&I Line, renamed the ISLE OF INNISFREE and introduced onto the Rosslare - Pembroke Dock service, replacing the MUNSTER (8093t, 1970). In 1993 she was transferred to the Dublin - Holyhead service. In early 1995 she was chartered to Lion Ferry. She was renamed the LION KING. In 1996 she was replaced by a new LION KING and renamed the STENA NAUTICA. During Summer 1996 she was chartered to Trasmediterranea of Spain but returned to Stena RoRo in the autumn and remained laid up during 1997. In December 1997 she was chartered to Stena Line and placed on the Halmstad - Grenaa route. This route ended on 31st January 1999 and she was transferred to the Varberg - Grenaa route. During Winter 2001/02 she was rebuilt to heighten the upper vehicle deck and allow separate loading of vehicle decks; passenger capacity was reduced. On 16th February 2004

Stena Flavia (*Sebastian Ziehl*)

Stena Saga (*John Bryant*)

she was hit by the coaster JOANNA and holed. Returned to service at the end of May 2004 after repairs at Gothenburg and Gdansk.

STENA SAGA Built as the SILVIA REGINA by Oy Wärtsilä Ab, Turku, Finland for *Stockholms Rederi AB Svea* of Sweden. She was registered with subsidiary company *Svea Line* of Turku, Finland and was used on *Silja Line* services between Stockholm and Helsinki. In 1981 she was sold to *Johnson Line* and in 1984 sold to a Finnish Bank and chartered back. In 1990 she was purchased by *Stena RoRo* of Sweden for delivery in 1991. In 1991 she was renamed the STENA BRITANNICA and took up service on the Hook of Holland - Harwich service for Dutch subsidiary *Stena Line BV*, operating with a British crew. In 1994 she was transferred to the Oslo - Frederikshavn route and renamed the STENA SAGA. During Winter 2002/03 rebuilt to increase passenger capacity by 200.

STENA SCANDINAVICA Ro-pax vessel built by Hyundai Heavy Industries, Ulsan, South Korea, for *Stena RoRo*. Launched and delivered in January 2003 as the STENA BRITANNICA II. Chartered to *Stena Line* for use on the Hook of Holland - Harwich service, replacing the 2000-built STENA BRITANNICA, now the FINNFELLOW of *FinnLink*. In March 2003 renamed the STENA BRITANNICA. In 2007 lengthened at Lloyd Werft, Bremerhaven. In September 2010 renamed the BRITANNICA. Between October 2010 and April 2011 refurbished and had 100 additional cabins added at Gdansk. In April 2011 renamed the STENA SCANDINAVICA IV and entered service on the Gothenburg - Kiel route. In May, after the previous STENA SCANDINAVICA had been renamed the STENA SPIRIT, she was renamed the STENA SCANDINAVICA.

STENA SCANRAIL Built by Van der Giessen-de Noord, Krimpen aan den IJssel, Rotterdam, The Netherlands. Launched as the STENA SEATRADER for *Stena AB* and entered service as the SEATRADER. In 1976 she was lengthened and then demise-chartered to *Bahjah Navigation* of Cyprus and renamed the BAHJAN. In 1981 the charter ended and she was renamed the STENA SEARIDER. In 1983 chartered to *Snowdrop Shipping* of Cyprus and renamed the SEARIDER. The charter ended the following year and she resumed the name STENA SEARIDER. Later in 1984 she was renamed the TRUCKER and in 1985 again reverted to the name STENA SEARIDER. In 1987 she was converted to a train ferry to operate between Gothenburg and Frederikshavn, chartered to *Stena Line* and renamed the STENA SCANRAIL.

STENA SPIRIT Built as the STENA SCANDINAVICA by Stocznia i Komuni Paryski, Gdynia, Poland for *Stena Line* for the Gothenburg - Kiel service (launched as the STENA GERMANICA and names swapped with sister vessel before delivery). There were originally intended to be four vessels. Only two were delivered to *Stena Line*. The third (due to be called the STENA POLONICA) was sold by the builders as an unfinished hull to *Fred. Olsen Lines* of Norway and then resold to *ANEK* of Greece who had her completed at Perama and delivered as EL VENIZELOS for service between Greece and Italy. The fourth hull (due to be called the STENA BALTICA) was sold to *A Lelakis* of Greece and was to be rebuilt as a cruise ship to be called REGENT SKY; however, the project was never completed. The hull was broken up in 2004. During the summer period on some days, the vessel arriving in Gothenburg overnight from Kiel operates a round trip to Frederikshavn before departing for Kiel the following evening. During Winter 1998/99 she was modified to increase freight capacity and reduce the number of cabins. In April 2011 replaced by the former STENA BRITANNICA (renamed the STENA SCANDINAVICA IV) and entered CityVarvet in Gothenburg for refurbishment. In June 2011 she was renamed the STENA SPIRIT and, in July 2011, transferred to the Karlskrona - Gydnia route.

STENA VISION Built as the STENA GERMANICA by Stocznia im Lenina, Gdansk, Poland for *Stena Line* for the Gothenburg - Kiel service. During the summer period on some days, the vessel arriving in Gothenburg overnight from Kiel operates a round trip to Frederikshavn before departing for Kiel the following evening. During Winter 1998/99 modified to increase freight capacity and reduce the number of cabins. In August 2010 replaced by the former STENA HOLLANDICA (renamed the STENA GERMANICA III initially) and entered CityVarvet in Gothenburg for refurbishment. In September she was renamed the STENA VISION and, in November, transferred to the Karlskrona - Gydnia route.

TRELLEBORG Train/vehicle ferry built by Öresundsvarvet AB, Landskrona, Sweden for *Svelast* of Sweden (an SJ subsidiary). In 1990 ownership transferred to *SweFerry*. She is used on the Trelleborg - Sassnitz service.

URD Built as the EASY RIDER by Nouvi Cantieri Aquania SpA, Venice, Italy, a ro-ro freight ferry, for *Delpa Maritime* of Greece and used on Mediterranean services. In 1985 she was acquired by *Sealink British Ferries* and renamed the SEAFREIGHT HIGHWAY to operate a freight-only service between Dover and Dunkerque. In 1988 she was sold to *SOMAT* of Bulgaria for use on *Medlink* services in the Mediterranean and renamed the BOYANA. In 1990 she was sold to *Blæsbjerg* of Denmark, renamed the AKTIV MARINE and chartered to *DSB*. In 1991 she was converted into a ro-pax vessel, renamed the URD and introduced onto the Århus - Kalundborg service. Purchased by *Scandlines* in 1997. Withdrawn at the end of May 1999 and, after modification, transferred to the *Balticum Seaways* (later *Scandlines Balticum Seaways*) Århus - Aabenraa - Klaipėda route. In 2001 lengthened and moved to the Rostock - Liepaja route. In Autumn 2005 this route became Rostock - Ventspils. Withdrawn from Rostock - Ventspils in November 2009. Vessel inaugurated new service Travemünde - Ventspils in January 2010. Replaced by the WATLING STREET in May 2011 and moved to the Travemünde - Liepaja route. In October 2012 sold to *Sol Dru A/S* (a subsidiary of *Swedish Orient Line*) and chartered to *Stena Line*.

STRANDFARASKIP LANDSINS

THE COMPANY *Strandfaraskip Landsins* is owned by the Faroe Islands Government.

ADDRESS Sjógøta 5, Postboks 30 FO-810, Tvøroyri, Faroe Islands.

TELEPHONE Administration +298 34 30 30, Reservations +298 34 30 00.

FAX Administration & Reservations +298 34 30 01.

INTERNET Email ssl@ssl.fo Website www.ssl.fo *(Faroese)*.

ROUTES OPERATED Passenger and Car Ferries Tórshavn (Streymoy) - Tvøroyri (Suduroy) (1 hr 50 mins; *SMYRIL*; up to 2 per day), Klaksvík - Syðradali (20 min; *SAM*; up to 6 per day), Skopun – Gamlarætt (30 mins; *TEISTIN*; up to 9 per day). Passenger-only Ferries Sørvágur - Mykines (1 hr 15 mins; *SILJA STAR/FROYUR (chartered ships)*; up to 3 per day), Hvannasund - Svínoy (40 mins) - Kirkja (20 mins) - Hatlarvik (10 mins) - Svínoy (30 mins; *RITAN*; up to 4 per day), Sandur - Skúvoy (35 mins; *SILDBERIN*; up to 5 per day), Tórshavn - Nólsoy (25 mins; *TERNAN*; up to 5 per day).

1p	RITAN	81t	71	10.5k	22.1m	125P	0C	0L	-	FO	
2	SAM	217t	75	9.7k	30.2m	115P	17C	-	A	FO	7602168
3p	SILDBERIN	34t	79	7.5k	11.2m	30P	0C	0L	-	FO	
4	SMYRIL	12670t	05	21.0k	135.0m	976P	200C	32L	A	FO	9275218
5p	SÚLAN	11t	87	-	12.0m	40P	0C	0L	-	FO	
6	TEISTIN	1260t	01	11.0k	45.0m	288P	33C	2L	BA	FO	9226102
7	TERNAN	927t	80	12.0k	39.7m	319P	0C	0L	BA	FO	7947154

RITAN Built by Monnickenda, Volendam, The Netherlands. Used on the Hvannasund – Svínoy-Kirkja- Hattarvik service.

SAM Built by Blaalid Slip & Mek Verksted, Raudeberg, Norway. Used on the Klaksvik - Syðradali route and the Leirvik - Syðradali route.

SILDBERIN Built at Tvøroyri, Faroe Islands. Used on the Sandur - Skúvoy route.

SMYRIL Built by IZAR, San Fernando, Spain for *Strandfaraskip Landsins*. Operates on the Tórshavn – Tvøroyri service.

SÚLAN Built by Faaborg Værft A/S, Faaborg, Denmark. Used on the Sørvágur - Mykines service.

TEISTIN Built by P/F Skipasmidjan a Skala, Skala, Faroe Islands for *Strandfaraskip Landsins*. Used on the Skopun – Gamlarætt service.

TERNAN Built by Tórshavnar Skipasmidja P/f, Tórshavn, Faroe Islands for *Strandfaraskip Landsins*. Used on the Tórshavn –Nólsoy service.

TALLINK/SILJA LINE

THE COMPANY *AS Tallink Grupp* is an Estonian private sector company. *Tallink Silja Oy* is a Finnish subsidiary, *Tallink Silja AB* is a Swedish subsidiary.

MANAGEMENT *AS Tallink Grupp:* **Chairman of Management Board** Enn Pant, *Tallink Silja Oy* **Managing Director** Margus Schults, *Tallink Silja AB* **Managing Director** Kadri Land.

ADDRESSES *AS Tallink Grupp* Sadama 5/7, Tallinn 10111, Estonia, *Tallink Silja Oy* P.O. Box 43, 02151 Espoo, Finland, *Tallink Silja AB* Box 27295, 10253 Stockholm, Sweden.

TELEPHONE *AS Tallink Grupp* +372 (0)640 9800, *Tallink Silja Oy* Administration +358 (0)9 18041, Reservations +358 (0)600 15700 and +358 (0)600 15700, *Tallink Silja AB* Administration +46 (0)8 6663330, Reservations +46 (0)8 222140.

FAX *AS Tallink Grupp* Administration + 372 (0)640 9810, *Tallink Silja Oy* Administration +358 (0)9 1804633, *Tallink Silja AB* Administration +46 (0) 8 7823982.

INTERNET www.tallinksilja.com *(English, Danish, Estonian, Finnish, German, Latvia, Norwegian, Swedish, Russian),* www.tallink.com (corporate site).

ROUTES OPERATED **Tallink branded services** *Passenger Ferries* Helsinki - Tallinn: *Shuttle* (2 hrs; *STAR, SUPERSTAR*; 5 per day), *Cruise Ferry* (3 hrs 30 mins; *SILJA EUROPA*; 1 per day), Stockholm - Långnäs (Åland) - Tallinn (14 hrs; *BALTIC QUEEN, VICTORIA I*; daily), Stockholm - Riga (Latvia) (16 hrs; *ISABELLE, ROMANTIKA*; daily), *Freight-only Ferries* Kapellskär - Paldiski (9 hrs - 11 hrs; *REGAL STAR*, 1 per day), Stockholm (Sweden) - Långnäs (Åland) - Turku (Finland) (10 hrs 45 mins; *SEA WIND*; 1 per day).

Silja Line branded services Helsinki (Finland) - Mariehamn (Åland) - Stockholm (Sweden) (16 hrs; *SILJA SERENADE, SILJA SYMPHONY*; 1 per day), Turku (Finland) - Mariehamn (Åland) (day)/Långnäs (Åland) (night) - Stockholm (11 hrs; *BALTIC PRINCESS, GALAXY*; 2 per day).

1	ATLANTIC VISION	30285t	02	27.9k	203.3m	728P	695C	110L	BA2	CY	9211509
2	BALTIC PRINCESS	48300t	08	24.5k	212.0m	2800P	300C	82T	BA	EE	9354284
3	BALTIC QUEEN	48300t	09	24.5k	212.0m	2800P	300C	82T	BA	EE	9443255
4	GALAXY	48915t	06	22.0k	212.0m	2800P	300C	82T	BA	SE	9333694
5	ISABELLE	35154t	89	21.5k	170.9m	2420P	364C	30T	BA	LV	8700723
6F	REGAL STAR	15281t	00	17.5k	156.6m	100P	-	120T	A	EE	9087116
7	REGINA BALTICA	18345t	80	21.3k	145.2m	1450P	500C	68T	BA	LV	7827225
8	ROMANTIKA	40803t	02	22.0k	193.8m	2178P	300C	82T	BA	LV	9237589
9F	SEA WIND	15879t	72	17.5k	154.4m	260P	55C	88Tr	BAS	SE	7128332
10	SILJA EUROPA	59912t	93	21.5k	201.8m	3000P	400C	68T	BA	EE	8919805
11	SILJA FESTIVAL	34414t	85	22.0k	170.7m	2000P	400C	80T	BA	LV	8306498
12	SILJA SERENADE	58376t	90	21.0k	203.0m	2641P	450C	70T	BA	FI	8715259
13	SILJA SYMPHONY	58377t	91	21.0k	203.0m	2641P	450C	70T	BA	SE	8803769
14	STAR	36249t	07	27.5k	185.0m	1900P	450C	120L	BA	EE	9364722
15	SUPERSTAR	36000t	08	29.0k	175.0m	1800P	600C	140T	BA	EE	9365398
16	VICTORIA I	40975t	04	22.0k	193.8m	2500P	300C	823T	BA	EE	9281281

ATLANTIC VISION Built as the SUPERFAST IX by Howaldtswerke Deutsche Werft AG, Kiel, Germany for *Attica Enterprises* for use by *Superfast Ferries*. She operated between Rostock and Södertälje from January until April 2002. In May 2002 she began operating between Rosyth and Zeebrugge (with the SUPERFAST X). In 2004 fitted with additional cabins and conference/seating areas. In 2005 transferred to the Rostock – Hanko (later Helsinki) route. In 2006 sold to *Tallink*. In October 2008 chartered to *Marine Atlantic* of Canada to operate on the North Sydney-Port aux Basques service and renamed the ATLANTIC VISION.

BALTIC PRINCESS Built by Aker Yards, Helsinki. A large part of the hull was built at St Nazaire, France. In August 2008 replaced the GALAXY on the Tallinn - Helsinki route. In February 2013 transferred to the Stockholm - Turku service.

Baltic Queen (*Mike Louagie*)

Star (*Miles Cowsill*)

BALTIC QUEEN Built by STX Europe, Rauma, Finland. Operates between Stockholm and Tallinn.

GALAXY Built by Aker Yards, Rauma, Finland to operate as a cruise ferry on the Tallinn - Helsinki route. In July 2008 transferred to the Stockholm - Turku route and rebranded as a *Silja Line* vessel.

ISABELLE Built as the ISABELLA by Brodogradevna Industrija, Split, Yugoslavia for *SF Line*. Used on the *Viking Line* Stockholm - Naantali service until 1992 when she was switched to operating 24-hour cruises from Helsinki and in 1995 she was transferred to the Stockholm - Helsinki route. During 1996 she additionally operated day cruises to Muuga in Estonia during the 'layover' period in Helsinki. In 1997 she was transferred to the Stockholm - Turku route. In January 2013 she was replaced by the VIKING GRACE. After covering for the AMORELLA during her refit period she was laid up. In April 2013 sold to *Hansa Link Limited*, a subsidiary of *AS Tallink Grupp* and renamed the ISABELLE. In May placed on the Stockholm - Riga service, replacing the SILJA FESTIVAL.

REGAL STAR Partly built by Sudostroitelnyy Zavod Severnaya Verf, St Petersburg. Work started in 1993 (as a deep-sea ro-ro) but was never completed. In 1999 the vessel was purchased, taken to Palumba SpA, Naples and completed as a short-sea ro-ro with accommodation for 80 drivers. In 2000 she was delivered to *MCL* of Italy and placed on a route between Savona and Catania. In September of that year she was chartered by *Grimaldi Ferries* and operated on a route Salerno – Palermo – Valencia. In late 2003 she was sold to *Hansatee Shipping* of Estonia and, in 2004, placed on the Kapellskär – Paldiski route, replacing the KAPELLA. From February 2006 she was transferred to the Helsinki – Tallinn service, replacing the KAPELLA due to the hard ice conditions. She continued in this service for the summer, but the returned to the Paldiski – Kapellskär service. In June 2010 moved to the *SeaWind Line* Stockholm – Turku service for the summer seasons and returned to the Kapellskär - Paldiski route in the autumn.

REGINA BALTICA Built as the VIKING SONG by Oy Wärtsilä Ab, Turku, Finland for *Rederi AB Sally* of Finland and used on the *Viking Line* service between Stockholm and Helsinki. In 1985 replaced by the MARIELLA of SF Line and sold to Fred. Olsen Lines. She was named BRAEMAR and used on services between Norway and Britain as well as Norway and Denmark. Services to Britain ceased in June 1990 and she continued to operate between Norway and Denmark. She was withdrawn in 1991 and sold to *Rigorous Shipping* of Cyprus (a subsidiary of *Fred. Olsen Lines*). She was chartered to the *Baltic Shipping Company* of Russia, renamed the ANNA KARENINA and inaugurated a service between Kiel and St Petersburg. In 1992 a Nynäshamn call was introduced. In 1996 the service ceased and she was returned to her owners and renamed the ANNA K. Later in 1996 she was sold to *Empremare Shipping Co Ltd* of Cyprus (a company jointly owned by *Nordström & Thulin* and *Estonian Shipping Company*), chartered to *EstLine* and renamed the REGINA BALTICA. In 2000 the charter transferred to *Tallink*; she continued to operate between Stockholm and Tallinn. Purchased by *Tallink* in 2002. In May 2006 replaced by the ROMANTIKA and succeeded the FANTAASIA on the Stockholm - Riga service. In May 2009 replaced by the ROMANTIKA and laid up. In May 2010 chartered to *Acciona Trasmediterranea*, of Spain and operated between Almeria (Spain) and Nador (Morocco). In October 2011 returned to Tallinn and laid up. In February 2012 chartered to *Scira* of Norway to act as an accommodation vessel for the Sheringham Shoal Offshore Wind Farm off the North Norfolk coast.

ROMANTIKA Built by Aker Finnyards, Rauma, Finland for *Tallink Grupp* to operate for *Tallink* between Tallinn and Helsinki. In Spring 2006 moved to the Tallinn - Stockholm route. In May 2009 transferred to the Stockholm - Riga route.

SEA WIND Train/vehicle ferry built as the SVEALAND by Helsingørs Skipsværft, Helsingør, Denmark for *Stockholms Rederi AB Svea* and used on the *Trave Line* Helsingborg (Sweden) - Copenhagen (Tuborg Havn) - Travemünde freight service. In 1981 she was sold to *TT-Saga Line* and operated between Travemünde and Malmö. In 1984 she was rebuilt to increase capacity and renamed the SAGA WIND. In 1989 she was acquired by *SeaWind Line*, renamed the SEA WIND and inaugurated a combined rail freight, trailer and lower-priced passenger service between Stockholm and Turku. This route is now freight-only.

SILJA EUROPA Built by Jos L Meyer, Papenburg, Germany. Ordered by *Rederi AB Slite* of Sweden for *Viking Line* service between Stockholm and Helsinki and due to be called EUROPA. In 1993, shortly before delivery was due, *Rederi AB Slite* went into liquidation and the order was cancelled. A charter agreement with her builders was then signed by *Silja Line* and she was introduced onto the Stockholm

- Helsinki route as SILJA EUROPA. In early 1995 she was transferred to the Stockholm - Turku service. In January 2013 she was transferred to the Helsinki - Tallinn route.

SILJA FESTIVAL Built as the WELLAMO by Oy Wärtsilä Ab, Helsinki, Finland for *EFFOA* for the *Silja Line* Stockholm - Mariehamn - Turku service. In 1990, following the sale of the FINLANDIA to *DFDS*, she was transferred to the Stockholm - Helsinki service until the SILJA SERENADE was delivered later in the year. In 1991 she was renamed the SILJA FESTIVAL. During Winter 1991/92 she was extensively rebuilt and ownership was transferred to *Silja Line*. In 1993 she was transferred to the Malmö - Travemünde service of *Euroway*, which was at this time managed by *Silja Line*. This service ceased in 1994 and she was transferred to the Vaasa - Sundsvall service. In 1994 and 1995 she operated on this route during the peak summer period and on the Helsinki - Tallinn route during the rest of the year. The Vaasa - Sundsvall service did not operate in Summer 1996 and she continued to operate between Helsinki and Tallinn. In 1997 she was transferred to the Stockholm - Turku route replacing the SILJA SCANDINAVIA (see the GABRIELLA, *Viking Line*). In Autumn 2008 transferred to the Stockholm - Riga route and operated under the *Tallink* brand. In May 2013 replaced by the ISABELLE and laid up.

SILJA SERENADE, SILJA SYMPHONY Built by Masa-Yards Oy, Turku, Finland for *Silja Line* for the Stockholm - Helsinki service. In 1993, SILJA SERENADE was transferred to the Stockholm - Turku service but in early 1995 she was transferred back to the Helsinki route.

STAR Built by Aker Yards, Helsinki, Finland for *Tallink* to operate as a normal ferry on the Tallinn - Helsinki route, reducing the crossing time to 2 hours.

SUPERSTAR Built by Fincantieri-Cantieri Navali Italiani SpA, Riva Trigoso, Italy to operate on the Tallinn - Helsinki route from May 2008.

VICTORIA I Built by Aker Finnyards, Rauma, Finland for *Tallink*. Operates between Tallinn and Stockholm.

TESO

THE COMPANY *TESO* is a Dutch private company, with most shares owned by inhabitants of Texel. Its full name is *Texels Eigen Stoomboot Onderneming*.

MANAGEMENT **Managing Director** C H S de Waal.

ADDRESS Pontweg 1, 1797 SN Den Hoorn, Texel, The Netherlands.

TELEPHONE **Administration** + 31 (0)222 36 96 00, **Reservations** Not applicable.

FAX **Administration** + 31 (0)222 36 96 59.

INTERNET **Email** info@teso.nl **Website** www.teso.nl *(Dutch, English, German)*.

ROUTE OPERATED Den Helder (The Netherlands) - Texel (Dutch Frisian Islands) (20 minutes; *DOKTER WAGEMAKER, SCHULPENGAT*; hourly).

1	DOKTER WAGEMAKER	13256t	05	15.6k	130.0m	1750P	320C	44L	BA2	NL	9294070
2	SCHULPENGAT	8311t	90	13.6k	110.4m	1750P	156C	25L	BA2	NL	8802313

DOKTER WAGEMAKER Built at Galatz, Romania (hull and superstructure) and Royal Schelde, Vlissingen (fitting out) for *TESO*.

SCHULPENGAT Built by Verolme Scheepswerf Heusden BV, Heusden, The Netherlands for *TESO*.

TT-LINE

THE COMPANY *TT-Line GmbH & Co KG* is a German private sector company.

MANAGEMENT **Managing Directors** Hanns Heinrich Conzen & Jens Aurel Scharner, **Sales Manager** Dirk Lifke.

ADDRESS Zum Hafenplatz 1, 23570, Travemünde, Germany.

Galaxy (*Miles Cowsill*)

Sea Wind (*Miles Cowsill*)

TELEPHONE Administration *Travemünde* +49 (0)4502 801 452, *Rostock* +49 (0)381 6707911, Reservations *Travemünde* +49 (0)4502 801 81, *Rostock* +49 (0)381 670790.

FAX Administration & Reservations *Travemünde* +49 (0)4502 801 407, *Rostock* +49 (0)381 6707980.

INTERNET Email info@ttline.com Website www.ttline.com (*English, German, Swedish*).

ROUTES OPERATED *Passenger Ferries* Travemünde (Germany) - Trelleborg (Sweden) (8 hrs 30 mins/9 hrs 30 mins; *NILS HOLGERSSON, PETER PAN*; 2 per day). *Ro-pax Ferries* Travemünde (Germany) - Trelleborg (Sweden) (7 hrs 30 mins/8 hrs 15 mins; *NILS DACKE, ROBIN HOOD*; 2 per day), Rostock (Germany) - Trelleborg (Sweden) (5 hrs 30 mins/6 hrs 30 mins/7 hrs 30 mins; *HUCKLEBERRY FINN, TOM SAWYER*; 3 per day, *Freight Ferries* Travemünde - Helsingborg (Sweden) (10 hrs; *NILS DACKE, ROBIN HOOD*; 1 per week).

1	HUCKLEBERRY FINN	26391t	88	18.0k	177.2m	400P	280C	121T	BAS2 SE	8618358
2	NILS DACKE	26790t	95	18.5k	179.7m	317P	-	157T	BA SE	9087477
3	NILS HOLGERSSON	36468t	01	18.0k	190.8m	744P	-	171T	BAS2 DE	9217230
4	PETER PAN	36468t	01	18.0k	190.8m	744P	-	171T	BAS2 SE	9217242
5	ROBIN HOOD	26796t	95	18.5k	179.7m	300P	-	157T	BA DE	9087465
6	TOM SAWYER	26478t	89	18.0k	177.2m	400P	280C	121T	BAS2 DE	8703232

HUCKLEBERRY FINN Built as the NILS DACKE by Schichau Seebeckwerft AG, Bremerhaven, Germany, as a ro-pax vessel. During Summer 1993 rebuilt to transform her into a passenger/car ferry and renamed the PETER PAN, replacing a similarly named vessel (31356t, 1986). On arrival of the new PETER PAN in Autumn 2001 she was renamed the PETER PAN IV. She was then converted back to ro-pax format, renamed the HUCKLEBERRY FINN and, in early 2002, transferred to the Rostock -Trelleborg route.

NILS DACKE, ROBIN HOOD Ro-pax vessels built by Finnyards, Rauma, Finland for *TT-Line*. Primarily freight vessels but accompanied cars - especially camper vans and cars towing caravans - are conveyed. They operate on the Travemünde - Trelleborg and Travemünde - Helsingborg routes.

NILS HOLGERSSON, PETER PAN Built by SSW Fähr und Spezialschiffbau GmbH, Bremerhaven, Germany for *TT-Line* for the Travemünde - Trelleborg route.

TOM SAWYER Built as the ROBIN HOOD by Schichau Seebeckwerft AG, Bremerhaven, Germany, as a ro-pax vessel. During Winter 1992/93 rebuilt to transform her into a passenger/car ferry and renamed the NILS HOLGERSSON, replacing a similarly named vessel (31395t, 1987) which had been sold to *Brittany Ferries* and renamed the VAL DE LOIRE. In 2001 converted back to ro-pax format and renamed the TOM SAWYER. Transferred to the Rostock - Trelleborg route.

UNITY LINE

THE COMPANY *Unity Line* is a Polish company owned by *Polish Steamship Company (Polsteam)*. The operator manages seven ferries on two routes: Swinoujscie – Ystad and Swinoujscie – Trelleborg. Three ships are owned by *Euroafrica Shipping* which was previously a partner in the company; the ships continue to be operationally managed by to *Unity Line*.

MANAGEMENT Chairman of the Board Jarosław Kotarski.

ADDRESS Plac Rodla 8, 70-419 Szczecin, Poland.

TELEPHONE Administration +48 091 35 95 795, Reservations +48 091 35 95 600.

FAX Administration +48 (0)91 35 95 885.

INTERNET Email unity@unityline.pl Website www.unityline.pl (*Polish, English, Swedish*).

ROUTES OPERATED **Passenger Service** Swinoujscie (Poland) - Ystad (Sweden) (6 hrs 30 mins (day), 9 hrs (night); *POLONIA, SKANIA*; 2 per day). **Freight Services** Swinoujscie (Poland) - Ystad (Sweden) (8 hrs (day), 9 hrs (night); *JAN NIADECKI, KOPERNIK*; 2 per day), Swinoujscie (Poland) - Trelleborg (Sweden) (6 hrs 30 mins (day), 9 hrs (night); *GALILEUSZ, GRYF, WOLIN*; 3 per day).

Nils Holgersson (*FotoFlite*)

Skania (*John Bryant*)

1F+	GALILEUSZ	15848t	92	17.0k	150.4m	160P	-	115L	A	CY	9019078
2F+	GRYF	18653t	90	16.0k	158.0m	180P	-	125L	BA	BS	8818300
3F+	JAN SNIADECKI	14417t	88	17.0k	155.1m	57P	-	70Lr	SA2	CY	8604711
4F+	KOPERNIK	13788t	77	18.0k	160.1m	360P	-	60Lr	SA2	PL	7527887
5	POLONIA	29875t	95	17.2k	169.9m	920P	440C	145Lr	SA2	BS	9108350
6	SKANIA	23933t	95	22.5k	173.7m	1400P	430C	140L	BA	BS	9086588
7F+	WOLIN	22874t	86	17.5k	188.9m	370P	-	110Lr	SA	BS	8420842

GALILEUSZ Built as the VIA TIRRENO by Van der Giessen-de Noord, Krimpen aan den IJssel, The Netherlands for *Viamare di Navigazione SpA* of Italy. Initially operated between Voltri and Termini Imerese. In 1998 transferred to the Genoa - Termini Imerese route and in 2001 to the Genoa - Palermo route. In 2006 sold to *Euroafrica Shipping*, renamed the GALILEUSZ and in November introduced onto the *Unity Line* Swinoujscie - Ystad service. In February 2007 transferred to the new Swinoujscie - Trelleborg route.

GRYF Built as the KAPTAN BURHANETTIN ISIM by Fosen Mekaniske Verksteder, Fevag, Norway for *Turkish Cargo Lines* of Turkey to operate between Trieste (Italy) and Derince (Turkey). In 2002 chartered to *Latlines* to operate between Lübeck and Riga (Latvia). In 2003 chartered to *VentLines* to inaugurate a new service between Travemünde and Ventspils. In 2004 sold to *Polsteam*, managed by *Unity Line* and renamed the GRYF. Entered service in 2005. In February 2007 transferred to the new Swinoujscie - Trelleborg route.

JAN SNIADECKI Built by Falkenbergs Varv AB, Falkenberg, Sweden for *Polish Ocean Lines* to operate between Swinoujscie and Ystad. Now operates for *Unity Line* on this route.

KOPERNIK Train/vehicle ferry built as the ROSTOCK by Bergens Mekaniske Verksted A/S, Bergen, Norway for *Deutsche Reichsbahn* of Germany (DDR). Used on freight services between Trelleborg and Sassnitz. In 1992 modified to increase passenger capacity in order to run in passenger service. In 1993 ownership transferred to *DFO* and in 1994 she opened a new service from Rostock to Trelleborg. In 1997 she was used when winds precluded the use of the new MECKLENBURG-VORPOMMERN. Following modifications to this vessel in late 1997, the ROSTOCK continued to operate to provide additional capacity until the delivery of the SKÅNE of *Scandlines AB*, after which she was laid up. In 1999 she was sold to *SeaWind Line*, renamed the STAR WIND and operated in freight-only mode between Stockholm and Turku. Initial plans to bring her passenger accommodation up to the standards required for Baltic night service were dropped. In October 2002 replaced by the SKY WIND and transferred to the Helsinki - Tallinn route. She carried a limited number of ordinary passengers on some sailings. In May 2005 returned to the Stockholm - Turku service, no longer carrying ordinary passengers, but was laid up after a few weeks. In October sold to *Euro Shipping OÜ* of Estonia, a company linked to *Saaremaa Laevakompanii*, and renamed the VIRONIA. In 2006 inaugurated a new service between Sillamäe (Estonia) and Kotka (Finland). In 2007 sold to *Euroafrica Shipping*, renamed the KOPERNIK and, in April 2008, placed on the Swinoujscie - Ystad route, replacing the MIKOLAJ KOPERNIK.

POLONIA Train/vehicle ferry built by Langsten Slip & Båtbyggeri A/S, Tomrefjord, Norway for *Polonia Line Ltd* and managed by *Unity Line*.

SKANIA Built as the SUPERFAST I by Schichau Seebeckwerft, Bremerhaven, Germany for *Superfast Ferries* of Greece. Operated between Patras and Ancona (Italy). In 1998 transferred to the Patras - Igoumenitsa (Greece) - Bari (Italy) route. In 2004 sold to a subsidiary of *Grimaldi Lines*, renamed the EUROSTAR ROMA and placed on the Civitavecchia (Italy) - Barcelona (Spain) service. In 2008 sold to *Polsteam* and renamed the SKANIA. After modifications, she was placed on the *Unity Line* Swinoujscie - Ystad service as second passenger vessel. In during the peak summer period in 2010 will operate a round trip between Ystad and Rønne for *Bornholmstrafikken*.

WOLIN Train/vehicle ferry built as the ÖRESUND by Moss Rosenberg Værft, Moss, Norway for *Statens Järnvägar (Swedish State Railways)* for the 'DanLink' service between Helsingborg and Copenhagen. Has 817 metres of rail track. Service ceased in July 2000 and vessel laid up. In 2001 sold to *Sea Containers Ferries* and in 2002 converted at Gdansk, Poland to a passenger ferry. She was chartered to *SeaWind Line*, renamed the SKY WIND and in Autumn 2002 replaced the STAR WIND on the Stockholm - Turku service. In 2007 sold to *Polsteam*, renamed the WOLIN and placed on the *Unity Line* Swinoujscie - Trelleborg service.

VIKING LINE

THE COMPANY *Viking Line Abp* is a Finnish company Listed on the Helsinki Stock Exchange since 1995.

MANAGEMENT President & CEO Mikael Backman, Executive Vice President/Sales, Marketing & Products Pavlos Ylinen.

ADDRESS Norragatan 4, 22100 Mariehamn, Åland.

TELEPHONE Administration +358 (0)18 27000, Reservations +358 (0)9 1235300.

FAX Administration +358 (0)18 16944.

INTERNET Email international.sales@vikingline.com Websites www.vikingline.fi *(Finnish, English, Swedish)* www.vikingline.ee *(Estonian)* www.vikingline.de *(German)*.

ROUTES OPERATED Stockholm (Sweden) - Mariehamn (Åland) - Helsinki (Finland) (14 hrs; *GABRIELLA, MARIELLA*; 1 per day), Stockholm - Mariehamn (day)/Långnäs (Åland) (night) - Turku (Finland) (9 hrs 10 mins; *AMORELLA, VIKING GRACE*; 2 per day), Kapellskär (Sweden) - Mariehamn (Åland) (2 hrs 15 mins; *ROSELLA*; up to 3 per day), Helsinki - Tallinn (2 hrs 30 mins; *VIKING XPRS*; 2 per day), Cruises from Stockholm to Mariehamn (21 hrs - 24 hrs round trip (most 22 hrs 30 mins); *VIKING CINDERELLA*; 1 per day).

1	AMORELLA	34384t	88	21.5k	169.4m	2450P	450C	53T	BA	FI	8601915
2	GABRIELLA	35492t	92	21.5k	171.2m	2420P	400C	50T	BA	FI	8917601
3	MARIELLA	37799t	85	22.0k	176.9m	2500P	400C	60T	BA	FI	8320573
4	ROSELLA	16850t	80	21.3k	136.0m	1700P	340C	40T	BA	SE	7901265
5	VIKING CINDERELLA	46398t	89	21.5k	191.0m	2500P	100C	-	BA	SE	8719188
6	VIKING GRACE	57000t	13	23.0k	214.0m	2800P	556C	90L	BA	FI	9606900
7	VIKING XPRS	34000t	08	25.0k	185.0m	2500P	250C	60L	BA	SE	9375654

AMORELLA Built by Brodogradevna Industrija, Split, Yugoslavia for *SF Line* for the Stockholm - Mariehamn - Turku service.

GABRIELLA Built as the FRANS SUELL by Brodogradiliste "Split", Split, Croatia for *Sea-Link AB* of Sweden to operate for subsidiary company *Euroway AB*, who established a service between Lübeck, Travemünde and Malmö. In 1994 this service ceased and she was chartered to *Silja Line*, renamed the SILJA SCANDINAVIA and transferred to the Stockholm - Turku service. In 1997 she was sold to *Viking Line* to operate between Stockholm and Helsinki. She was renamed the GABRIELLA.

MARIELLA Built by Oy Wärtsilä Ab, Turku, Finland for *SF Line*. Used on the Stockholm - Helsinki service. During 1996 additionally operated short cruises to Muuga in Estonia during the 'layover' period in Helsinki.

ROSELLA Built by Oy Wärtsilä Ab, Turku, Finland for *SF Line*. Used mainly on the Stockholm - Turku and Kapellskär - Naantali services until 1997. From 1997 operated 21 to 24-hour cruises from Stockholm to Mariehamn under the marketing name 'The Dancing Queen', except in the peak summer period when she operated between Kapellskär and Turku. In Autumn 2003 transferred to a new twice-daily Helsinki - Tallinn ferry service. In May 2008 placed on the Mariehamn - Kapellskär route under the Swedish flag. In 2011 she was extensively rebuilt at Balti Laevaremondi Tehas in Tallinn, Estonia. Cabin capacity was lowered from 1184 to 418 and the restaurant and shop areas were increased.

VIKING CINDERELLA Built as the CINDERELLA by Wärtsilä Marine Ab, Turku, Finland for *SF Line*. Until 1993 provided additional capacity between Stockholm and Helsinki and undertook weekend cruises from Helsinki. In 1993 she replaced the OLYMPIA (a sister vessel of the MARIELLA) as the main Stockholm - Helsinki vessel after the OLYMPIA had been chartered to *P&O European Ferries* and renamed the PRIDE OF BILBAO. In 1995 switched to operating 20-hour cruises from Helsinki to

Jan Sniadecki *(John Bryant)*

Viking Grace *(Mike Louagie)*

Estonia in the off peak and the Stockholm - Mariehamn - Turku service during the peak summer period (end of May to end of August). From 1997 she remained cruising throughout the year. In Autumn 2003 she was transferred to the Swedish flag, renamed the VIKING CINDERELLA and transferred to Stockholm - Mariehamn cruises. She operates these cruises all year round.

VIKING GRACE Built by STX Europe, Turku, Finland. She operates between Stockholm and Turku. She is powered by LNG. Entered service in January 2013.

VIKING XPRS Built by Aker Yards, Helsinki to operate between Helsinki and Tallinn.

WAGENBORG PASSAGIERSDIENSTEN

THE COMPANY Wagenborg Passagiersdiensten BV is a Dutch private sector company.

MANAGEMENT Managing Director G van Langen.

ADDRESS Postbus 70, 9163 ZM Nes, Ameland, The Netherlands.

TELEPHONE Administration & Reservations +31 (0)519 546111.

FAX Administration & Reservations +31 (0)519 542905.

INTERNET Email info@wpd.nl Website www.wpd.nl (Dutch, English, German)

ROUTES OPERATED Car Ferries Holwerd (The Netherlands) - Ameland (Frisian Islands) (45 minutes; OERD, SIER; up to 14 per day), Lauwersoog (The Netherlands) - Schiermonnikoog (Frisian Islands) (45 minutes; MONNIK, ROTTUM; up to 6 per day). Passenger Ferries (Summer only) Esonstad - Lauwersoog – Schiermonnikoog (1 hr; ESONBORG up to 5 per day).

1p	ESONBORG	98t	99	20.0k	30.5m	130P	0C	0L	-	NL	-
2	MONNIK	1121t	85	12.2k	58.0m	1000P	46C	9L	BA	NL	8408961
3	OERD	2286t	03	11.2k	73.2m	1200P	72C	22L	BA	NL	9269673
4	ROTTUM	1121t	85	12.2k	58.0m	1000P	46C	9L	BA	NL	8408959
5	SIER	2286t	95	11.2k	73.2m	1200P	72C	22L	BA	NL	9075761

ESONBORG River Runner 150 catamaran built as the AQUA-RUNNER by Damen Shipyards, Gorinchem, The Netherlands (under licence to NQEA Australia Pty Ltd) for the Doeksen Group of The Netherlands. Chartered to Aqualiner BV of The Netherlands. Operated between Damen and Gorinchem. In 2007 chartered to Wagenborg, renamed the ESONBORG and placed on the summer-only Esonstad - Lauwersoog – Schiermonnikoog route.

MONNIK Built by Scheepswerf Hoogezand, Hoogezand, The Netherlands for Wagenborg Passagiersdiensten BV as the OERD. In 2003, on delivery of the new OERD, she was renamed the MONNIK. Used on the Lauwersoog - Schiermonnikoog route.

OERD Built by Scheepswerf Bijlsma Lemmer, Lemmer, The Netherlands for Wagenborg Passagiersdiensten BV. Used on the Ameland - Holwerd route.

ROTTUM Built as the SIER by Scheepswerf Hoogezand, Hoogezand, The Netherlands for Wagenborg Passagiersdiensten BV and used on the Holwerd - Ameland route. In 1995 renamed the ROTTUM and transferred to the Lauwersoog - Schiermonnikoog route.

SIER Built by Shipyard Bijlsma, Wartena, The Netherlands for Wagenborg Passagiersdiensten BV. Used on the Ameland - Holwerd route.

WASALINE

THE COMPANY *Wasaline* is the trading name of *NLC Ferry Oy Ab*, a Finnish company, jointly owned by the cities of Vaasa and Umeå.

ADDRESS *Finland* Skeppsredaregatan 3, 65170 Vasa, Finland *Sweden* Blå Vägen 4, 91322 Holmsund, Sweden.

TELEPHONE Administration & Reservations *Finland* +358 (0)207 716 810, *Sweden* +46 (0)90 185 200.

FAX Administration & Reservations

INTERNET *Email* marketing@nlcferry.com *Website* www.wasaline.com *(English, Finnish, Swedish)*.

ROUTE OPERATED Vaasa (Finland) - Umeå (Sweden) (4 hrs; *WASA EXPRESS*; 1/2 per day).

1	WASA EXPRESS	17053t	81	17.0k	140.8m	1100P	450C	84T	BAS2 FI	8000226

WASA EXPRESS Built by Oy Wärtsilä AB, Helsinki, Finland as the TRAVEMÜNDE for *Gedser-Travemünde Ruten* of Denmark for their service between Gedser (Denmark) and Travemünde (Germany). In 1986 the company's trading name was changed to *GT Linien* and in 1987, following the takeover by *Sea-Link AB* of Sweden, it was further changed to *GT Link*. The vessel's name was changed to the TRAVEMÜNDE LINK. In 1988 she was purchased by *Rederi AB Gotland* of Sweden, although remaining in service with *GT Link*. Later in 1988 she was chartered to *Sally Ferries* and entered service in December on the Ramsgate - Dunkerque service. She was renamed the SALLY STAR. In 1997 she was transferred to *Silja Line*, to operate between Vaasa and Umeå during the summer period, and operated under the marketing name WASA EXPRESS (although not renamed). She returned to *Rederi AB Gotland* in Autumn 1997, was renamed the THJELVAR and entered service with *Destination Gotland* in January 1998. Withdrawn and laid up in December 2003. In 2004 chartered to *Color Line* to inaugurate a new service between Larvik and Hirtshals. Renamed the COLOR TRAVELLER. Operated in reduced passenger mode on this service but in summer peak period operated between Frederikshavn and Larvik in full passenger mode. In December 2006 returned to *Rederi AB Gotland*. In 2007 renamed the THJELVAR, chartered to *Scandlines* and placed on the Gedser – Rostock route. Renamed the ROSTOCK. In Autumn 2008 withdrawn and laid up. In June 2009 sub-chartered to *Comarit* of Morocco for two months. In September she resumed the name THJELVAR. In August 2008 she was chartered to *Fred. Olsen SA* of Spain, renamed the BETANCURIA and placed on the Las Palmas - Puerto del Rosario - Arrecife service. In September 2012 laid up. In October 2013 purchased by *NLC Ferry Oy Ab* and, in November, renamed the WASA EXPRESS. Entered service in January 2013.

Amorella and **Baltic Queen** (*Matthew Punter*)

Viking Cinderella (*Miles Cowsill*)

The following passenger vessels are, at the time of going to print, not operating and are owned by companies which do not currently operate services or are used on freight -only services. They are therefore available for possible re-deployment, either in the area covered by this book or elsewhere. Passenger vessels operating freight-only services outside the scope of this book are also included here. Exceptionally we have included two freight-only vessels possibly to be chartered to an operator serving the UK. Withdrawn vessels not yet disposed of and owned by operating companies are shown under the appropriate company and marked '•'.

Rederi AB Gotland

1	GUTE	7616t	79	15.0k	138.8m	88P	-	60T	BA	SE	7802794

GUTE Built as the GUTE by Falkenbergs Varv AB, Falkenberg, Sweden for *Rederi AB Gotland* of Sweden. Used on service between Gotland and the Swedish mainland. In 1988 chartered to *Brambles Shipping* of Australia and used between Port Melbourne (Victoria) and Burnie (Tasmania). In 1992 she was renamed the SALLY SUN and chartered to *Sally Ferries*, operating between Ramsgate and Dunkerque. In 1994 she inaugurated a Ramsgate - Vlissingen service, which was later changed to Dartford - Vlissingen. In 1995 she was chartered to *SeaWind Line*, renamed the SEAWIND II and operated between Stockholm and Turku. In 1997 she was chartered to *Nordic Trucker Line* for the Oxelösund - St Petersburg service and in 1998 she returned to *SeaWind Line*. In 1998, after *Rederi AB Gotland*-owned *Destination Gotland* regained the franchise to operate to Gotland, she was renamed the GUTE and resumed her summer role of providing summer freight back-up to the passenger vessels, but with a number of short charters during the winter. In Autumn 2002 chartered to *Amber Lines* for the Karlshamn - Liepaja service. In February 2003 chartered to *NATO* for the Iraq crisis. Returned to *Destination Gotland* in Summer 2003. In Autumn 2003 chartered to *Scandlines Amber Lines* to operate between Karlshamn and Liepaja. In 2004 lengthened by 20.3m by Nauta Shiprepair, Gdynia, Poland. In Autumn 2004 chartered to *Riga Sea Line* to inaugurate a freight service between Riga and Nynäshamn. In Autumn 2005 the service ended and the vessel was laid up. In January 2006 chartered to *Lisco* and placed on the Klaipėda - Karlshamn route, also undertaking two trips from Klaipėda to Baltiysk. In May 2006 chartered to *SeaWind Line*. In March 2007 chartered to *Baltic Scandinavian Line*. Charter ended September 2007. Apart from a trip to Cameroon, conveying Swedish UN Troops for Chad, she remained laid up until October 2008 when she was chartered to *Baltic Scandinavian Line* to operate between Härnösand and Kaskinen. In 2009 this service closed and she was laid up. She is currently laid up at Norrkoping, Sweden.

Sadco International Ltd

1»	EMERAUDE FRANCE	3012t	90	35.0k	74.3m	350P	80C	-	BA	BB	8903703

EMERAUDE FRANCE Incat 74m catamaran built as the SEACAT TASMANIA at by Incat,Hobart, Tasmania for *Sea Containers* subsidiary *Tasmanian Ferry Services* of Australia to operate between George Town (Tasmania) and Port Welshpool (Victoria). In 1992 chartered to *Hoverspeed* to operate Dover - Calais and Folkestone - Boulogne services. Returned to Australia after the 1992 summer season but returned to Britain in Summer 1993 to operate Dover - Calais and Folkestone - Boulogne services during that summer. She was repainted into *Hoverspeed* livery and renamed the SEACAT CALAIS. In 1994 chartered for five years (with a purchase option) to *Navegacion Atlantida* for *Ferry Linas Argentinas AS* of Uruguay's service between Montevideo (Uruguay) and Buenos Aires (Argentina) and renamed the ATLANTIC II. The purchase option was not taken up and in 1999 she was returned to *Sea Containers* and operated for *Hoverspeed* between Dover and Calais. In 2000 she was chartered to *SNAV Aliscafi* of Italy to operate between Ancona (Italy) and Split (Croatia) in a joint venture with *Sea Containers* and was renamed the CROAZIA JET. This operation was repeated in 2001. In 2002 she was renamed the SEACAT FRANCE and transferred to operate between Dover and Calais. At the end of the 2002 summer period she was laid up for sale or charter in Birkenhead. Returned to Dover in Summer 2004 to operate the during peak summer period. In February 2005 chartered to *Emeraude Jersey Ferries* and renamed the EMERAUDE FRANCE. In early April the charter ended (following the ending of the one-year agreement with *Sea Containers Ferries* to provide a fast ferry) and she returned to *Sea Containers Ferries*. Laid up for sale. In 2007 sold to *Maritime Charter Sales* of the Isle of Man and chartered to *IOMSP*. Returned to lay-up at Tilbury in September 2007. In May 2011 sold to *Sadco International Ltd* of the British Virgin Islands.

Sea Containers

1»	THE PRINCESS ANNE	-	69	50.0k	56.4m	360P	55C	-	BA	UK	-
2»	THE PRINCESS MARGARET	-	68	50.0k	56.4m	360P	55C	-	BA	UK	-

THE PRINCESS ANNE, THE PRINCESS MARGARET British Hovercraft Corporation SRN4 type hovercraft built at Cowes, UK for *Seaspeed*. Built to Mark I specification. In 1978/1979 respectively lengthened to Mark III specification. They underwent complete refurbishment at the beginning of 1999. Withdrawn in 2000 and laid up at the Hovercraft Museum at Lee-on-Solent.

TransEuropa Ferries (in administration)

1	GARDENIA	8097t	78	18.4k	118.1m	105P	-	52L	BA2	CY	7711139
2	LARKSPUR	14458t	76	17.5k	143.8m	1150P	314C	55L	BA2	CY	7500451

GARDENIA Built as the EUROPEAN ENTERPRISE by Schichau-Unterweser AG, Bremerhaven, Germany for *European Ferries*. In 1988 she was renamed the EUROPEAN ENDEAVOUR. She was used on freight services between Dover and Calais and Dover and Zeebrugge. If space were available, a small number of passengers was sometimes conveyed on the Zeebrugge service, although the sailings were not advertised for passengers. This ceased with the withdrawal of passenger services on this route at the end of 1991. During the summer period she provided additional freight capacity on the Dover - Calais service and has also served on other routes. In Autumn 1995 she was transferred to the Cairnryan - Larne service. In 1998 her accommodation was raised to provide extra freight capacity. In March 1999 she also began operating from Larne to Ardrossan but this ceased later in the year. Withdrawn from service in July 2002 and sold to *Odyssy Maritime Co Ltd* and renamed the GARDENIA. In 2003 she began operating for *TEF* between Ramsgate and Ostend. In April 2013 laid up.

LARKSPUR Built as the GEDSER by Schichau-Unterweser AG, Bremerhaven, Germany for *Gedser-Travemünde Ruten* of Denmark for their service between Gedser (Denmark) and Travemünde (Germany). In 1986 she was purchased by *Thorsviks Rederi A/S* of Norway and chartered to *Sally Ferries*, re-registered in The Bahamas, renamed the VIKING 2 and entered service on the Ramsgate - Dunkerque service. In early 1989 she was renamed the SALLY SKY and during Winter 1989/90 she was lengthened by 20.4 metres. At the end of 1996 she was withdrawn from the Dunkerque service. In 1997 she was renamed the EUROTRAVELLER, transferred to *Holyman-Sally Ferries* and, in March, was introduced onto the Ramsgate - Ostend route. In 1998, when *Holyman-Sally Ferries* came to an end, she operated in a freight-only role for *Sally Line* under the *Sally Freight* name. Passenger services were resumed in May, under the name of *Sally Direct*. All *Sally Line* operations ended in November 1998 and she was withdrawn for sale and laid up. In 1999 sold to *Forsythia Maritime Co Ltd* and renamed the LARKSPUR. She was given a major refit at Dunkerque, including the provision of 60 drivers' cabins with private facilities. She entered service with *TEF* in August 2000. Passengers were conveyed from July 2004. In April 2013 laid up.

Volkswerft Stralsund

1	BERLIN	24000t	-	20.5k	169.0m	1500P	480C	96L	BA2	DK	9587855
2	COPENHAGEN	24000t	-	20.5k	169.0m	1500P	480C	96L	BA2	-	9587867

BERLIN, COPENHAGEN Partly built by Volkswerft Stralsund, Stralsund, Germany for *Scandlines* to operate on the Gedser - Rostock route. The propulsion system allows for adaption to LNG. Originally due to enter service in Spring 2012, the construction of these vessels was seriously delayed and it was found that the vessels did not meet the specification and the order was cancelled. The builders are currently seeking a buyer for the vessels. The BERLIN is 90% finished and has undertaken sea trials; the COPENHAGEN has been launched and is 50% finished.

Larkspur (*Miles Cowsill*)

Gardenia (*Miles Cowsill*)

The following vessels are sisters or near sisters. This refers to 'as built' condition; some ships will subsequently have been modified and become different from their sister vessels.

AMORELLA *(Viking Line)*, ISABELLE *(Tallink Silja Line)*, GABRIELLA *(Viking Line)*, CROWN OF SCANDINAVIA *(DFDS Seaways)*.

ARGYLE, BUTE *(Caledonian MacBrayne)*.

ASK, URD *(Stena Line)*.

ATLANTIC VISION *(Tallink)*, DIEPPE SEAWAYS *(DFDS Seaways)*, STENA SUPERFAST VII, STENA SUPERFAST VIII *(Stena Line)*.

AURORA AF HELSINGBORG, HAMLET *(Stena Line)*, TYCHO BRAHE *(Scandlines)*.

CELTIC HORIZON *(Celtic Link)*, NORMAN ASTURIAS *(LD Line)*, NORMAN VOYAGER *(DFDS Seaways France)*, STENA LAGAN, STENA MERSEY, SCOTTISH VIKING, STENA FLAVIA *(Stena Line)*.

BALTIC QUEEN, BALTIC PRINCESS, GALAXY *(Tallink Silja Line)*.

BASTØ I, BASTØ II *(Bastø Fosen)*.

BEN-MY-CHREE *(Isle of Man Steam Packet Company)*, COMMODORE CLIPPER *(Condor Ferries)*, HAMMERODDE *(Bornholmstrafikken)* (Near sisters).

BERLIOZ, RODIN *(MyFerryLink)*.

CANNA *(Rathlin Island Ferry Ltd)*, CLEW BAY QUEEN *(Clare Island Ferry Company)*, COLL *(Arranmore Island Ferries)*, EIGG *(Caledonian MacBrayne)*, MORVERN *(Arranmore Fast Ferries)*, RAASAY *(Caledonian MacBrayne)*, RHUM *(Arranmore Island Ferries)*.

CARRIGALOE, GLENBROOK *(Cross River Ferries)*.

COLOR FANTASY, COLOR MAGIC *(Color Line)*.

COLOR VIKING *(Color Line)*, STENA NAUTICA *(Stena Line)*.

CÔTE D'ÂLBATRE, SEVEN SISTERS *(DFDS Seaways France)*.

DAGALIEN, DAGGRI *(Shetland Islands Council)*.

DELFT SEAWAYS, DOVER SEAWAYS, DUNKERQUE SEAWAYS *(DFDS Seaways France)*.

DEUTSCHLAND, SCHLESWIG-HOLSTEIN *(Scandlines)*.

EARL SIGURD, EARL THORFINN *(Orkney Ferries)*.

ECKERÖ *(Eckerö Linjen)*, POVL ANKER *(Bornholmstrafikken)*.

ERNEST BEVIN, JAMES NEWMAN, JOHN BURNS *(Woolwich Free Ferry)*.

EUROPEAN CAUSEWAY, EUROPEAN HIGHLANDER *(P&O Ferries)*.

EUROPEAN ENDEAVOUR *(P&O Ferries)*, STENA ALEGRA *(Stena Line)*.

FENJA, MENJA *(Færge)*.

FINNCLIPPER, FINNEAGLE, FINNFELLOW *(Finnlines)*, STENA GERMANICA *(Stena Line)*.

FINNLADY, FINNMAID, FINNSTAR, NORDLINK *(Finnlines)*.

FINNPARTNER, FINNTRADER, TRANSEUROPA *(Finnlines)*.

FRIGG SYDFYEN, ODIN SYDFYEN *(Færge)*.

FRISIA I, FRISIA V *(Reederei Norden-Frisia)*.

GOTLAND, VISBY *(Destination Gotland)*.

HARILAID, KÖRGELAID *(Saaremaa Laevakompanii)*.

HIIUMA, MUHUMAA, SAAREMAA *(Saaremaa Laevakompanii)*.

Bute (*Miles Cowsill*)

St Cecilia and **St Helen** (*Miles Cowsill*)

HJALTLAND, HROSSEY *(NorthLink Ferries)*.

HUCKLEBERRY FINN, TOM SAWYER *(TT-Line)*.

KAUNAS SEAWAYS *(DFDS Seaways)*, PETERSBURG *(Sassnitz - Ust Luga Ferry)*, VILNIUS SEAWAYS *(DFDS Seaways)*.

KING SEAWAYS, PRINCESS SEAWAYS *(DFDS Seaways)*.

KONG HARALD, NORDLYS, RICHARD WITH *(Hurtigruten)*.

KRONPRINS FREDERIK, PRINS JOACHIM *(Scandlines)*.

LANGELAND, LOLLAND *(Færge)*.

LOCH DUNVEGAN, LOCH FYNE *(Caledonian MacBrayne)*.

LOCH LINNHE, LOCH RANZA, LOCH RIDDON, LOCH STRIVEN *(Caledonian MacBrayne)*.

LYNHER II, PLYM II, TAMAR II *(Torpoint Ferries)*.

MARIELLA *(Viking Line)*, PRINCESS ANASTASIA *(St. Peter Line)*.

MERCANDIA IV, MERCANDIA VIII *(Stena Line)*.

MIDNATSOL, TROLLFJORD *(Hurtigruten)*.

MIDSLAND, WESTFALEN *(Rederij Doeksen)*.

MONNIK, ROTTUM *(Wagenborg)*.

MÜNSTERLAND, OSTFRIESLAND *(AG Ems)*.

NILS DACKE, ROBIN HOOD *(TT-Line)*.

NILS HOLGERSSON, PETER PAN *(TT-Line)*.

NORBANK, NORBAY *(P&O Ferries)*.

NORDKAPP, NORDNORGE, POLARLYS *(Hurtigruten)*.

OERD, SIER *(Wagenborg)*.

OILEAN NA H-OIGE, SANCTA MARIA *(Bere Island Ferries)*.

PRIDE OF BRUGES, PRIDE OF YORK *(P&O Ferries)*.

PRIDE OF CANTERBURY, PRIDE OF KENT *(P&O Ferries)*.

PRIDE OF HULL, PRIDE OF ROTTERDAM *(P&O Ferries)*.

PRINCESS MARIA *(St. Peter Line)*, STENA SAGA *(Stena Line)*.

PRINS RICHARD, PRINSESSE BENEDIKTE *(Scandlines)*.

RED EAGLE, RED FALCON, RED OSPREY *(Red Funnel Ferries)*.

ROMANTIKA, VICTORIA I *(Tallink Silja Line)*.

SILJA SERENADE, SILJA SYMPHONY *(Tallink Silja Line)*.

SOUND OF SANDA, SOUND OF SCALPAY *(Western Ferries)*.

SOUND OF SCARBA, SOUND OF SHUNA *(Western Ferries)*.

SOUND OF SEIL, SOUND OF SOAY *(Western Ferries)*.

SPIRIT OF BRITAIN, SPIRIT OF FRANCE *(P&O Ferries)*.

ST CECILIA, ST FAITH, ST HELEN *(Wightlink)*.

STENA ADVENTURER, STENA SCANDINAVICA *(Stena Line)*.

SECTION 8 – SISTERS

STENA BRITANNICA, STENA HOLLANDICA *(Stena Line).*

STENA SPIRIT, STENA VISION *(Stena Line).*

SUPERSPEED 1, SUPERSPEED 2 *(Color Line).*

WIGHT LIGHT, WIGHT SKY, WIGHT SUN *(Wightlink).*

Fast Ferries

CONDOR EXPRESS, CONDOR RAPIDE, CONDOR VITESSE *(Condor Ferries).*

FJORD CAT *(Fjord Line)*, MAX MOLS *(Mols-Linien).*

KATEXPRESS 1, KATEXPRESS 2 *(Mols-Linien).*

MAI MOLS, MIE MOLS *(Mols-Linien).*

RED JET 1, RED JET 2 *(Red Funnel Ferries).*

WIGHT RYDER I, WIGHT RYDER II *(Wightlink).*

Freight Ferries

ADELINE *(CLdN/Cobelfret Ferries)*, WILHELMINE *(P&O Ferries).*

AEGEAN BREEZE, ARABIAN BREEZE, ASIAN BREEZE, BALTIC BREEZE *(UECC).*

AMANDINE, OPALINE *(CLdN/Cobelfret Ferries).*

ANGLIA SEAWAYS *(Seatruck Ferries)*, FLANDRIA SEAWAYS *(DFDS Seaways).*

ANVIL POINT *(Foreland Shipping)*, BEACHY HEAD *(DFDS Seaways France)*, EDDYSTONE, HARTLAND POINT, HURST POINT*(Foreland Shipping)*, LONGSTONE *(DFDS Seaways).*

ARROW, CLIPPER RANGER *(Seatruck Ferries)*, HELLIAR, HILDASAY *(NorthLink Ferries).*

AUTO BALTIC, AUTO BANK, AUTO BAY *(UECC).*

AUTOPREMIER, AUTOPRESTIGE, AUTOPRIDE, AUTOPROGRESS *(UECC).*

AUTORACER, AUTORUNNER *(UECC).*

AUTOSKY, AUTOSTAR, AUTOSUN *(UECC).*

BEGONIA SEAWAYS, FICARIA SEAWAYS, FREESIA SEAWAYS *(DFDS Seaways).*

BIRKA CARRIER, BIRKA TRADER *(Transfennica).*

BOTNIA SEAWAYS, FINLANDIA SEAWAYS *(DFDS Seaways)*, FINNHAWK, FINNKRAFT *(Finnlines).*

BRITANNIA SEAWAYS, SELANDIA SEAWAYS, SUECIA SEAWAYS *(DFDS Seaways).*

CAPUCINE, SEVERINE *(Stena Line).*

CAROLINE RUSS *(Finnlines)*, FRIEDRICH RUSS, PAULINE RUSS, SEAGARD *(Transfennica).*

CELANDINE, CELESTINE, CLEMENTINE, MELUSINE, VALENTINE, VICTORINE *(CLdN/Cobelfret Ferries).*

CLIPPER PENNANT *(Seatruck Ferries)*, CLIPPER POINT *(DFDS Seaways)*, SEATRUCK PACE, SEATRUCK PANORAMA *(Seatruck Ferries).*

CYMBELINE, UNDINE *(CLdN/Cobelfret Ferries).*

FINNBREEZE, FINNMILL, FINNPULP, FINNSEA, FINNSKY, FINNSUN, FINNTIDE, FINNWAVE *(Finnlines)*, CORONA SEAWAYS, FIONIA SEAWAYS, HAFNIA SEAWAYS, JUTLANDIA SEAWAYS *(DFDS Seaways).*

GENCA, KRAFTCA, PLYCA, PULPCA, TIMCA, TRICA *(Transfennica).*

Berlioz (*Andrew Cooke*)

Condor Vitesse (*Andrew Cooke*)

SECTION 8 – SISTERS

MAGNOLIA SEAWAYS, PETUNIA SEAWAYS, PRIMULA SEAWAYS *(DFDS Seaways)*.

MAZARINE, PALATINE, PEREGRINE, VESPERTINE *(CLdN/Cobelfret Ferries)*.

NORSKY, NORSTREAM *(P&O Ferries)*.

OBBOLA, ORTVIKEN, ÖSTRAND *(SCA Transforest)*.

PAULINE, YASMINE *(CLdN/Cobelfret Ferries)*.

SCHIEBORG, SLINGEBORG, SPAARNEBORG *(CLdN/Cobelfret Ferries)*.

SEATRUCK POWER, SEATRUCK PROGRESS *(Seatruck Ferries)*, STENA PERFORMER, STENA PRECISION *(Stena Line)*.

STENA CARRIER, STENA FREIGHTER *(Transfennica)*.

STENA FORECASTER, STENA FORERUNNER, STENA FORETELLER *(Transfennica)*.

STENA TRANSIT, STENA TRANSPORTER *(Stena Line)*.

Stena Performer (*Gordon Hislip*)

Begonia Seaways (*Peter Therkildsen*)

SECTION 8 – SISTERS

DISPOSALS

The following vessels, listed in *Ferries 2013 - British Isles and Northern Europe* have been disposed of - either to other companies listed in this book or others. Company names are as used in that publication.

AMBER *(Sea-Cargo)* In February 2013 charter terminated.

ASK *(Scandlines (Denmark & Germany))* In September 2012 sold to *Stena Line*.

AURORA *(Scandlines (Denmark & Germany))* In September 2012 sold to *SOL Continent Line* (who took over the Rostock - Hanko freight service) and renamed the VIKINGLAND.

AURORA AF HELSINGBORG *(Scandlines(Sweden))* Now listed under *Stena Line*.

BALTIC EXCELLENT *(UPM-Kymmene Seaways)* In January 2013 charter terminated.

BALTICBORG *(Mann Lines)* The arrangement whereby *Mann Lines* part-chartered the northbound capacity of this vessel has ceased.

BIRKA CARRIER *(Finnlines)* In January 2013 charter ended. Chartered to *Transfennica*.

BIRKA EXPRESS *(Finnlines)* In February 2013, charter ended. Chartered to *Med Cross Lines* of Italy for operation in the Mediterranean.

BIRKA TRADER *(Finnlines)* In January 2013 charter ended. Chartered to *Transfennica*.

BERLIN, COPENHAGEN *(Scandlines (Denmark & Germany))* In November 2012 the order was cancelled. Now shown in Section 7 under *Volkswerft Stralsund*.

BOTHNIABORG *(Mann Lines)* The arrangement whereby *Mann Lines* part-chartered the northbound capacity of this vessel has ceased.

CAPUCINE *(Cobelfret Ferries)* In September 2012 chartered to *Stena Line* to operate between Rotterdam and Harwich. Transferred to UK registry.

CAROLINE RUSS *(Transfennica)* In January 2013 charter ended. Chartered to *Finnlines*.

CIMBRIA *(DFDS/LD Lines joint venture)* In August 2012 sold to *Asian Marine Transport Corp* of the Philippines.

CLIPPER POINT (Seatruck Ferries) In May 2012 chartered to *DFDS Seaways* and placed on the Immingham-Cuxhaven route.. In May 2013 began operating for *DFDS Seaways* in the Baltic.

DEAL SEAWAYS *(DFDS/LD Lines joint venture)* In November 2012 returned to *Brittany Ferries* and reverted to the name BARFLEUR.

DOLPHIN JET *(Kattegat-Ruten)* The fast ferry service lasted less than a month due to operational problems and she was laid up. In May 2013 she returned to the Mediterranean.

EGLANTINE *(CLdN/Cobelfret Ferries)* In March 2013 sold to *Namma International Trading* of Saudi Arabia and renamed the ALNAWA EXPRESS.

EUROPALINK *(Finnlines)* In October 2012 sold to *Atlantica Navigazione* of Italy, another company within the *Grimaldi Group*, for Mediterranean service.

HUMBER VIKING *(DFDS Seaways)* In October 2012 sold to *Atlantica SpA Di Navigazione* (*Grimaldi Group*), At the end of January 2013, charter ended. Absorbed into the *Grimaldi* fleet and renamed the EUROCARGO SICILIA. She operates in the Mediterranean.

ISABELLA *(Viking Line)* In April 2013 sold to *Hansalink Limited*, part of the *Tallink Grupp*. Renamed the ISABELLE.

KAPELLA *(Tallink/Silja Line)* In September 2012 sold to *Universal Logistic System* of Estonia and renamed the ULS FERRY 1. She operates between Sillamäe (Estonia) and Ust-Luga (Russia).

LOUISE RUSS *(Transfennica)* In January 2013 charter terminated.

Pride of Dover *(Miles Cowsill)*

Nordstjernen *(Hurtigruten)*

MAAS VIKING *(DFDS Seaways)* In September 2012 sold to *CLdN* of Luxembourg and renamed the KENT. In January 2013 renamed the HATCHE and chartered to *Ekol Lojistik* of Turkey.

MAESTRO SEA *(Van-Uden RoRo)* In January 2013 charter ended.

MERCANDIA IV *(HH-Ferries)* Now listed under *Stena Line*.

MERCANDIA VIII *(HH-Ferries)* Now listed under *Stena Line*.

MECKLENBURG-VORPOMMERN *(Scandlines (Denmark & Germany))* In autumn 2012 sold to *Stena Line*.

MERCHANT *(Scandlines (Denmark & Germany))* In September 2012 sold to *SOL Continent Line* (who took over the Rostock - Hanko freight service).

MIRANDA *(UPM-Kymmene Seaways)* In January 2013 charter ended.

MISANA *(UPM-Kymmene Seaways)* In July 2013 charter transferred to *Finnlines*.

MISIDA *(UPM-Kymmene Seaways)* In July 2013 charter transferred to *Finnlines*.

MISTRAL *(UPM-Kymmene Seaways)* In July 2013 charter ended.

MONNIK*(UPM-Kymmene Seaways)* In January 2013 charter ended.

NORDSTJERNEN *(Hurtigruten)* In December 2012 sold to *Vestland Rederi AS* and used by *Indre Nordhordland Dampbåtlag* of Bergen on cruises from Bergen.

NORMAN TRADER *(Daybreak Shipping)* In April 2013 sold to *Stena RoRo*. Renamed the STENA ALEGRA and in July 2013 chartered to *Stena Line* and placed on the Karlskrona - Gdynia service.

NORQUEEN *(P&O Ferries)* In February 2013 charter ended. Sold to *Golden Anchor Enterprises* of Greece. Renamed the MEDQUEEN.

OLEANDER *(TransEuropa Ferries)* In April 2013 sold to *Novgorod Shipping Company* of Russia. Renamed the SHERBATSKIY. Continued to be chartered to *Acciona Trasmediterranea*.

PAULINE RUSS *(Transfennica)* In January 2013 charter ended.

PRIDE OF DOVER *(P&O Ferries)* In November 2012 sold to German interests and in December 2012 delivered for scrapping to Alagia, Turkey.

RG-1 *(RG Line)* In February 2013 sold to Fornaes Shipbreaking, Grenaa, Denmark. However, she may be sold for future use.

SASSNITZ *(Scandlines (Denmark & Germany))* In September 2012 sold to *Stena Line*.

SCOTTISH VIKING *(Scandlines (Denmark & Germany))* In September 2012 charter transferred to *Stena Line*.

SKÅNE *(Scandlines(Sweden))* Now listed under *Stena Line*.

SEAFRANCE BERLIOZ, SEAFRANCE RODIN *(SeaFrance (in administration))* In June 2012 sold to *Eurotransmanche*. In July 2012 renamed the BERLIOZ and the RODIN. In August 2012 chartered to *My Ferry Link* and resumed operation between Calais and Dover.

SEAFRANCE MOLIERE *(SeaFrance (in administration))* In July 2012 sold to *Scapino Shipping Ltd* of Monaco and renamed the MOLIERE. In October 2012 chartered to *DFDS/LD Lines* joint venture and, in November, renamed the DIEPPE SEAWAYS and introduced onto the Dover - Calais service.

SEAFRANCE NORD PAS-DE-CALAIS *(SeaFrance (in administration))* In June 2012 sold to *Eurotransmanche*. In July 2012 renamed the NORD PAS-DE-CALAIS. In November 2013 chartered to *My Ferry Link* and resumed operation between Calais and Dover.

SEATRUCK PERFORMANCE, SEATRUCK PRECISION *(Seatruck Ferries)* In September 2012 chartered to *Stena Line* and renamed the STENA PERFORMER and STENA PRECISION respectively. They operate between Heysham and Belfast.

SEVERINE *(Cobelfret Ferries)* In September 2012 chartered to *Stena Line* to operate between Rotterdam and Harwich. Transferred to Dutch registry.

SNAEFELL *(Isle of Man Steam Packet Company)* In June 2012 sold to *Taxyploa Maritime Co* and renamed the MASTER JET. Operates for *SeaJets* in the Aegean.

STENA BALTICA *(Stena Line)* In February 2013 sold to *SNAV* of Italy and renamed the SNAV ADRIATICO.

STENA FERONIA *(Stena RoRo)* July 2012 chartered to *FRS* to operate between Algeciras and Tangiers

STENA HIBERNIA *(Stena Line)* In September 2012 transferred to *Stena RoRo.*

STENA SCOTIA *(Stena Line)* In September 2012 transferred to *Stena RoRo.*

STENA VOYAGER *(Stena Line)* In May 2013 towed to Landskrona, Sweden for demolition and recycling.

SYMPHORINE *(CLdN/Cobelfret Ferries)* In October 2012 sold to *Sunlink Maritime* of Northern Cyprus and renamed the DEEP KARPAZ.

THOR SYDFYEN *(Færgen)* In June 2012 withdrawn for sale. In January 2013 sold to *Petersen & Sørensen A/S* of Denmark and renamed the THOR S. In February 2013 resold to *Ugtrans Terminal Co. Of Cyprus.*

TRANSLANDIA *(Eckerö Line)* In March 2013 sold to *Salem Al Makrani Cargo Co*, United Arab Emirates.

TRELLEBORG *(Scandlines(Sweden))* Now listed under *Stena Line.*

URD *(Scandlines (Denmark & Germany))* In September 2012 sold a subsidiary of *Swedish Orient Line* and chartered to *Stena Line.*

WATLING STREET *(Scandlines (Denmark & Germany))* In September 2012 charter transferred to *Stena Line.* In April 2013 renamed the STENA FLAVIA.

Stena Voyager *(Miles Cowsill)*

Eglantine *(Nick Widdows)*

WILHELMINE (CLdN/Cobelfret Ferries) In January 2013 chartered to P&O Ferries to operate between Tilbury and Zeebrugge. After three weeks moved to the Middlesbrough - Rotterdam service.

VESSELS RENAMED

The following vessels have been renamed since the publication of Ferries 2012 - British Isles and Northern Europe without change of operator.

CROWN OF SCANDINAVIA (DFDS Seaways) In January 2013 renamed the CROWN SEAWAYS.

DANA SIRENA (DFDS Seaways) In March 2013 renamed the SIRENA SEAWAYS.

FINNARROW (Finnlines) In April 2013 chartered to Grimaldi Line of Italy for five years and, in July, renamed the EUROFERRY BRINDISI.

FREEDOM (Eckerö Line) In June 2012 renamed the FINLANDIA.

NORMAN SPIRIT (DFDS Seaways/LD Lines joint venture) In March 2013 renamed the CALAIS SEAWAYS.

PRIDE OF CALAIS (P&O Ferries) In December 2012 chartered to TransEuropa Ferries for three years and renamed the OSTEND SPIRIT. Entered service on the Ostend - Ramsgate route in January 2013. In April 2013 re-possessed by P&O Ferries and returned to lay up at Tilbury.

TOR BEGONIA (DFDS Seaways) In July 2012 renamed the BEGONIA SEAWAYS.

TOR BOTNIA (DFDS Seaways) In January 2013 renamed the BOTNIA SEAWAYS.

TOR FREESIA (DFDS Seaways) In August 2012 renamed the FREESIA SEAWAYS.

TOR FINLANDIA (DFDS Seaways) In December 2012 renamed the FINLANDIA SEAWAYS.

TRANSLUBECA (TransRussia Express) Now shown under Finnlines.

TRANSRUSSIA (TransRussia Express) Now shown under Finnlines.

COMPANY CHANGES

DFDS/LD Lines joint venture Now shown as DFDS Seaways France.

Doolin Ferries This company has been absorbed by Doolin2Aran Ferries.

North Sea RoRo In March 2013 this operator ceased trading.

RG Line (Sweden) In November 2011 the company went into liquidation. The service was taken over by NLC Ferry Oy Ab trading as RG Line until 31st December 2012. From 1st January 2013 the company traded as Vaasanlaivat (Finnish) and Vasabåtarna (Swedish). In May 2013 the trading name was changed to Wasaline.

SeaFrance (in administration) During 2012 company liquidated and all assets disposed of.

Scandlines (Sweden) During 2012 incorporated into Stena Line, who took over all Scandlines (Denmark and Germany) Baltic routes. The Helsingborg - Helsingør route continues to be jointly operated and branded as Scandlines.

TransEuropa Ferries In April 2013 the company ceased trading and filed for bankruptcy.

UPM-Kymmene Seaways In July 2013 this operator ceased trading and transferred the charter of two of its vessels to Finnlines.

Calais Seaways (*Andrew Cooke*)

Ostend Spirit (*William Barham*)

LATE NEWS

Eckerö Line In June 2013 *Rederiaktiebolaget Eckerö* sold the NORDLANDIA to an unknown company called *Isabella Cruise Co Ltd*, registered in Belize. She was renamed the ISABELLA 1.

Scandlines In July 2013 *Scandlines* and STX Finland Oy signed a Letter of Intent for two new ferries for the Rostock-Gedser route for delivery in spring 2015. They will be double ended and construction will allow the ferries to be used on the Puttgarden-Rødby route as well. Each ferry will have a capacity of 1,300 passengers and 72 trucks or 382 cars. The ferries will use LNG fuel.

Viking Grace (*Viking Line*)

FERRIES ILLUSTRATED

Note: Date of construction is stated for vessels not listed. Interior pictures of the Viking Grace are not included.

EIGG	55	FIONIA SEAWAYS	62	GRYF	190
EILEAN DHIURA	99	FIVLA	89	GUTE	197
EMERAUDE FRANCE	197	FJORD CAT	162	GYLEN LADY	105
EMILY	134	FLANDRIA SEAWAYS	62	HAFNIA SEAWAYS	62
ERNEST BEVIN	113	FOYLE RAMBLER	106	HALLAIG	55
ESONBORG	193	FOYLE VENTURE	106	HAMLET	172
ESTRADEN	120	FRAM	164	HAMMERODDE	158
EUROFERRY BRINDISI	159	FREEDOM 90	134	HAMNAVOE	74
EUROPEAN CAUSEWAY	80	FREESIA SEAWAYS	62	HAPPY HOOKER	133
EUROPEAN ENDEAVOUR	80	FRIEDRICH RUSS	126	HARILAID	171
EUROPEAN HIGHLANDER	80	FRIESLAND	152	HARTLAND POINT	120
EUROPEAN SEAWAY	80	FRIGG SYDFYEN	158	HATCHE	115
EXPRESS	80	FRISIA I	168	HEBRIDEAN ISLES	55
EYNHALLOW	76	FRISIA II	168	HEBRIDES	55
FASTCAT SHANKLIN	137	FRISIA IV	168	HELGOLAND	157
FBD TINTERN	108	FRISIA V	168	HELLIAR	74
FENCER	133	FRISIA VI	168	HENDRA	89
FENJA	158	FRISIA VII	168	HERM TRIDENT V	138
FERRY DAME	137	FRISIA IX	168	HIGHER FERRY	131
FICARIA SEAWAYS	62	FRISIA X	168	HIIUMAA	171
FILLA	89	GABRIELLA	191	HILDASAY	74
FINLAGGAN	55	GALAXY	183	HJALTLAND	74
FINLANDIA SEAWAYS	62	GALICIA	125	HOLGER DANSKE	174
FINLANDIA	155	GALILEUSZ	190	HOTSPUR IV	134
FINNBREEZE	118	GARDENIA	198	HOY HEAD	76
FINNCLIPPER	159	GEIRA	89	HROSSEY	74
FINNEAGLE	159	GELLAN	110	HUCKLEBERRY FINN	188
FINNFELLOW	159	GENCA	126	HURRICANE CLIPPER	137
FINNHAWK	118	GIRL GRAY	99	HURST POINT	120
FINNKRAFT	118	GLENACHULISH	109	IKOM K	108
FINNLADY	159	GLENBROOK	104	ISABELLE	183
FINNMAID	159	GLÓR NA FARRAIGE	133	ISLAND EXPRESS	134
FINNMARKEN	164	GOD MET ONS III	110	ISLAND PRINCESS	133
FINNMILL	118	GOLDEN MARIANA	76	ISLAND TRADER	133
FINNPARTNER	159	GOOD SHEPHERD IV	89	ISLE OF ARRAN	55
FINNPULP	118	GOSPORT QUEEN	134	ISLE OF CUMBRAE	55
FINNSAILOR	159	GOTLAND	148	ISLE OF INISHMORE	70
FINNSEA	118	GOTLANDIA II	148	ISLE OF LEWIS	55
FINNSKY	118	GOTLANDIA	148	ISLE OF MULL	55
FINNSTAR	159	GRAEMSAY	76	IVAN	125
FINNSUN	118	GRAN CANARIA CAR	125	JACK B	133
FINNTIDE	118	GREAT EXPECTATIONS	134	JAMES NEWMAN	113
FINNTRADER	159	GRONINGERLAND	157	JAN SNIADECKI	190
FINNWAVE	118	GRY MARITHA	105	JENACK	110

JOHN BURNS	113	LOCH STRIVEN	55	NILS DACKE	188
JONATHAN SWIFT	70	LOCH TARBERT	55	NILS HOLGERSSON	188
JOSEPHINE	137	LOCHINVAR	60	NO 5	131
JUTLANDIA SEAWAYS	62	LOCHNEVIS	55	NOORD-NEDERLAND	152
KAITAKI	70	LOFOTEN	164	NORBANK	80
KANHAVE	158	LOLLAND	158	NORBAY	80
KATEXPRESS 1	167	LONGSTONE	62	NORD PAS-DE-CALAIS	73
KATEXPRESS 2	167	LORD OF THE ISLES	55	NORDKAPP	164
KATTEGAT	163	LORELEY	133	NORDLANDIA	155
KAUNAS SEAWAYS	148	LYNHER II	132	NORDLICHT	157
KING HARRY FERRY	131	LYONESSE LADY	105	NORDLINK	159
KING SEAWAYS	62	MACDARA	133	NORDLYS	164
KINGSWEAR PRINCESS	133	MAGNOLIA SEAWAYS	62	NORDNORGE	164
KINTYRE EXPRESS II	134	MAI MOLS	167	NORMAN ASTURIAS	166
KINTYRE EXPRESS III	134	MAID OF GLENCOUL	104	NORMAN VOYAGER	67
KINTYRE EXPRESS IV	137	MALLARD	131	NORMANDIE EXPRESS	47
KINTYRE EXPRESS	134	MANANNAN	73	NORMANDIE	47
KIRSTY M	102	MARIELLA	191	NORRLAND	121
KOEGELWIECK	152	MARIN MARIE	137	NORRÖNA	175
KONG HARALD	164	MAX MOLS	167	NORSKY	80
KOPERNIK	190	MAZARINE	115	NORSTREAM	80
KÖRGELAID	171	MECKLENBURG-		OBBOLA	121
KRAFTCA	126	VORPOMMERN	176	ODIN SYDFYEN	158
KRONPRINS FREDERIK	174	MELUSINE	115	OERD	193
KYHOLM	158	MENJA	158	OFELIA	171
L'AUDACE	125	MERCANDIA IV	176	OILEAN NA H-OIGE	102
LA SURPRISE	125	MERCANDIA VIII	176	OLDENBURG	137
LANGELAND	158	MERI 3	106	OPALINE	115
LARKSPUR	198	METEOR CLIPPER	137	OPTIMA SEAWAYS	148
LEIRNA	89	MIDNATSOL	164	ORCOMBE	134
LEONORA CHRISTINA	158	MIDSLAND	152	ORTVIKEN	121
LINGA	89	MIE MOLS	167	OSCAR WILDE	70
LIVERPOOL SEAWAYS	148	MISANA	118	OSTEND SPIRIT	80
LOCH ALAINN	55	MISIDA	118	OSTFRIESLAND	157
LOCH BHRUSDA	55	MONNIK	193	ÖSTRAND	121
LOCH BUIE	55	MONSOON CLIPPER	137	PALATINE	115
LOCH DUNVEGAN	55	MONT ST MICHEL	47	PAQIZE	115
LOCH FYNE	55	MOON CLIPPER	137	PATRIA SEAWAYS	149
LOCH LINNHE	55	MORVERN	99	PAULINE RUSS	126
LOCH PORTAIN	55	MUHUMAA	171	PAULINE	116
LOCH RANZA	55	MUIRNEAG	55	PEARL SEAWAYS	149
LOCH RIDDON	55	MÜNSTERLAND	157	PENTALINA	85
LOCH SEAFORTH	60	MY QUEEN	134	PENTLAND VENTURE	134
LOCH SHIRA	55	NEW ADVANCE	102	PEREGRINE	116

STAR	183	TAMAR II	132	VIKING CINDERELLA	191
STAVANGERFJORD	162	TEISTIN	182	VIKING GRACE	191
STENA ADVENTURER	90	TENERIFE CAR	126	VIKING XPRS	191
STENA ALEGRA	176	TERNAN	182	VILLUM CLAUSEN	158
STENA BRITANNICA	90	THE LISMORE	99	VILNIUS SEAWAYS	149
STENA CARISMA	176	THE ODYSSEY	106	VISBY	148
STENA CARRIER	126	THE PRINCESS ANNE	198	VLIELAND	152
STENA DANICA	176	THE PRINCESS		WAPPEN VON BORKUM	157
STENA EUROPE	90	MARGARET	198	WAPPEN VON	
STENA EXPLORER	90	THE SECOND SNARK	133	NORDENEY	168
STENA FLAVIA	176	THE TOM AVIS	132	WARRIOR	133
STENA FORECASTER	126	THE TOM CASEY	132	WASA EXPRESS	194
STENA FORERUNNER	126	THORA	89	WAVERLEY	138
STENA FORETELLER	126	THORSVOE	79	WAWEL	170
STENA FREIGHTER	126	TIGER	152	WESTERN ISLES	133
STENA GERMANICA	176	TIMCA	126	WIGHT LIGHT	96
STENA HOLLANDICA	90	TOCQUEVILLE	137	WIGHT RYDER I	96
STENA JUTLANDICA	176	TOM SAWYER	188	WIGHT RYDER II	96
STENA LAGAN	90	TORNADO CLIPPER	137	WIGHT SKY	96
STENA MERSEY	90	TRANQUILITY	137	WIGHT SUN	96
STENA NAUTICA	176	TRANS CARRIER	121	WILHELMINE	80
STENA NORDICA	90	TRANSEUROPA	159	WOLIN	190
STENA PERFORMER	90	TRANSLUBECA	159	WYRE ROSE	134
STENA PRECISION	90	TRANSPULP	62	YASMINE	116
STENA SAGA	176	TRANSRUSSIA	159	YOKER SWAN	137
STENA SCANDINAVICA	176	TRELLEBORG	178		
STENA SCANRAIL	176	TRICA	126		
STENA SPIRIT	176	TRIDENT VI	138		
STENA SUPERFAST VII	90	TROLLFJORD	164		
STENA SUPERFAST VIII	90	TWIN STAR	137		
STENA TRANSIT	90	TYCHO BRAHE	174		
STENA TRANSPORTER	90	TYPHOON CLIPPER	137		
STENA VISION	178	ULYSSES	70		
STORM CLIPPER	137	UNDINE	116		
STRANGFORD FERRY	110	URD	178		
SUAR VIGO	126	VALENTINE	116		
SUECIA SEAWAYS	62	VARAGEN	79		
SÚLAN	182	VENTURER	106		
SUN CLIPPER	137	VESPERTINE	116		
SUPERSPEED 1	146	VESTERÅLEN	164		
SUPERSPEED 2	146	VICTOR HUGO	137		
SUPERSTAR	183	VICTORIA I	183		
SWIFT LADY	105	VICTORIA SEAWAYS	149		
SYLT EXPRESS	164	VICTORINE	116		

Other books from Ferry Publications

Brittany Ferries - 40 Memorable Years

Had you seen a vessel of Brittany Ferries heading across the Channel from France in 1973 it would not only have been carrying ferry passengers but fresh produce, grown by Breton farmers and on its way to the daily markets of south-west England. From this unlikely enterprise has flourished one of Europe's most successful shipping companies. Today, Brittany Ferries is not only the leading ferry operator on the Western Channel but also renowned for an extensive choice of hotel and self-catering holidays in France and Spain. This new book tells and superbly illustrates the whole fascinating story. Now avaiable. Price £17.50 plus p&p.

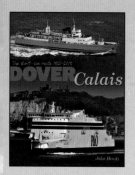

Dover-Calais

This will be an updated version of the Dover-Calais 2009 edition. Written by John Hendy, it covers the history of the most famous ferry crossing in the world but looks in detail at the development and expansion of the ferry operations and the new tonnage which has been introduced since the opening of the tunnel. The book will be richly illustrated in colour and black and white. It will include DFDS and Myferrylink operations. Published November 2013. Price £18.95 plus p&p.

TT Line

Since the introduction of the first Nils Holgerssonin 1962, this German ferry has been both an innovative and reliable player in the southern Baltic ferry market. Their core Travemunde Trelleborg route has seen no less than six different generations of ferries so far. TT-Line is also known for Olau Line and for a service between Rostock. In 2012 TT-Line celebrated its 50th anniversary. This book captures the fascinating history of TT-Line, their routes and their ships. Price £18.95 plus p&p. Published October 2013.

Order online from
www.ferrypubs.co.uk
By telephone on
+ 44 (0)1624 898445
By post from
PO Box 33, Ramsey, Isle of Man IM99 4LP
Please telephone or email for current postage costs.

Stena Line - Celebrating Years of Service

This book brings together a selection of outstanding photographs of Stena Line's operations of both the Baltic No Sea and the UK. Compiled by Br Peter with complimenting text o lining the companies history and operations. Over 200 photograph in both colour and black & white Hardback, 128 pages, A4 size. Now available. Price £19.50 plus p&

The SeaFrance Years

SeaFrance came into bein on New Years Day 1996 aft splitting with former partners Stena Line. Although a late starter in the operation of vehicle ferries across the Channel, the fleet that eventually developed was a fine collection of purpose-built ships embodying the best examples of French design and technical advancement that frequently eclipsed their British contemporaries. This book traces the post-war development of French participation in the English Channel, also briefly looking at the Dieppe Newhaven and Dunkirk - Dover operations which played such an important part in cross-Channel communications. 120 pages, Now avaiable. Price £18.00 plus p&p.

Silja Line

Silja Line and Tallink are two of the world's best known ferry companies. This book gathers together for the first time in English their entire histories, from humble beginnings with small steamers to the leisure-oriented cruise ferries of today. Partial bilingual text in Finnish. Price £24.50 plus p&p. Published October 2013.

Irish Ferries

In 1973, a newcomer to the Irish ferry scene began sailings between Rosslare and Le Havre. This company would grow from a single ship operator to become Irish Ferries.. Today the company is market leader on the Irish Sea to the UK and France. Price £19.75 plus p&p.